ALCOHOLISM

A Matter of Choice

*A Twenty-First Century
View of Addiction*

ALCOHOLISM

A Matter of Choice

A Twenty-First Century
View of Addiction

JIM HEWITT

Schenkman Books, Inc.
Rochester • Vermont

Copyright ©1999

Schenkman Books, Inc.
P.O. Box 119
Rochester, Vermont 05767

Library of Congress Cataloging-in-Publication Data

Hewitt, Jim, 1930 -
   Alcoholism: a matter of choice: a twenty-first century view of
   addiction / by Jim Hewitt.
         p. cm.
   Includes bibliographical references and index.
   ISBN 0-87047-107-4 (cloth)
   1. Alcoholism. 2. Compulsive behavior. I. Title.
   HV5035.H48 1988
   362.29'2--dc21

                                             97-27008
                                             CIP

ISBN 0-87047-107-4 cloth

For my beautiful twin daughters, Kathy and Patti. If I accomplished little else in life, being their father is enough. Devoted wives, superb mothers, and loving daughters! I cherish them endlessly.

A special gratitude to their mother, Mary, who guided them through their ordeal with compassion and courage.

Contents

Preface

The day after my release from a county hospital detoxification unit, I became a student of alcoholism. That was fifteen years ago. I was fifty-two years old when I finally put the cork in the bottle. But I was not content with the great miracle of my recovery; I had to know what happened and why. During these years of recovery from twenty-two years of alcohol abuse, I have scoured public libraries, college libraries, bookstores, and relevant journals for information about the behavior that distorted most of my adult life.

I had left behind a crooked trail of careers—former Jesuit, senior New York newspaper executive, bartender, teacher of Latin and Greek. These were major stopping-off points amidst various excursions. I have been husband and father, suburban homeowner, and client of several psychotherapists. For most of my life I was an ego but not a self. For much of my life I was a successful counterfeit, loved and trying to love.

According to Jellinek's descriptions (*The Disease Concept of Alcoholism*), I am a Gamma alcoholic. Gamma alcoholics start drinking early in life, stay in control for many years, and toward mid-life gradually slip over into uncontrollable drinking . My type was believed—before drugs speeded up the process—to make up the majority in Alcoholics Anonymous (AA).

At one of my first beginners' meetings in AA, fresh out of the hospital, I annoyed the leader when I said that I didn't think I had a disease; I said that I thought I had a *disorder*. I hadn't the least notion of what I was talking about, but that was the feeling I had about my problem. My dissatisfaction with the disease concept was vague but nettlesome. It seemed too physically oriented. One of the first things I realized in my work, however, was that

AA is not interested in alcoholism as such—just the alcoholic. Later, twentieth-century science would help me understand the experiential truth of AA's insights.

My recovery in AA led me to discover deeper issues in my life—issues I had buried (or drowned) with alcohol. I read about "second-stage sobriety." My suspicion grew that I had more to understand about the roots of this enormous affliction. I joined Alanon to learn more about my relationship with my deceased alcoholic father. I joined Coda [Codependents Anonymous] to learn more about the self-destructive adaptations I had made in my relationships.

It was in Coda that I met people addicted to things other than alcohol. At a meeting one night a tense young man sat down near me. He was quite frightened and upset. When it came his turn to say something he said he had just gotten out of a four-week rehabilitation program, he was terrified, and he needed telephone contacts. I tried to guess whether it was alcohol or drugs. When I asked him, his answer shocked me. He said "credit cards."

I never forgot that. There were no ingestive substances, no chemicals involved in this young man's deep disturbance, but he was obviously suffering from a powerful disorder of some kind. The idea of addiction took on a different dimension for me. My uneasiness with the prevalent ideas about alcoholism increased. There was a profound common experience between me and that young man—an alcoholic and a credit card junkie. Was there some unitary factor, although one disorder involved chemicals and one did not?

There was a growing literature at that time on addictions other than alcoholism, but it was largely clinically oriented. It proposed no etiological theories. So I established a base at a local college library and went to work. I chose to focus on alcoholism. That was the most heavily studied addiction—and I had a volume of personal data.

I saw that the principles underlying AA's success were ignored by the experts. I learned that AA was more than a "support group." I believed AA somehow knew the secret of alcoholism—and all addiction! We'll see about that later in this book.

I was uncomfortable about the many differing claims to ownership of the puzzle. Medical men, psychiatrists, sociologists, pharmacologists, and psychologists are pursuing the demon down the familiar trails of their own science without talking to one another. Thomas S. Kuhn, in his classic *The*

Structure of Scientific Revolutions helped me to understand the flaw in the academic assault upon addiction.

No one has yet penetrated the nature of alcoholism. No one is heading in the right direction in research. The reason? Not one of the experts is considering the nature of the subject—the human being! I propose to unmask the demon addiction where it hides inside our humanity.

What has pulled everything together for me is the radical change in the physicists' worldviews in the twentieth century. There can be no understanding of addiction without the grounding supplied by modern physics.

If I were to choose a central theme for this book it would be Mark Engel's in the preface of Gregory Bateson's *Steps to an Ecology of Mind:* "The central idea in this book is that we create the world that we perceive, not because there is no reality outside our heads, but because we select and edit the reality we see to conform to our beliefs about what sort of world we live in."

My central task is to show why and how alcoholics create the world they perceive. To do that we have to look first at the nature of humankind and human feelings. In this book we will come as close as we can get to a conceptual grounding for the nature of addiction.

I hope that I can push the frontier of research and discovery another step along the way. The most important work is not in brain chemistry or genetics, or related medical and physical fields, nor in conventional psychology and sociology. The most important work to be done for alcoholism lies in understanding and teaching what I call the formative symbolic processes of meaning and feelings; in explaining family systems and shame; and in inquiring into the reality offered by the first three Steps of Alcoholics Anonymous.

A special note of gratitude is reserved for John Bradshaw, the peripatetic evangelist of the recovery movement. It required a total immersion in the Bradshaw message for me to find out what had happened to the child who fathered the adult. Not a single word of this book would have been written had I not by chance tuned in Bradshaw one night on television.

Today I am safe and secure in my home filled with books. My time is filled with those who love me and whom I love. I don't know personally the men and women who wrote these books on my shelves, but I am deeply grateful for the deliverance they provided. Oddly, the maps to the lair of my demon have not been drawn by the specialists in addiction! You will find the names of the mapmakers in my select and general bibliography. They write not only with luminous intellects but with passion and generosity. I hope that I am reflecting a ray or two of their brilliance into the murky origins of addiction. I will introduce many of them as we go along.

Aldous Huxley was a wise prophet when he called Bill Wilson, cofounder of AA, the most important social architect of the twentieth century. It has made me uneasy that most of the experts look upon AA as merely a helpful adjunct to professional efforts. In my view, AA alone has seized upon the human nature of alcoholism.

Introduction

What causes alcoholism? This has been a most perplexing question because it is not the right question. What causes water to boil? That is a good question because it is an appropriate question. But asking what causes alcoholism is like asking what causes divorce. The appropriate question about divorce, or about alcoholism, or about any human behavior, is not what causes it, but why do people do it?

The twentieth century has been a period full of a dizzying array of events. It has also been the century when addiction shared the stage with a host of social maladies. There is a plague upon the land. We are at last aware that addictions are a widespread and devastating scourge on the well-being of our societies.

Society became aware first of addiction to alcohol, then to drugs and cigarettes. Finally, toward the end of the century, we learned about addictions to gambling, food, sex, work, and quite a few other mood-altering behaviors. Alcohol reached center stage with the enactment of Prohibition, but that movement made no attempt to understand *why* we drink. Our attention was drawn to the problem of addiction during the 1930s with the founding of Alcoholics Anonymous. Simultaneously, scientists took up the challenge in increasing numbers. But we have yet to understand that the commonly recognized addictions are just a few faces of a many-headed monster. It is no longer only the drunk who looks in the mirror in the morning and sees despair. It is no longer only the gambler thinking of suicide because his home is about to be taken by the bank. Our society is looking in the mirror today and seeing child abusers, wife beaters, incest victims, Wall Street spoilers, rapists, scheming politicians, hate mongers, and religious zealots. It has been a shock. It is, we hope, a wake-up call.

This book is about alcoholism, but it is also about all of the above. The maladies that are inherent in being a complex human organism on this planet have a common origin—what the historian of science Morris Berman calls "the basic fault." We can use alcoholism as a model for the behavioral ills that beset us individually and as a society. It is vitally important that we understand the nature of alcoholism, for in unmasking the alcoholic we will see the same demon hiding behind the face of the child abuser, the gambler, the spender, the wife-beater.

In this book I unfold a map and lay it on the table. Together we will make a journey to the lair of the demon. Once there we can decide whether we have solved the mystery of alcoholism's origins—and possibly the origin of all our maladies. Then we can figure out what to do about it.

Throughout the last half of the twentieth century, an unprecedented effort has been launched within several scientific and academic communities to uncover the origins of what some call the disease of alcoholism. As you will see in the pages ahead, our efforts to date have been unselfconsciously fragmented. Different communities of experts see alcoholism as a puzzle to be solved within the conventions of their own disciplines. Sociologists and behavioral psychologists spurn the biological determinists; some psychiatrists emphasize the cognitive features, and others emphasize the biophysical features. To a layperson, the search for the origins of addiction appears to be in chaos.

TWO MAJOR ISSUES

My investigation has revealed two major problems. First, I find no unified, controlling image of the subject guiding the varied research. They are talking about human behavior, but what is a human being?

The two distinguishing characteristics of the human organism are never considered in addiction research: (1) We are symbol-producing creatures. We write plays, plan vacations, read newspapers, save money, dedicate buildings, argue philosophy, play games, listen to music, paint pictures, design clothes, go to church, and so on. And (2) we are aware of our mortality. We are aware of a life cycle—of past, present, and future. We know we are going to die. Both of these human features must be figured into a concept of addiction.

Second, we have been looking at alcoholism from a 300-year-old Cartesian-Newtonian clockwork view of the world. Let's take this second problem first.

From Cartesian Mechanics to Quantum Mechanics

As a result of the seventeenth-century revolution begun in science by Descartes and Newton, it is second nature to look for the causes of behavior, as if human beings were machines. Physicist F. David Peat says we have been "hypnotized" by the notion of the clockwork universe. Under the Cartesian-Newtonian mindset—which has governed Western inquiry into reality for 300 years—disciplines from the hard sciences to the social sciences have been developed from the mechanical notions of separate parts, and cause and effect.

Has something occurred in the twentieth century that enables us to escape from Cartesian-Newtonian mechanics as the only explanation of the world and human behavior? The answer is emphatically yes.

In a 1990 review of a book called *The Quantum Self*, by Danah Zohar, Christopher Lehmann-Haupt said in the *New York Times*, "Something important is clearly going on as a result of the public's tardy but accelerating grasp of an intellectual revolution now over seventy years old." The revolution to which Lehmann-Haupt is referring is quantum mechanics, the most stunning development (so far) in the history of knowledge. In 1964 another shock wave hit with Bell's theorem of nonlocal causality.

The vast majority of us know nothing about these revolutions. But as Lehmann-Haupt observed, the implications are slowly seeping into public consciousness. Such books as *The Dancing Wu Li Masters* (National Book Award for Science, 1979) by Gary Zukav and *The Tao of Physics* by Fritjov Capra have sold well and still grace the shelves of bookstores.

The most significant implication for alcoholism research from this scientific revolution has been the realization that the Cartesian-Newtonian mechanical worldview is not the ultimate explanation of reality, nor of human behavior. The meaning for alcoholism flowing from the implications of quantum theory is now inevitable, and we'll explore that meaning in this book.

Systems Theory

Fundamental to the proposition of this book—that alcoholism is a matter of choice—is systems theory. When quantum mechanics superseded Cartesian mechanics as the ultimate view of reality, our world and everything in it had to be seen as a vast interdependent system. Our world now is no longer a giant clock, but a complex system. Systems theory enables us to cast a radically new model of human action and motivation.

WHOLE AND PART

The atoms and molecules that constitute my makeup are concrete. They are real. But the principle that organizes them into the various levels of life is not real. It is abstract. This is a key fact for us to examine. Stay with me at this critical point; this book will take you out of a lifetime of Cartesian-Newtonian thinking about cause and effect, matter, observable realities, and common sense logic. We are going into the brand-new world of twentieth-century physics. Most important is the notion of the whole and the part.

We are uncomfortable with the abstract in this technological society, but in fact we deal familiarly every day with the abstract. Take the idea of arrangement, for example. We know that when musical notes are arranged, they mean something to us that they do not mean without being arranged. And yet we cannot weigh, or measure, or see this arrangement under a microscope. Although the musical notes themselves can be quantified by various scientific instruments, we cannot quantify the arrangement. It remains abstract; it is an abstract arrangement of the same atoms and molecules that account for the difference between me and a lizard. It is the abstract whole that gives meaning to the concrete parts.

A quick and painless glance at modern science—quantum mechanics, nonlocal causality, dialectical biology, systems theory—will introduce us to principles of organization. We can describe them even if we don't completely understand them.

One can describe the affliction of addiction by approaching it from a ground-up examination. We begin with subatomic reality and go right up through atoms and molecules, and organisms, finally arriving at the top. At the top, specific organizing principles make collections of atoms into behaving organisms. Addictions are formed at the top.

The twentieth century has seen scientific revolutions and paradigm shifts. The mechanical worldview has been superseded by quantum mechanics. Importantly for alcoholism studies, there has been a radical shift in depth psychology. I hope to provide a synthesis of these shifts to come up with a new understanding of the human organism and its "basic fault." Throughout this book I attempt to weave into a whole fabric the threads of key notions from several modern scientists and thinkers. To journey to the land of the demon we must first understand the journey the physicists have taken to the abstract world of subatomic reality. From this abstract world we get our fundamental notions of wholes and connections. Thankfully, these ideas have been made simple for us by scientists who took time to write gentle primers, which can be found in any bookstore. A modest tutorial in modern physics is quite important. The cardinal flaw in scientific alcoholism studies hovers around what physicists call "level confusion."

In the chapters ahead we will be wondering how a collection of blood, flesh, and bone can plan a vacation—and we will see that ultimate matter is not matter at all, but mysterious fields of potential full of "unreal" forms and symmetries. Hang on!

We have consulted the physicists for their notions of whole and part, causality, determinism, reductionism, and free will, all of which are essential to the thesis of this book—that alcoholism is a matter of choice.

The limits of reductionism have been clearly marked by quantum mechanics, giving support to notions of holism and systems. This universe is now indisputably a participatory universe, consisting of a vast complex of networks and relations, as well as observable causes and effects. Heisenberg maintains that ultimate matter is not matter at all, but abstract forms and symmetries. We can indulge in the idea that the human organism is (so far) the ultimate expression of the systems in the universe. In that context, the alcoholic is desperately trying to fit in, to stabilize himself or herself at the center of things.

THE CONTROLLING IMAGE

Throughout this book I will frequently be using the term *controlling image*. Robert Jay Lifton says, "My basic premise is that we understand man through paradigms or models. The choice of the paradigm or model becomes extremely important, because it determines what might be called the *controlling image* or central theme of our psychological theory."

When we want to understand something or learn about it, we build a model of it, to see if it will work. But building a model to understand the psychology of a human being is not the same as building a physical, real model. The psychological process is intangible, unquantifiable, unmeasurable. It is simply experienced. To build a model for psychological processes we will have to use metaphors or concepts. Freud's model of ego, id, and superego were taken from Latin pronouns. Freud had not surgically opened up someone's skull and laid out an ego, an id, and a superego on the specimen table. What is important to note here is that these terms, although not real, *do* offer new knowledge.

Because of these artificial descriptions of parts we can develop a system that works. In other words, by understanding the conceptual relationships among the parts we can gain useful knowledge of the psychological process itself. For example, rational animal is a controlling image. Those two terms will control the full explanation of what it means to be a human. A model, or paradigm, will be built flowing from the meanings inherent in the notions rational and animal. These relationships will, it is hoped, mimic the internal dynamics of the reality we are attempting to understand.

How can we explain the behavior of humankind if we fail to establish and agree on a model of the human being? Several disciplines—or at least many practitioners—have assumed jurisdiction in the question of alcoholism, as if all the pieces of the puzzle were in their box alone for them to put together. The question is never asked—is this a problem our particular specialty can solve? They have no controlling image of the subject that can help them raise and answer that question. Thus we find pharmacologists, biopsychiatrists, anthropologists, psychologists, sociologists, neuroscientists, biologists, nutritionists, et al., weighing in with books claiming the last word on the problem, with barely a nod to other investigators. The tendency of anthologists of this material is to welcome it as a good thing. But no one is concerned about a controlling image of the subject, humankind. Suggesting that the field is chaotic is not an exaggeration.

To develop my controlling image for alcoholism I make use of the specific features of human beings—first, that we are symbol-producing organisms, and second, that we are aware of mortality.

The controlling image I have chosen for my work is the human as symbolic-affective organism-in-environment. I start my narrative with a new look at the human as a living organization of atoms and molecules. Everything in the universe, both organic and inorganic, consists of particles, atoms, and molecules. What makes me different from a rock or a tree is not different atoms and molecules, but the increasingly complex arrangement or pattern of those atoms and molecules. The notion of myself as an organization of some kind seems to be about as basic as you can get.

THE SYMBOLIC ANIMAL

Thinkers used to define the human as the rational animal, in Latin, *animal rationale*. Then in the later half of this century we thought better about that, and came up with the definition *animal symbolicum*. This description was proposed by Ernst Cassirer because it became obvious that our principal distinction from higher animals is our symbolic capacity. Monkeys can fashion a stick to poke around in ant holes, but only humans can write novels, compose symphonies, act in plays, plan vacations, and write and read about our history. We must not forget, however, that this symbolic activity is centered within the task to survive! Accordingly, I add another word to Cassirer's definition, calling man *animal symbolicum moriturum*. We are compelled to acknowledge that the most important activity of humankind has to do with symbolic immortality, or a sense of being alive.

In the pages ahead I employ the thought of Robert Jay Lifton. Lifton, emphasizing our species' need for a sense of life's continuity, gave us a revolutionary concept to understand our basic psychological processes. It is Lifton's work that ultimately illuminates the power of addiction.

The Mortal Animal

We have to face up to the second feature of humankind—a pretty grim feature. We know we are going to die. The other organisms don't seem to know about this. Our awareness, as we shall see, is a most critical factor in our behavior as humans. Possibly even before we are born the tension between life and death is immanent in every cell of our bodies. If you think about it for a moment, the term *life* cannot even be understood without simultaneously understanding the term *death*. Life has no meaning except in terms of death. When we shake hands and say, "You're looking pretty good, buddy," that remark is meaningful only because we could look pretty poorly.

In conventional thought, life and death are regarded as a duality. In Lifton's work, however, we find no duality; life and death are instead a unified polarity. Death, therefore, is animating. The life-death polarity is at the heart of alcoholism.

Organism-in-Environment

We shall see that this organism we are talking about, this *animal symbolicum moriturum*, cannot be viewed in a vacuum. We used to think we could completely understand organisms by understanding their organismic features only. But many authors are educating us to the fact that organisms exist in an environment, in a kind of tension with that environment, and therefore cannot be completely understood except as organisms-in-environments. Human beings are not passive receivers in the environment, but interact with the environment in such a way that human and environment codetermine each other. Biologists call this relationship a *dialectic*. I explain this later when I describe human organismic life in the environment as a kind of poker game.

Here is where we are sneaking up on the problem of alcoholism. Picture the alcoholic as an active participant who has been dealt a hand to play.

IMAGES AND FEELINGS

How do we know the environment? Cats look around and "know" that luscious mouse. Cats look at a mouse and think "mouse." We can not only look at a mouse and think mouse, but we can think about mice, what they are, and how they fit into the scheme of things. We can discuss mice with other humans. We know not only mouse but that there is a kind of thing called mouse. So when we know our environment we also can know it symbolically. Then we can take that symbolic thought and express it in a word that another human understands. *Symbolic Interaction*

That is a simple introduction to the most mysterious feature of the human organism—how do we represent external realities inside our heads? If you reflect for a moment, you will realize that your waking life is a never-ending stream of images and feelings. Inside our heads there is a constant collapse and re-creation of images, some merging with others instantaneously, being replaced, changed, renewed, enhanced, diminished, and so on without interruption. Along with this goes an undertone of feeling, sometimes muted, sometimes enhanced, as the parade of images goes on. Even as we are taking in impressions through our senses we are sifting through associated images from memory, always accompanied by variable murmurs of feeling. This undertone of feeling may be a sense of well-being, or a sense of unease.

What I am talking about here has been scientific fallow ground for much of this century. Cognitive science revolted against decapitation by behaviorism in the 1940s and 1950s, and has since screwed the head back on the model of the human being. As Silvan Tomkins described behaviorism: "Psychology has lost its mind!"

THE FEELING COMPLEX

The feeling complex is a complex of perception, intellection, feeling, and decision making. I describe it as the organism's interface with the environment. It is the feeling complex that reads the environment, that is programmed to find meanings of life and death equivalents in the images it forms. Life and death are the only two meanings to an organism, but they do not always confront the individual in immediate forms; that is, the human feeling complex reads the environment for equivalents of life and ✓ death. These equivalents are most often in symbolic forms. For example, our sight of a small child bending to pet a cat is read by the feeling complex as a life equivalent. The sight adds to our vitality, our joy at being alive. Then there is the sight of a burned-out slum. It detracts from our vitality. These are symbolic life and death equivalents.

Some people go through life seeing the glass half full; others see it always half empty. How we see life depends upon the vast inventory of associated image feelings we have stored up about life and death equivalents. I explain this in detail when we talk about Lifton's ideas. It is important to understand that the human organism negotiates its existence in the environment through image feelings of life and death equivalents—and this will lead you to some idea of what alcoholism is all about.

Because we are *animal symbolicum moriturum*, our specific human activity— the activity that marks us as human—will be activity around symbolic immortality, or continuity. The principal task of the organism is to survive as what it is. We pursue a sense of *ongoingness* through symbolic modes of continuity. For example, we look to family, children, and grandchildren for a sense of continuity; or to the books we write or the paintings we do; or to the religious beliefs we cherish; or to the businesses we build, or the homes we leave behind. Monkeys and parrots do not buy billions of dollars of life insurance to see to the continuity of their kind.

We are coming closer to that feature of the human organism where the demon lives. In the most important level of human organization, the feeling complex, we can suffer deficits, or failures. If the glass is always half empty, something has gone awry in the feeling complex. We are forming too many death equivalents when we are symbolizing the meanings around us. Why?

SHAME

The most interesting part of our narrative describes the origins of alcoholic and addictive behavior—a recently resurrected emotion called shame. Shame is the most powerful death equivalent the feeling complex can come up with. In explaining this we will work from the thoughts of Silvan Tomkins, Gershen Kaufman, and Robert Firestone. We'll pull it all together with Lifton's model of death and the continuity of life.

Shame arises from broken connections with primary caregivers. Broken connection is the fundamental death equivalent. The importance of connection has been amply researched, especially by Bowlby, Mahler, Erikson, et al. The overarching importance of connection has been demonstrated by modern physics.

The experience of broken connection—shame—is often internalized; it becomes part of the repertory of image feelings dominating the symbolizing process in connections (relationships). Shaming during the developmental stages causes (1) distrust, (2) self-dependence, and (3) painful confusion. Shamed people are highly defended people, a state which Firestone maintains is the single greatest obstacle to relationships.

Shame is probably the most frequent setup for addiction. The principal effect of alcohol is the restoration of a sense of connection with self, others, and the world (or the numbing of separation). When we have discovered shame in this book we will have cornered the demon in his lair. When we have uncovered the dynamics of shame we will have discovered the dark secret of the man who walks into a school with an automatic weapon and kills teachers and children. We will have discovered the secret behind the compulsive midnight raids upon the refrigerator; we will have discovered the secret of the rapist, the child abuser, and the wife-beater.

FREE WILL OR CHOICE?

The title of this book catches a lot of folks by surprise: *Alcoholism: A Matter Of Choice*. Although no one chooses to be alcoholic, alcoholics *do* repeatedly choose to drink in spite of the consequences. That may sound heretical in the light of today's disease concept, but the capacity to choose is a specific characteristic of human organization. We will find alcoholism located at the level of choice.

I will be unraveling a highly controversial problem as we examine the nature of choice. Alcoholism is not simply a question of will power, or lack of character, or moral failure. Choosing to drink self-destructively is not like choosing between ice cream or yogurt. For the alcoholic, choosing alcohol is felt as choosing life over death. Life and death equivalents lurk at the core of every choice we make. Thus we need to take a look at the nature of choice and free will.

I make a distinction between free will and choice. As organisms we do not have free will, but we do have the capacity to choose within the limits of our organismic tasks. It is vitally important that we understand choice in the context of alcoholic behavior. The correct notion of choice is what is missing in alcoholism studies.

THE BASIC FAULT

What I hope for most as a result of these propositions is a refocusing of interest on the "basic fault" in our society. The basic fault is the vulnerability of the young human to disharmony between parents and child. Alice Miller champions this view that too many of our children are forced to build defenses in their connections from the beginning of their lives, and that is the core of all our social ills. Once society learns to believe it, we can begin to focus on the heart of the matter.

For the reader of these pages, I hope that whatever clarity these ideas provide about addictions helps you understand the appropriate tasks that must be undertaken to renew a life. A human being is not "a bundle of bad habits," although, unfortunately, many psychologists will tell you this. *Habits* are not specifically human behavior. *Addictions* are. All of us suffer from issues around distrust, self-dependence, and confusion in varying degrees of intensity. These are the specifically human afflictions that must be confronted.

For generations, the power of addiction has eluded us. It was not until Lifton developed his paradigm shift in the basic psychological process that the origin of addiction burst into light. As you will read, Freud and the neo-Freudians could not help us with addiction, nor could the behavioral psychologists and sociologists. Many dedicated scientists have come up with exhaustive peripheral information. They have surrounded the demon, but they haven't forced him out of hiding. Until now, no one has illuminated the power of addiction.

PREVAILING VIEWS

In Chapter 12, I pause in the narrative to take an intensive look at the ideas of other authors on the subject of addiction. I call these the prevailing views, since they are generally accepted by society, insurance companies, universities, and government agencies. These authors lack understanding of the origins of addiction; they are engaged by the Cartesian-Newtonian view of the world.

If you have been reading current books about alcoholism and addiction, you will get a lot of information about the conditions under which alcoholism may occur, but they will not be able to pinpoint for you the nature of alcoholism. Alcoholism is a matter of genes and heredity, they tell you; or else it's a matter of physiological, psychological, and sociological causes added up to make folks drink abusively (the "multifactorial" concept); or some say it's largely a matter of neurochemical anomalies affecting the brain, or that alcoholism is first and foremost a physiological disease process that can be complicated by psychological and sociological factors.

Still other strong voices will insist that alcoholism is in no way a disease process, but simply a matter of bad habits, bad learning, and loss of values. Others disagree. Bright and cheery books trumpet revelations of advances in genetic and neuroscientific investigations. Eager publishers use words like *revolutionary*, *groundbreaking*, and *at the cutting edge* to describe their products. There have been no breakthroughs, no revolutions, and no cutting edge in understanding alcoholism! (This is a deliberately strong statement. Sometimes you have to strike a blow to get attention!)

ALCOHOLICS ANONYMOUS

A major part of this book is about the way out of the demon's lair. Many, many people do escape. There are all kinds of escape routes running off in different directions, but this book is about the organic nature of alcoholism, and so I limit myself to a description of the organic way out. We will take a look at the program of Alcoholics Anonymous (AA), which I call a pre-rational program of commitment to reality. An examination of the principles of AA provides an opportunity to understand AA in the light of the scientific revolutions of the twentieth century. I examine with particular scrutiny the first three Steps of Alcoholics Anonymous. They are the bedrock of recovery from addiction.

When we have reached the final point on our map to the lair of the demon, we will find the outposts of Alcoholics Anonymous already encamped there. Oddly, these men and women are not trained explorers of any kind. They are actually just survivors of pain, confusion, and despair who are coming back to life. Now they are at last, triumphantly, authentic organisms-in-environment.

A TRIP TO THE LIBRARY

The books that enabled me to write this book are waiting on the bookstore shelves for you; I will introduce you to them as we go along.

Don't be discouraged, fellow layperson, if at first they appear somewhat incomprehensible. They once were to me, but to my surprise and delight, many of these gifted scientists are also entertaining writers!

First, I was profoundly affected by the implications in quantum mechanics for our understanding of our world. As a result, I am able to see now a universe of vast interdependencies and relationships, a far different view from that of the universe as a giant clockwork. I have to thank for that the books I have read by Werner Heisenberg, Gary Zukav, Paul Davies, F. David Peat, David Bohm, Nick Herbert, Richard Feynmann, Danah Zohar, and Fritjof Capra.

Second, I came upon systems theory and cybernetics in the work of Gregory Bateson, Ervin Laszlo, and Eric Jantsch. These authors have also suggested modes of inquiry into reality that include experience as well as subject-object distancing of rationalism.

Third, I discovered a new trend in biology from pure analysis to a concern about synthesis—a concern about the phenomena of patterns under the microscope. Biologist Rupert Sheldrake nudged me away from a biology of composition of discrete parts into a living world of relationships and fields. In this area, a dialectic of wholes in the environment has been proposed by Lewontin, Rose, and Kamin. These authors reject determinism and pure interactionism. Their work led me to a new understanding of the human whole in its environment.

Fourth, I became fascinated with the story of cognitive science as told by Howard Gardner. Gardner's narrative, combined with Owen Flanagan's work on the science of mind, put more nails in the coffin of behaviorism as an explanation of human action. Cognitive scientists have re-established the notion of the image, or internal representation, as crucial to understanding the mind. As we shall see, the image is crucial to an understanding of alcoholism. The image we speak of is nothing more than what fills your head in all your waking moments.

Fifth, my world was re-enchanted by the work of Morris Berman, a historian of science who has undertaken to uncover "our hidden history" (our emotional life) as human beings, and somatize the human enterprise. Berman emphasizes the pitfalls of an exclusively rational-scientific world view.

Finally, Ernest Becker's *The Denial of Death* (Pulitzer Prize, 1979) prepared the way for my readings of Robert Jay Lifton's *The Broken*

Connection. Lifton has shifted the depth psychological model from Freudian instinct and defense to a model of death and the continuity of life. Lifton's thought provides at last a model for the power of addiction—the most powerful model in the history of psychology.

CODEPENDENCY

Appendix A covers the hugely popular recovery movement and codependency. The codependency movement looks to the principles of Alcoholics Anonymous. The Twelve Step movement has increasingly vociferous opponents and champions. We'll review the controversy in terms of our controlling image of mankind.

SHAME AND GUILT

Appendix B addresses a rising interest in the difference between shame and guilt. Understanding this difference is important in the processes of recovery from addiction.

The narrative you are about to read is unlike anything you have ever read about human nature. I hope it provides food for thought in the management of your own life. It is so much more rewarding to confront our dissatisfactions, disappointments—and even our depressions—when we understand their nature. Then we can understand the way out. Welcome to the twenty-first century!

PART ONE:

HUMAN ORGANIZATION

1

The Cartesian-Newtonian Worldview

Whenever we face a personal problem, or a problem in the family, in the workplace, or in a laboratory, someone will inevitably say, "Let's analyze that." Analyze means to break something down into its constituent elements. The hope is that, seeing the elements laid out, we can change one or more, so that the problem can be solved. This method was introduced to science in the seventeenth century by René Descartes.

We will not understand the nature of alcoholism or any addiction until we consider the radically new scientific viewpoint about the nature of reality. We have been approaching alcoholism from a three-hundred-year-old point of view about reality. The experts agree we still do not know the nature of alcoholism. We never will until we adapt to the major shifts in scientific views that have broken away from what is called the Cartesian-Newtonian view of the world, which saw our world as a vast clockwork, a huge machine run by immutable physical laws. It is most important that the human being be carefully located within these revolutions.

Current alcoholism studies make no attempt to include an understanding of the nature of human beings. We observe humankind "objectively," as something whose physical properties can be analyzed, and treated with surgery and drugs; whose behavior can be observed, statistically described, and predicted mathematically; and whose conduct can be changed by techniques to replace bad habits with good ones. These approaches are governed by the old Cartesian-Newtonian tradition, but the human being has been left out of the equation.

You hardly expected to be treated to a scientific treatise when you picked up a book about alcoholism and choice. Ten years ago I hardly expected to be writing one. Ten years ago I had only a vague notion of the Cartesian-Newtonian worldview. It is necessary, however, to know something about the tremendous shifts in human understanding if we are to finally confront the addictions that plague our society. Books being written today on alcoholism and addiction are written from a point of view established in the Cartesian-Newtonian tradition. This is true whether the authors are "hard scientists" (e.g., biologists) or "soft scientists" (e.g., sociologists).

Reflecting upon my own alcoholism, I felt a conflict between my experience and what the experts were telling me. I needed to know about the mind and the brain; about perception; about feelings and emotion; about the development of humankind; about the influence of the early years and the developmental tasks; about the organism in its environment; about how we know things; about meaning and the emotions, and so on.

I did not bury myself in research libraries, reading documents available only in academia. Most of the material I needed I found in the bookstores and in my local libraries. When I realized how very accessible this information was, I wondered why the various experts on alcoholism did not bother to read the same material I was reading. But then Thomas Kuhn, who wrote the classic *The Structure of Scientific Revolutions,* explained it to me. Experts start college at eighteen, lock on to a major, go to graduate school where they deepen and intensify their interest, do postdoctoral work, and then go on to teach in the universities where they generally publish on subjects within their major. Their working lives are spent in a community of people with similar interests. It is not the practice to cross over disciplines to solve puzzles. Very few experts develop syntheses from other major disciplines. This would account for the lack of a controlling image in alcoholism literature.

THE SCIENTIFIC REVOLUTION

The way Western people look at things today began to take shape after medieval science was replaced. Medieval science, emerging from the Dark Ages when there had been no science to speak of, had inquired into the universe to find meanings, significance, and the signs of God in all things. It was based on both reason and faith. Its purpose was to establish the natural laws by which human beings could guide their conduct. The scientific attitude had been one of understanding and participation.

The scientific revolution that followed had as its purpose prediction, and particularly, control and manipulation of nature. Note the remarkable language of Francis Bacon in the seventeenth century, who wrote that nature had to be "hounded in her wanderings," "bound into service," and made a "slave." He said that nature was to be "put in constraint," and the scientist was to "torture nature's secrets from her." Bacon's viewpoint flowed from the notion that the entire universe and everything in it was a giant machine. (Bacon's attitude is also an example of the reigning patriarchy.)

The key point of the scientific revolution is that a mathematical description of nature was the crucial novelty. Galileo postulated that scientists must restrict their investigations to the properties of material objects only—shapes, numbers, movement—which they could measure and quantify. This was heady stuff. All kinds of mental activity had to be banned from scientific curiosity. The result of the quantification of science was the abandonment of experience as a valid mode of knowing or inquiring. Cast into limbo were aesthetics, ethical sensibilities, values, quality, intentions, feelings, motives, soul, and spirit. While the success of mathematical quantification has been spectacular, at the same time condemning experience has been a disaster from which we are just beginning to recover. Measurement and quantification took on the character of obsession. Direct experience was sneered at.

Capra tells us,

> From the time of the ancients the goals of science had been wisdom, understanding the natural order and living in harmony with it . . . In the seventeenth century this attitude changed into its polar opposite; from yin to yang, from integration to self assertion.

This shift,

> which was to become of overwhelming importance for the further development of Western civilization, was initiated and completed by the two towering figures of the seventeenth century, Descartes and Newton.

Descartes set out to construct a new system of inquiring into the nature of things. He was passionately driven, believing that God had ordained him to communicate a new science to humankind, that his vocation was to distinguish truth from error in all fields of learning. He resolved to develop a philosophy in which only those things are to be believed that are perfectly known "and about which there can be no doubts." (Heisenberg points out that Descartes got off to a bad start. Modern physics has shown us that we cannot have absolute certainty. We must accept partial and approximate truth.)

Descartes' analytical method was also the beginning of the scientific division between mind and matter. Descartes concluded that the body and mind were fundamentally disconnected, a decree that has had a profound and lasting effect upon Western thought.

Capra says, "[T]he Cartesian division has led to endless confusion about the relation between mind and brain, and in physics made it extremely difficult for the founders of quantum theory to interpret their observations of atomic phenomena." Capra further quotes Heisenberg: "This partition has penetrated deeply into the human mind during the three centuries following Descartes and it will take a long time for it to be replaced by a really different attitude toward the problem of reality." Perceptions about the realities of alcoholism have been affected by this partition. It will take time before alcoholism is generally understood.

Descartes established two fundamentally different and independent domains in his worldview: one the domain of mind—the *res cogitans*—and the other the domain of matter—*res extensa*. Descartes believed that both mind and matter were created by God. *In following centuries, however, science split off from notions of God and the* res cogitans *to concentrate on the* res extensa. This was a natural development because mathematics could be applied only to observable matter, to *res extensa*, and not to the things of the mind.

For Descartes, the human body was indistinguishable from a machine. Descarte said, "I consider the human body as a machine. . . . My thought . . . compares a sick man and an ill-made clock with my idea of a healthy man and a well-made clock." Unfortunately, this viewpoint still prevails in modern medicine (but with increasing protests from physicians like Bernie Siegel and Deepak Chopra). Human beings were inhabited by a rational soul, said Descartes, connected with the body through the pineal gland located in the center of the brain. Understandably, this thinking had a strong influence on our attitudes toward our bodies and the world. Our attitudes since have been those of objectivity, control, and manipulation.

Descartes was a brilliant mathematician and philosopher, the inventor of analytic geometry. The Cartesian method immediately captured the thought of the Western world. There is a price to be paid for this legacy, however. You have heard the expression, "He couldn't see the forest for the trees"? In a sense, a mechanical world is a world of trees with no one noticing the forest. Patterns, organization, and designs escaped Descartes' interest, and they escaped our interest for three hundred years. Wholes were, of course, recognized, but they were of no significance to science. A whole as such was abstract. It could not be measured or quantified for mathematics. Organisms were simply collections of atoms and molecules arranged so that they could ingest, metabolize, and excrete. Descartes' method prevails in alcoholism studies, which never approaches the human being as a whole. We have "multifactorial" causes of alcoholism: genetic factors, chemical imbalances in the brain, and so on. Students of alcoholism have no conceptual tools to describe the affliction properly. We find in both the physical and psychological approaches to addiction a relentless analysis of the mechanisms that determine alcoholic behavior. The idea of cause and effect dominates the addiction literature.

The second intellectual giant who shared the crowning achievement of seventeenth- century science was Isaac Newton. Descartes had died knowing his system was incomplete, but he had left the world his method of analytic reasoning and his mechanical view of the universe. Newton came upon the scene gifted with the most powerful mathematical mind of his time. He invented a new method to describe the motion of solid bodies, known as *differential calculus*. Einstein considered this achievement the "greatest advance in thought that a single individual was ever privileged to make."

We know the story of Newton sitting under the apple tree, getting his basic insight from the falling apple. Newton discovered gravity. Using his mathematical skills, he was able to formulate the laws governing the falling apple, and all bodies. Descartes was thereby confirmed. The universe was one vast mechanical system, operating according to exact mathematical laws. Newton presented his findings in his well-known *Principia Mathematica Philosophiae Naturalis,* or simply *The Principia*, as the work is commonly called.

Prior to Newton, Bacon had left us the inductive method of reasoning from experimentation, and Descartes the deductive method from clear ideas. Newton went beyond both men and combined both methods, which has been the basis of natural science ever since. Capra gives us a succinct description of Newtonian mechanics:

> In Newtonian mechanics all physical phenomena are reduced to the motion of material particles, caused by their mutual attraction, that is, by the force of gravity. The effect of this force on a particle or any other material object is described mathematically by Newton's equations of motion, which form the basis of classical mechanics.

These were considered fixed laws according to which material objects moved, and were thought to account for all changes observed in the physical world.

During the eighteenth and nineteenth centuries, Newtonian mechanics were employed with the greatest success. The picture of the world as a perfect machine was now an accepted and proven fact.

With the tremendous success of the Newtonian viewpoint, it was only natural that Newtonian physics would become the basis of all the sciences. Up until the mid-twentieth century, no inquiry into nature or behavior could gain respectability unless it emulated Newtonian physics. Even psychologists took their lead from the mechanists. There was simply no other way to investigate reality in any of its manifestations.

The Newtonian explanation of the universe was a strictly rational approach, completely objective, and left no place for the experiences of the individual. The Cartesian-Newtonian worldview was firmly established during the eighteenth century, so much so that it became the Age of Enlightenment for historians. Also around this time, late in the seventeenth century, John Locke came upon the stage. Locke focused on the nature of the human being within the new rational, mechanistic viewpoint. His best known phrase is *tabula rasa*, a blank slate, which he used to describe the human mind at birth—a blank slate upon which knowledge is impressed through the senses. The human being was a product of environment, pure and simple. It was therefore of utmost importance that a rational environment be established for societies.

Locke believed that the same laws of nature that governed the material world also governed the behavior of the human being, so that mankind was by nature always seeking a balanced state—just as atoms in a gas were determined to do. Thus governments, according to Locke, should not make up arbitrary laws but simply discover and enforce the natural laws that pre-empted government. Locke's ideas about these natural laws became the value system of the Enlightenment, contributing significantly to the thinking of Thomas Jefferson. Surely the Declaration of Independence and the American Constitution reflect Lockean ideals. Locke's ideas, though mechanical and deterministic, are benign.

In obscure laboratories, however, work on the nature of nature continued. A cloud loomed over the perfect scheme of the Cartesian-Newtonian universe. The discovery of electric and magnetic phenomena was found to involve a new type of force. It could not be described by the mechanistic model. Faraday and Maxwell replaced the concept of force with the much subtler concept of a field of force. Fields of force had their own reality. They could be studied without reference to material bodies.

This theory was called *electrodynamics*. It produced the first cracks in the Cartesian-Newtonian mechanical structure. Maxwell himself did not realize he had damaged the mechanical model. Einstein was the first to declare emphatically that electromagnetic fields were entities in their own right—that they could travel through space and could not be explained mechanically.

EVOLUTION

At the same time that electromagnetism bloodied the mechanistic viewpoint, another major upheaval was gathering. This was the notion of change, growth, and development—completely contradictory to a fixed and immutable clockwork universe. Great intellectuals were pondering the obvious problem of *becoming*. Lamarck was the first to propose a coherent theory of evolution, a change so radical and dramatic that Gregory Bateson compared it to the Copernican revolution. Several decades later, Darwin's *Origin of Species* synthesized the ideas of earlier thinkers. Darwinism has shaped all subsequent biological thought.

Darwinian evolution is one of the greatest intellectual achievements. Most followers of modern Darwinism are philosophical materialists. This point of view impacts on our image of ourselves as compassionate and truly spiritual. Darwinism leaves many intellectuals puzzled: how can a purely material organism have spiritual qualities? The problem is cleared up when our controlling image of the human is brought to bear. Darwinism does not allow for notions of a self-regulating whole negotiating its connections in its environment. But the subject requires more attention than space allows in this book.

Summary: This chapter has presented the background for the analytic method that prevails in alcoholism studies. Analysis, also known as reductionism, has been humankind's most powerful tool to uncover the elements of nature. We knew of no other effective way, but with the advent of quantum mechanics, we now must look at the forest as well as the trees.

2

The New Worldview: Quantum Mechanics and Systems Theory

> Thus relativity theory has taught us the same lesson as quantum mechanics. It has shown us that our common notions of reality are limited to our ordinary experience of the physical world and have to be abandoned whenever we extend this experience.
>
> —Fritjof Capra, *The Turning Point*

By the end of the nineteenth century, Cartesian-Newtonian mechanics had lost its role as the ultimate theory of natural phenomena. Electrodynamics—fields having their independent existence outside the mechanistic structure—and the powerful idea of evolution awakened sharply in scientists the realization that the universe was far more complex than the straightforward model of Descartes and Newton. Even so, Cartesian-Newtonian ideas were still believed to be basically correct—until the first three decades of the twentieth century changed all that. Two developments in physics, relativity theory and quantum theory, smashed the principal concepts of the worldview of Descartes and Newton.

Albert Einstein stood alone at the frontier of the new physics. In 1905, Einstein published the papers that began the twentieth-century revolution in scientific thought. One paper was concerned with establishing a framework for unifying electrodynamics and mechanics, the two separate theories of classical physics. The framework is known as the special theory of relativity. Ten years later, Einstein proposed his theory of general relativity in which he extended the special theory to include gravity. In both of these propositions Einstein changed our concepts of space and time, thus drastically undermining the Newtonian worldview.

In another development, Einstein theorized that energy itself is quantized. What he meant is that light comes in packets of energy, so that a beam of light, rather than continuous, is actually like a stream of bullets. Each bullet is called a photon. This discovery was to lead to the development of the theory of quantum mechanics. What brought about intense interest in quantum theory was the apparent contradiction between Einstein's discovery that light is made of photons, or particles, and Thomas Young's proof, one hundred years earlier, that light consists of waves. Particles and waves are mutually exclusive concepts—one cannot be the other. And yet subsequent experiments showed that light could be either a wave or a particle, depending upon how you set up your experiment. Then still later, experiments showed scientists that they could not get a fix on the momentum and the position of the electron at the same time. You can set up your experiment to measure either the velocity of an electron or its position, but at the same time you can never know. This became an enormous problem for physicists. Its resolution would change forever the way we look at our world.

To make some sense of the particle-wave contradiction, physicists had to accept an aspect of reality that subverted the very foundations of the mechanistic worldview. They had to accept that ultimate matter is not real. Subatomic particles, it was found, are not "things"; they are interconnections *between* things. Capra says, "In quantum theory you never end up with things; you always deal with interconnections." Heisenberg says, "The world thus appears as a complicated tissue of events, in which connections of different kinds alternate or overlap, or combine and thereby determine the texture of the whole." Henry Stapp of the University of California says, "An elementary particle is not an independently existing unanalyzable entity. It is, in essence, a set of relationships that reach outward to other things."

To come to the quantum conclusion about the ultimate nature of reality cost the physicists a great intellectual and emotional price. All of the early investigators were stunned by their conclusions. Einstein said he felt as if the ground had been taken from beneath him. Heisenberg said he walked through woods at night in despair. Zukav said, "In 1927 the most famous assemblage of physicists in history decided that it might not ever be possible to construct a model of reality," i.e., to explain the way things "really are behind the scenes."

Some present-day intellectuals (the classical philosopher Mortimer Adler, for one) see no problem here. For these intellectuals the conditions of the experiment itself disturb the reality of the electron; we are not getting a true reading about its actuality. Many physicists, including Heisenberg himself for a while, believed in the disturbance view of the apparent contradiction. But most physicists today, according to Nick Herbert (*Quantum Reality*), have discarded the disturbance viewpoint and embrace what is known as the *Copenhagen Interpretation.*

Herbert says, "In brief, the Copenhagen Interpretation holds that in a certain sense, the unmeasured atom is not real: its attributes are created or realized in the act of measurement." (This is totally unacceptable to classic philosophy.) This is the position of Heisenberg, who won the Nobel Prize for his famous Uncertainty Principle. Heisenberg holds that the ultimate particle is not a particle at all. It is actually a potency, which is brought into actuality by the act of measurement. Fields of potency, which some call quantum fields, lie outside the limits of our capacity to know them. What quantum reality is, no one knows.

The shift from objects (concrete) to relationships (abstract) has had a profound impact on many thinkers, as you might expect. Most of us, of course, have been blissfully unaware of these developments in science. But powerful thinkers like Gregory Bateson, for example, taught that a thing should not be defined by what it is in itself but by its relation to other things. He argued that this should be taught to our children in elementary school.

Living now with quantum theory for several decades, many authors are working with the implications of quantum mechanics. Physicist F. David Peat (*Synchronicity*) says, "Rather than nature and the heavens being *reduced* to 'mere matter', the reverse has in fact taken place." We need no longer think of reduction in our search but instead we can think of extension. We can actually cross over on the spectrum of reality from the tangible to the intangible, into deeper and deeper regions of reality without limit. "The order of matter has therefore become far removed from that of the billiard balls and falling apples of the Newtonian world. Rather than nature being *reduced* to the material, the whole notion of the material has been extended into regions of indefinite intangibility."

Deepak Chopra (*Quantum Healing*) says,

"To a physicist, all size stops at a specific number . . . an inconceivable fraction that can be written out as 1/10 followed by 32 zeros; this is known as Planck's limit, a kind of absolute zero for space. . . . But what is it that lies beyond after this limit of size has been reached?" Heisenberg said, "I think that modern physics has definitely decided in favor of Plato. In fact the smallest units of matter are not physical objects in the ordinary sense; they are forms, ideas which can be expressed unambiguously only in mathematical language."

What this means is that the abstract world is as real as the physical world—and actually more so. The physical world emerges from the abstract world. This validation of the abstract is important. When we try to talk about the patterns or organizing principles of the whole that make a collection of atoms into a human organism, we must be comfortable with the notion of the abstract realities at work.

What is the meaning of all this for our study of alcoholism? Quantum theory means that the world and everything in it is *not* a giant machine. There are limitations to the notions of cause and effect. Classical science can no longer explain the nature of reality. Our notions about alcoholism are based on classical science and psychology, but today we have to proceed from another point of view to understand alcoholism. The abstract principles that make me different from a dog must now be figured into the human equation. Nor can human behavior be reduced any longer to the physical levels of organization.

Nonlocal Causality

Nonlocal Causality is a discovery so outlandish that even Einstein could not accept it. It is a proven fact, however, with profound implications for our propositions about humankind and alcoholism. Physicists refer to nonlocal causality as *quantum inseparability*. As Herbert observes, this was the greatest surprise to come out of the quantum worldview. For physicists, locality means that when one body at location A acts on another body at location B, the interaction between the two must traverse the intervening distance. Also, it must traverse the distance at speeds no greater than the speed of light. In nonlocality, the force travels instantly from location A to location B without traversing the intermediate space. It travels at speeds *greater* than the speed of light. (In *Elemental Mind,* pp. 179-183, Herbert gives a brief and clear explanation of nonlocal causality.)

The discovery of nonlocal connections in the atomic world delivers a new notion of causality. Whereas in classical Cartesian science the world was analyzed into parts arranged according to causal laws—the clockwork, deterministic notion of the universe—quantum theory has shown us conclusively that we cannot analyze the world into independent elements. The notion of separate parts is an idealization. Separate parts are only aspects of reality; we are unable to perceive with our senses the actual indivisibility of the universe. This revelation from quantum mechanics and nonlocal causality has tremendous implications for our study of the human organism. Although we can analyze and take apart the organism, as an organism it is inseparable into parts. Alcoholism is the behavior of a whole within a whole system. The specific behavior of the whole will be influenced by its interdependencies in the greater whole. Specific behavior cannot be determined by the parts of the whole. We can see why science and psychology have failed to locate alcoholism in the human.

SYSTEMS THEORY

When quantum mechanics displaced the Cartesian view of the world as a giant machine, it became immediately apparent that another view was needed. If the world is not a machine, a giant clockwork, then obviously it is a *system* of some kind. Systems theory is a rational and necessary response to the inevitable implications of quantum mechanics. Systems theory states: First, the world is a dynamic system of interacting and interdependent relationships. Second, our knowledge of the world occurs at higher levels in the human whole than Cartesian rationality and objectivity. If the world is a system, then we are a part of it—not merely observers. Third, there are three levels of human inquiry into reality.

Jantsch illustrates the three levels of inquiry by picturing a man and a flowing river. In level one of inquiry, the person stands on the shore watching the river go by. Jantsch calls this *subject-object distancing.* This is the principal poise of the rational scientific view. At the second level the person is in a canoe on the fast-moving river. This is a subjective view because the man is involved with the river and must negotiate his way on it. At the third level of experience with the river, the person is caught up with the flow of the river, and is now interested in being part of the movement. He is no longer negotiating his passage on it, but flowing along with it, his eyes ahead.

Quantum mechanics had a profound impact on epistemology —the way we perceive reality. For the first time, scientists realized that we are not merely rational observers of the world but an integral part of the system. We are embedded in the system. We can no longer stand back in subject-object distancing. That meant that other levels of our connection within the system had to be re-examined. Systems theory illuminates three levels:

> The rational first level is the poise of the observer, the organizer, the communicator. It is characterized by objectivity.
>
> The second level is connective, feeling, interactive. It is characterized by subjectivity. The meaning-feeling process predominates.
>
> The third level is unitary. It is grounded in the first two levels, but transcends them. It is characterized by a profound awareness of unity. (The alcoholic yearns for this level of transcendence, but without being grounded in the first two.)

Morris Berman, a historian of science, says: "The great irony of quantum mechanics" is that it "established subjectivity as the cornerstone of objective knowledge," instead of being a Cartrtesian attempt to wipe out subjectivity once and for all. Jantsch says that rationality "constitutes the lowest level in a hierarchy of knowledge for human purposes." Jantsch believes that the rational approach "impoverishes and narrows down" reality.

David Finklestein, Director of the School of Physics at the Georgia Institute of Technology, says that experience is not bound by the rules of classical logic. He refers to a more permissive set of rules, quantum logic, which is not based on the way we think of things, but on the way we *experience* them.

In *The Dancing Li Masters* (National Book Award for Science, 1979) Gary Zukav says, "When we try to describe experience with classical logic— which is what we have been doing since we learned to write—we put on a set of blinders, so to speak, which not only restricts our field of vision, but also distorts it. . . ." In 1936 the mathematician John von Neumann and his colleague, Garrett Birkoff, published the paper that laid the foundations for quantum logic. Physicists acknowledge that they "demonstrated mathematically that it is impossible to describe experience with classical logic because the real world follows different rules. . . ." Jantsch remarks,

"Rationality, as it turns out, begins to play a role only after the knowledge has been obtained viscerally."

From the point of view of a cognitive scientist, Howard Gardner, in *The Mind's New Science*, we have the following: "Empirical work on reasoning over the past thirty years has severely challenged the notion that human beings—even sophisticated ones—proceed in a rational manner, let alone that they invoke some logical calculus in their reasoning. . . ."

Such statements affirm our position that we innately transform our perceptions into image-feelings of meaning before our rational capacities coherently organize these experiences.

Danah Zohar *(The Quantum Self)* supports this when she says, "All definite answers—all logic, all reason—are classical structures. They arise at the point where the wave function of thought collapses, that is, after the moment of choice."

Zukav writes, "[W]e are approaching the end of science. The end of science means the coming of Western civilization, in its own time, and in its own way, into the higher dimensions of human experience." Max Planck, the father of quantum mechanics, says, "Science means unresting endeavor and continually pressing development toward an aim which the poetic intuition may apprehend, but which the intellect can never fully grasp." In the same vein, G.F. Chew, Chairman of the Physics Department at Berkeley, says, "Our current struggle (with certain aspects of advanced physics) may thus be only a foretaste of a completely new form of intellectual endeavor, one that will lie not only outside physics but will not even be describable as scientific. . . ."

 In our present mechanistic conception of the world, we believe that the only mode of inquiry into our realities is the rational mode—subject-object distancing. But we have come to recognize other levels of inquiry into reality—what I like to call "somatic inquiry"—which includes subject-object distancing but goes beyond into the more fundamental inquiries initiated by the body through the meaning-feeling process. The nonrational levels of inquiry are well described by Jantsch and by Berman (in *Coming to Our Senses* and *The Reenchantment of the World)*. Quantum mechanics, quantum logic, systems theory, and organicism suggest the radical implications that include these new, nonclassical inquiries into reality.

One of the startling implications from quantum mechanics is that subject-object distancing, the rational-scientific view, is no longer a completely adequate probe into reality. The most vocal person I have found on this point is physicist John Wheeler of Princeton, who is fascinated by our participation in bringing about the reality of the electron through our measurements. It seems we are never simply the person on the shore; we are also in the river at the same time.

Following the discoveries of quantum mechanics and nonlocality, the notions of the whole, subjectivity, and participation have taken on fresh meaning. The Age of Enlightenment—of reason—is receding. We see ourselves now as deeply involved participants in a system, with a capacity to organize and prioritize our experience. Subjectivity, feeling, and commitment to experience are ascendant. As a result, honesty and responsibility have become indispensable characteristics of well-being in the quantum age. We look for wisdom rather than rationality.

Bateson remarked: "[T]he nonalcoholic world has many lessons which it might learn from the epistemology of systems theory and the ways of AA." We shall confirm that in later chapters.

3

The Whole and the Part

A fourth new feature of quantum mechanics, which was against
mechanism, was that the whole organizes the parts, even in ordinary
matter. One can see it doing so in living matter, in organisms, where
the state of the whole organizes the various parts in the organism.

—Physicist David Bohm
Post Modern Science and a Post Modern World

Classical science starts with the assumption that reality
is made up of separate parts—that taken all together, separate parts
constitute reality. Since the very beginning, classical science has concerned
itself with the relationships among these separate parts. Now we can no
longer look at ultimate reality from the point of view of the existence of
separate parts.

David Bohm explains that quantum physics is based upon a perception
of a new order. Bohm says, "We must turn physics around. Instead of
starting with parts and showing how they work together (the Cartesian
order), we start with the whole."

Working from quantum mechanics and nonlocal causality, Bohm asserts
that the universe and everything in it is an *unbroken wholeness*. If information
is moving faster than light (nonlocality), then the universe must be an
unbroken whole. It turns out, then, that our observations about events on
earth must be based on a new way of looking. In addition to looking at parts
and what links them together, we must look at wholes and how the whole
gives meaning to the parts. The implications for alcoholism research are
clear. No one currently considers the alcoholic as a whole informing its

parts; there is no consideration of the nature of the subject (no controlling image) except that of the alcoholic as the recipient of multiple causalities.

Quantum mechanics, with nonlocal causality, has "irreparably smashed Newton's clockwork," says physicist Herbert in *Quantum Reality*. "We are now certain that the world is not a deterministic mechanism. But what the world is, we cannot truly say. The search for quantum reality is a search for a single image that does justice to our knowledge of how the world actually works."

In the search for the image of how the world works, physicist Capra says that several paradigm shifts have been established in scientific inquiry into reality. "The first criterion of new paradigm science is the shift from the parts to the whole. . . . Ultimately there are no parts at all. What we call a part is merely a pattern in the web of relationships."

The enigma of alcoholism's origins can be understood if we work from this key notion of the whole and the part. Before we go any farther in building upon this idea, however, I am going to assume that most of us need a short refresher course in the notion of the whole. Everyone remembers the dictum that the whole is greater than the sum of the parts. Consider some simple examples of the significance of the whole. One of the most well known is the demonstration of the relations between tones and melodies. Single tones, or notes, identical in isolation, may be functionally different within distinct melodic wholes. The kid next door practicing the scale on his trumpet can drive us nuts, but if he blows the same notes *arranged differently* in the high school band, we applaud. The tones are heard in a relationship, a pattern, and mean something entirely different to the listener than they did in the scale. In the same vein, the young woman upstairs gets on our nerves playing the same extended note on her cello. But if that same note is the lingering final note in a melodic arrangement, we are thrilled. To have meaning, the note must be included in an arrangement of notes.

A different picture of wholes is presented by the concerted activity of an ant colony. No single ant, a whole organism in itself, is responsible for the design that emerges from the activity of the collection of ants. The secret of the purposeful activity of the whole colony cannot be learned by taking the individual ants apart and examining their nervous systems.

Still another picture of the whole is the human being. The human is made up of many individual parts, or organs, each with its own organic activity, but they are meaningless unless included in a greater whole. In themselves none of these parts has any features of the whole, so that adding up, or simply connecting these parts cannot deliver the features of the whole. We cannot, for example, account for mathematical thought by adding up the features of blood, flesh, and bone. And yet when blood, flesh, and bone are arranged in a certain way, mathematical thinking is a feature of the whole collection. There is nothing in the carbon, nitrogen, and oxygen out of which an architect is made that can account for the shopping center she just designed. Science does not understand how a beautiful design emerges from the furious firing of billions of neurons in the architect's brain. (Sir Arthur Stanley Eddington, the physicist, once remarked that we will never find the square root of a sonnet.)

A vivid example of the abstract principle of organization in the human being occurs in the case of a burn on my body. A certain number of atoms, molecules, and cells must become scar tissue in the healing process. I haven't the slightest idea how to direct that process in my own body, how to pick the cells, or how many cells to pick for the job—and no individual cell directs itself into the process of becoming scar tissue. An abstract principle of organization carries out the task, neither overdoing it, nor failing to do it economically and satisfactorily. As Capra points out, the healing process is beyond the ken of medical science.

Because it is beyond the measuring techniques known to science, the fascinating implications of the whole have been ignored, but quantum theory and nonlocal causality have made study of the nature of the whole the most fruitful inquiry into our reality. Considering the human individual as a whole provides the most productive inquiry into the nature of alcoholism.

Biologist Paul Weiss says, "[T]here is no phenomenon in a living system that is not molecular, but there is none that is only molecular either." Sidney Brenner says, "I think in the next twenty-five years we are going to have to teach biologists another language." Brenner goes on to say that what we have to aim at now "is the fundamental problem of the theory of elaborate systems. . . . We may need to get beyond the clock mechanisms."

An article in the October 13, 1992 "Science Times" section of the *New York Times* says:

"The new (biomolecular) research also points to the pitfalls of reductionism, the scientific method that depends on analyzing nature by reducing it to its simplest components," said Dr. James Shapiro. . . . Shapiro,

a molecular biologist says, "But we are entering a period in which, in some cases, we have come to the limit of that approach. *We need to understand more about how the properties of wholes arise"*
    I wish Dr. Shapiro were investigating alcoholism! This type of thinking is precisely what is missing in alcoholism research.

THE SELF-ORGANIZING WHOLE

    Beginning in the 1960s, the human being came to be regarded as a self-organizing whole. First of all, the human organism is not dependent upon its environment for its characteristic integrity. Because it is a whole, the human is autonomous. It has self-organizing capacities that are innate—not determined by external causes, nor explainable by the properties of its parts.
    The idea that the human organism is self-organizing was not meaningful to those earliest scientists describing organisms. Their descriptions were reductive. Organisms were defined as unitary entities that ingested, transformed, and excreted matter. Their organizing principle, like life itself, was not of interest. But since the advent of modern physics we are more comfortable now in talking about different levels of organisms. Now we can use both material and *abstract* descriptions of organisms. We can discuss their abstract organizing principles. Some of the awkwardness in saying the features of a whole are greater than the sum of the parts, is gone.
    The human organism is *self-healing*. The infinite complexities of spontaneous organization that meet the challenge of a wound are beyond our comprehension. The information and decisions that flow at the cellular level when a wound occurs are thoroughly mysterious.
    The human organism is also *self-renewing*. It is continuously recycling its components while at the same time maintaining the integrity of the overall structure. When I chance upon someone I know at the ballpark after several years of not seeing him, I recognize him immediately even though there is hardly a single cell left of the person I knew years ago.
    The human organism is also *self-transcending*. In the processes of learning, development, and evolution, the human organism is ever capable of being more than it was an instant before.
    By pointing out these autonomous characteristics of the organism we are not implying in the least that it is independent of its environment. Quantum mechanics and nonlocal causality imply instead that the organism is a whole in a vast interdependent web of wholes. Bateson and others have insisted

that organisms cannot be understood in isolation. Neither organism nor environment means anything without the other.

In the next chapter I examine the idea of organism-in-environment. This is the controlling image that I believe can lead to a synthesis of our viewpoints about the origin of alcoholism. Just what is the relationship between the self-organizing, self-renewing, self-healing, self-transcending organism and its indispensable environment?

4

The Organism-in-Environment

We do not live in an order of control, but rather in an order of complexity.

—Modern physicists

The basic principle we establish is that the human organism behaves in an environment, not *because* of an environment. This notion is crucial in grasping the essence of addiction. Perspectives on organism-in-environment are offered in Capra's *Turning Point*, and most elaborately in *Not in Our Genes*, by Lewontin, Rose, and Kamin— respectively an evolutionary geneticist at Harvard, a neurobiologist at the Open University in England, and a psychologist at Princeton.

In their views, we do not see an *order of control* between environment and organism, such as in the Cartesian-Newtonian view, but rather an *organization of overall complexity*. (Later we will compare this basic view to the so-called multifactorial view of alcoholism.) Capra says, "The unfolding of complexity arises not from adaptations of organisms to a given environment, but rather from the co-evolution of organism and environment at all system levels."

With this view, alcoholism does not result from an interaction between predisposition and environment, as if the environment were triggering the predisposition. While the prevailing views about alcoholism are based on the Cartesian-Newtonian notion that the alcoholic is reacting within an order of control, there is no order of control at work in alcoholism. The alcoholic is *responding* within an organization of overall complexity, not *reacting* within an order of control. It is our task in this book to uncover the individual's mechanisms of response.

(The premise of this book is that alcoholism—all addiction—is a matter
of choice; we are examining the difference between reacting and responding.)

DIALECTICAL BIOLOGY

Lewontin, Rose, and Kamin (LRK) offer the view of the organism in
its environment that is compatible with the physicists' views of wholeness
and interdependence. The crucial point developed by LRK is the upgrading
of the notion of interaction. In moving away from the mechanical, linear
determinism of the Cartesian-Newtonian world, some scientists have been
picking up on the notion of interactionism between the organism and its
environment. In moving away from pure biological (nature) and cultural
(nurture) determinism of human behavior, interactionism has beckoned to
quite a few scientists. LRK: "According to this view (interactionism) it is
neither the genes nor the environment that determines an organism, but a
unique interaction between them. Interactionism is the beginning of
wisdom." The *beginning* of wisdom.

At first, interactionism would seem to be the correct alternative to
biological and cultural determinism, but with our new views from quantum
mechanics and evolution, we cannot accept interactionism as it is proposed.
It is still tinged with the mechanistic view of the world. It takes the older
view from evolution, which is that *environment makes the organism* , while
forgetting that organism *also* makes environment. Interactionism draws "a
clean line" between organism and environment, retaining a kind of
Newtonian mechanistic force between them. We now know, however,
that the organism is an active participant in an inseparable whole, a complex
web of interdependencies. Interactionism cannot explain the dynamics
between the organism and the whole in which it participates.

Instead of interactionism, what we have is a *dialectic.* The idea of dialectics
is most compatible with our new worldviews from physics and evolution.
LRK make the case that the organism is not a separate, isolable entity
completely autonomous in its environment. Instead they see the organism
as a *respondent in a dialectical relationship* that is determined *neither by genes nor
environment,* but by an *interpenetration* of organism and environment.

> Against this (biological determinism) we counterpose a view not of
> organism and environment insulated from one another or
> unidirectionally affected, but of a constant and active interpenetra-
> tion of the organism with its environment. Organisms do not

merely receive a given environment, but actively seek alternatives or change what they find.

An analogy with an all-night poker game goes a long way in helping us picture organic dialectics. A poker game is not created by *interacting* parts or players. The game is created by a *dialectic* among the players. One player's move does not *determine* another player's move, although it does set the conditions and limitations for everyone else's *response*.

The human organism has been dealt a hand that it must play. The trouble with books on alcoholism is that they are so busy analyzing the hand we have been dealt that they neglect the most important part of the game—how we play it. Give ten poker players the same lousy hand and some will win with it, some will lose. We must ask ourselves, why did some win and why did some lose—all playing a bad hand? No point in looking at the hands they were dealt—they all had poor hands. Experts say that alcoholism is a matter of a lousy hand; if enough conditions build up—family trouble, work trouble, genetic predisposition—they have a cumulative effect and make the individual drink alcoholically. Not so. Alcoholism can result under these conditions but only if the hand is played badly.

The Card Game

Let's get a little closer to the viewpoint of dialectical biology, the viewpoint that explains the so-called interaction between the organism and its environment. As dialectical biologists say, we live in a causal universe, but our actions are not determined by sets and subsets of causes within the overall determination of organic life. Let's make believe that life in environment is a card game. Let's assume that everyone at the table likes the game and wants to participate. If there is to be a game, a common experience that all want, every player must strive against the other players. It appears as a striving against and it is—but more deeply it is actually cooperation. If someone were not trying his best to beat me, I would be upset. He would not be cooperating in making the game.

None of the moves of the players in the game is determined, but they are limited (1) by the rules of the game, (2) by the hands dealt, and (3) by the decisions made by others in the game. If the moves of each player were *determined* by all these conditions, then obviously there could be no game. Unfortunately, the prevailing views on alcoholism do not understand the choice of the alcoholic in this way. We are organisms in a dialectic with our environment, operating under biological rules, dealing with external circumstances. But we do not react; we *respond* in the dialectic.

The response the human organism makes is made at the level of mind, which brings up again one of the major points of inquiry about our humanity. What is the relationship of the body and the mind? Are they really one and same thing? Or are they separate entities?

5

The Mind-Body Question

Mind and body are not two components of a duality but two entirely different concepts drawn from different levels in a hierarchy of description. . . . Many of the old problems of a dualism fall away once it is appreciated that abstract, high level concepts can be equally as real as the low level structures that support them.

—Physicist Paul Davies

Let's continue with our examination of the whole. Remember that wholes are made up of particles, atoms, molecules; there are no differences between these elements in me and in a rock. What makes the difference is the pattern of *organization*. When we tackle this aspect of the whole we approach one of the most controversial issues about human life. The argument boils down to the mind-body question—still a burr under the saddle for many authors and experts. It comes up in free will, in intentionality, in propositional language, and so on. It is a most prominent question in our inquiry into the nature of alcoholism. Is alcoholism located at the level of brain or mind?

Descartes, the designer of the great machine viewpoint, had no idea about organic wholes organized by abstract principles. He solved the mind-body problem by calling for a strict dualism between mind and body. Many, if not most, experts today still balk at the suggestion that mind is anything other than as-yet-unknown complexities of the neurochemical activity of the brain. Mind is what biologists call an emergent feature of the material brain—or else it is a function of the material brain. Somehow or other, they believe, the mind must be explained materially. Today, however, thanks to modern physics, we can approach the problem with new concepts.

A grasp of the mind-brain controversy is important to an understanding of alcoholism. Later in the book I will describe alcoholism at the *level* of mind rather than brain, so I will spend some time now on this particular inquiry into the characteristics of the human whole.

LEVEL CONFUSION

The term *level confusion*, first described for me by the physicist Paul Davies, may well be the most helpful description of the puzzle about mind and brain. It is safe to suggest that level confusion is the single most serious impediment to the scientific discovery of the etiology of alcoholism. What do we mean by level confusion? Its preeminent manifestation in alcoholism studies is the dogged belief that neuroscience and genetic predispositions must eventually explain alcoholism—but alcoholism cannot be explained at the physiological level of human organization.

The prevailing views insist that activities of the brain can be reduced to electrochemical neurotransmitters, and the firing of billions of neurons. But Richard M. Restak, in his book *The Brain* (1984), puts the question very simply: "Does that mean the music I hear at the symphony is *nothing more than* the activity of certain neurons? . . . A symphony isn't a configuration of neurons; it exists in its own right and cannot be *explained* or *equated* with brain activity." And, Restak adds, if a brain scan were taken while he was listening to the symphony, the scan would not document "anything other than my-brain-responding-to-a-concert." A scan will not tell us anything about the symphony, or whether it is a sonata or a concerto.

Even though there is no electrochemical or neurological level on which the symphony exists, we cannot deny we experienced the symphony in all its glorious complexities of musical patterns. This phenomenon introduces us to the idea of *levels of description*. (Note that when we speak of levels of description we are not saying what a thing *is*; we are only describing it. Since quantum mechanics, scientists have learned to live with approximate, descriptive knowledge.) Certainly it would appear that the experience of the symphony exists at some level of reality other than the physiological, and it surely needs to be described, not ignored. The shocking concepts of quantum theory give some comfort here. Davies says quantum mechanics "provides the most convincing scientific evidence that consciousness plays an essential role in the nature of physical reality." In other words, the highly abstract world of mind, so ignored by behaviorists and mechanists, can now be regarded as the distinguishing characteristic of human organization.

Particular stress on this question of mind and brain is necessary because it is going to be hard, almost impossible, to convince the vast majority of experts working on the problem of alcoholism that addictions originate at the species-specific level of human organization—the level of mind. As Kuhn has pointed out, new ideas sometimes take a generation before they are accepted by those in given scientific communities. My concern is that this new model of addiction take hold within a reasonable period of time. We are spending enormous sums of money on research based on the old paradigms. For example, the Seventh Special Report to the United States Congress on Alcoholism and Health (1990) by the Secretary of Health and Human Resources forecasts that the most significant progress will be made in neuroscience and genetic research. This effort is misguided to the degree that it believes the nature of alcoholism can be described at the physiological levels of human organization.

The national consciousness must be raised about the nature of addiction. We have to snap out of our hypnotic preoccupation with Cartesian mechanics. Distinguishing correctly between mind and brain is a good place to start.

To begin with, Cartesian dualism is not necessary; brain and mind do not inhabit separate worlds. Many authors insist that mental experiences have as their only reality the activities of the brain, that they are purely material. They correctly reject a dualism of mind and brain, but the problem with the "brain only" position is that it is blind to levels of description. Instead of a brain-only description, we can describe mind as an extension of material reality into a nonmaterial reality. Mind and brain are both aspects of a whole activity arising out of a common quantum ground. (The point at which the quantum wave collapses into material reality remains one of the major questions in quantum theory.) The aspect of brain does not have the features of mental events, and cannot account for mental events. Mental events are accounted for by the features of the whole.

In our own organisms, therefore, the notion of formative capacities is not unreasonable. These formative capacities emerge from brain levels; they are mind. Often people say this sounds like mysticism, but it is, on the contrary, hardheaded reality. It will be helpful to listen to physics in this regard. Physicist Paul Davies says:

> Mind and body are not two components of a duality but two entirely different concepts drawn from different levels in a hierarchy of

description. . . . Many of the old problems of a dualism fall away once it is appreciated that abstract, high level concepts can be equally as real as the low level structures that support them.

We are already familiar with the reality of the abstract. F. David Peat, another physicist, says:

> Heisenberg (the Uncertainty Principle) argued that ultimate reality is to be found not in electrons, mesons, and protons, but in something that lies beyond them, in abstract symmetries that manifest themselves in the material world and could be taken as the scientific descendants of Plato's ideal forms.

Physicist David Bohm (*Wholeness and the Implicate Order*) maintains that intelligence is an unconditioned act of perception (a notion that we will amplify when we take up feeling and perception later on). Bohm says:

> If intelligence is to be an unconditioned act of perception, its ground cannot be in structures such as cells, molecules, atoms, elementary particles, etc. . . . So we see that the ground of intelligence must be in the undetermined unknown flux. Intelligence is thus not deducible or explainable on the basis of any branch of knowledge (e.g., physics or biology). Its order is deeper and more inward than any knowable order that could describe it.

Several other writers have picked up on aspects of this notion. Zohar (*The Quantum Self*) believes that thoughts spring from a different order of being, regarding them as collapsed wave functions of quantum levels of reality. Zohar's quantum levels and Bohm's undetermined flux would both seem to be part of the unknowable level of quantum reality.

In ideas such as these about thought and intelligence we see a clear-cut regard for orders or levels in the human whole. For these scientists it has become imperative that a level other than the physical be recognized in human organization. We must hope that eventually alcoholism research will become oriented to these new models of human activity.

Physicist (and Nobel laureate) Eugene Wigner, in his essay "Remarks on the Mind-Body Question," points out that most physical scientists have returned to the recognition that thought—meaning the mind—is primary. Wigner says, "It was not possible to formulate the laws of quantum mechanics in a fully consistent way without reference to the consciousness." Exploring Wigner's view, Harold J. Morowitz ("Rediscovering the Mind," *Psychology Today*, August 1990) sums up the levels in the concept of mind:

First, the human mind, including consciousness and reflective thought, can be explained by activities of the central nervous system, which, in turn, can be reduced to the biological structure and function of that physiological system. Second, biological phenomena at all levels can be totally understood in terms of atomic physics, that is, through the action and interaction of the component atoms of carbon, nitrogen, oxygen, and so forth. Third and last, atomic physics, which is now understood most fully by means of quantum mechanics, must be formulated with the mind as a primitive component of the system.

Here we have a circle, beginning and ending with mind. Morowitz believes that "the closing of this circle provides the best possible approach for psychological theorists."

When Morowitz talks of the mind as a primitive component of the whole system, he is referring to the most remarkable feature of quantum mechanics—the role of the mind in choosing the reality of the atom. As we have seen, in the Copenhagen interpretation of the wave/particle paradox, the electron is not real; it is brought to reality as either a wave or a particle by the observer's choice. Thus we can understand the circle Morowitz talks about. Mind itself springs from an indeterminate level, supported by physical systems in whose reality mind plays a role!

My purpose here is not to introduce Zeno-like paradoxes, but to show the intense interest in the mind–body question and the recognition of the level of mind.

Once we have accepted the unity of body and mind—real and abstract aspects—we are prepared to talk about aspects and attributes of human activity in terms of level descriptions. We will describe the brain and its activities at the level of physical description. We will describe the mind and its activities at the level of organization of the whole. Keep in mind that alcoholism research is bogged down in level confusion, an attempt to describe the attributes of mind at the physiological level.

In speaking of wholes we use two approaches: We can speak of the "parts" of wholes, and we speak of the "levels of organization." Under Cartesian rules we could formerly speak only of parts. Now, when we speak of the activity or behavior of the whole—its specific behavior—we can no longer look only at parts. *The activity of the whole must be described instead at the appropriate level of organization—the level that informs the activity of the parts.*

We are setting the groundwork here for our contention that alcoholism cannot be described at the neurological level of description. No specifically human behavior can be described at the neurological level. Designing a building, arranging flowers, writing a novel, planning a vacation, researching a problem—all of these activities must be described at two levels. First, there is the complex firing of millions of neurons, and second, there are the forms, symbols, feelings, and ideas that give rise to and inform the physical activity of the neurons. The level of mind actually gives rise to and emerges from the level of brain activity. Endocrinologist Deepak Chopra, in his book *Quantum Healing,* says that a thought, emerging out of the quantum potential, actually creates the neuropeptides that give it physical expression.

Richard Restak (*The Brain*) relates the well-known story about the neurosurgeon Wilder Penfield, who started out believing that "brain studies if properly conducted would lead inevitably to an understanding of the mind." Restak tells this story about Penfield:

> Two years before his death at age eighty-four, neurosurgeon Wilder Penfield was writing his final book, *The Mystery of the Mind.* During moments away from his desk, Penfield continued to ponder the theme of his book: the relationship of mind, brain, and science. One weekend while at his farm outside of Montreal, Penfield took up a small basket containing old cans of house paint. Proceeding to the slope of a nearby hill, he began painting on a huge rock. On one side he painted a Greek word for "spirit" along with a solid line connect-ing it to an Aesculapian torch, which represented science. The line continued around the rock to the other side, where he drew an outline of a human head with a brain drawn inside, which con-tained, at its center, a question mark. At this point, Penfield was satisfied: brain studies, if properly conducted, would lead inevitably to an understanding of the mind.

> But as Penfied progressed, he became less certain that the study of the brain, a field in which he had done pioneering work earlier in his career, would ever lead to an understanding of the mind. Finally, six months before he died, he reached a conclusion.

> Donning six sweaters to protect himself from the harsh Canadian wind, Penfield returned to the rock and with shaking hands con-verted the solid line connecting the spirit and brain into an inter-rupted one. This alteration expressed, in a form for all to see, Penfield's doubts that an understanding of the brain would ever lead to an explanation of the mind.

I would like to think that if Penfield had spent some leisure hours with physicists like David Bohm, F. David Peat, Fritjof Capra, or Paul Davies, he might have been satisfied by their encounter with levels of description, which allow for both the material and abstract characteristics implied in quantum mechanics. Peat says, "It should therefore be clear that while mind does in fact contain certain mechanical orders of operation, these all emerge out of a much deeper non-mechanical ground. The order of mind is therefore particularly subtle and can never be reduced to that of a machine." Peat is reflecting the thought of Heisenberg (the Uncertainty Principle) who believed that ultimate matter was not matter at all, but fields of potential, forms, and symmetries.

In studying the whole, physics underlies the need for two levels of description. Both levels are real—one physical, one abstract. (For those who are uncomfortable with the notion of an abstract reality, you are not alone. Quantum physicists had to realize that language is not possible for the phenomenon they encountered. The problem is not *in* the language; the problem *is* the language. Actually, only mathematical language is suitable for quantum reality. Quantum mechanics rules out objectivity, and either/ or propositions of classical logic.)

Physicist Davies points out:

> Life is a holistic concept, the reductionistic perspective (neuroscience) revealing only inanimate atoms within us. Similarly mind is a holistic concept, at the next level of description. *We can no more understand mind by reference to brain cells than we can understand cells by reference to their atomic constituents.* " (my emphasis)

We can begin to understand the futility of attempting to describe alcoholism by relentlessly probing the brain for the answers to human behavior. Davies goes on to say:

> The brain consists of billions of neurons, buzzing away, oblivious of the overall plan. This is the physical, mechanical world of electrochemical hardware. On the other hand we have thoughts, feelings, emotions, volitions, and so on. This higher level, holistic, *mental* world is equally oblivious of the brain cells; we can happily think while being totally unaware of any help from our neurons.

Hofstadter presents a vivid example of neural-mental complementarity:

> Say you are having a hard time making up your mind whether to order a cheeseburger or a pineapple cheeseburger. Does this imply that your neurons are also balking, having difficulty deciding whether or not to fire? Of course not. Your hamburger confusion is a high-level state which fully depends upon the efficient firing of thousands of neurons in very organized ways.

In other words, your confusion cannot be described at the neurological level. There is no confusion among the firing neurons; your confusion must be described at the abstract level of mind.

It should be clear that in any attempt to describe the nature of alcoholism—the behavior of a whole—both types of description must be recognized. There is the neurological level of the brain and the organizing level of mind. Interestingly enough, we have a wonderful example of a scientist recognizing these different descriptions, but without realizing he is doing so. Mark Gold, a biopsychiatrist, states in his book, *The Good News About Drugs and Alcohol,* "Any medical drug treatment program in 1991 that fails to include a Twelve Step strategy is not a serious program and simply will not work. Period."

SPECIES-SPECIFIC BEHAVIOR

Once we have begun to understand the notion of levels of description for organic wholes, we are in a position to describe what we call the whole's species-specific behavior, or characteristics. The species-specific characteristics of any organism are those attributes or features of the organism's behavior that clearly distinguish it from other organisms. Species-specific characteristics originate at the organizing level of the whole, which in the case of humans would be the mind. We will describe the species-specific characteristics of the human being in the chapters ahead.

We have taken time with the notion of the whole in order to get at the idea of levels of description (mind and body) and species-specific behavior. Alcoholism is species-specific behavior. No other organism besides the human can be an alcoholic. Not understanding this has been a cardinal mistake in alcoholism research. Beginning about the 1960s in this country, laboratory experiments on specially bred animals got under way. This was at the time when scientific attention, probably given a boost by Jellinek's work on the disease concept of alcoholism, was gathering momentum. There are two things to be said about laboratory experiments on animals and alcoholism. First, they are quite helpful in revealing the physical mechanisms that accompany alcoholic behavior. Second, they are no help whatever in revealing or describing the nature of alcoholism.

Laboratory studies are based on Cartesian notions of cause and effect; they yield mechanistic information. They do not include human choice. Furthermore, when applied to human beings, these studies suffer from level confusion. As we shall see later, other animals do not share our species-specific characteristics. Recently a Harvard scientist told me, "We have alcoholic rats and dogs." I responded, "Does that mean they wake up in the morning, study themselves in the mirror, apologize to their wives, go to the doctor, and swear they will never do that again?"

SUMMING UP

We started out with a review of the old worldview we inherited from Cartesian-Newtonian mechanics-mathematics. We saw that this view has been superseded by quantum mechanics, nonlocality, and sytems theory. Out of this revolution has come a new view of wholes and parts, in which the world is viewed as a vast and incomprehensible web of interdependencies. The objective view of reality is no longer absolute. The Copenhagen interpretation (the most popular) view of quantum mechanics tells us that ultimate matter is not real in view of the fact that the particular reality of the atom is chosen by the observer. The real nature of reality is an unknown, but can be described as fields of potential. Classical logic fails us in describing this reality in ordinary language. Only mathematical language is adequate.

The study of human activity must now be looked at as the activity of a whole in its environment. We observe every day that certain arrangements of the same atoms and molecules result in wholes. There appear to be principles of organization, or patterns, as the physicists say, that make collections of atoms and molecules able to behave at different levels of complexity. What is it that makes my collection of atoms and molecules behave differently from the same atoms that make up a rock or a lizard?

Human activity can no longer be studied only as the activity of its parts, or as the result of external, mechanical causes. We saw instead that human activity is not an interaction with the environment; it is a dialectic. Then we took a close look at the mind-body question. We can no longer describe the activities of the whole at the physiomechanical level of body. We must describe the activities of mind. We saw that mind is actually at the organizing level of the whole, and as such reveals the species-specific characteristics of the organism. The characteristics of mind will differentiate the human from other species.

Alcoholism must be described at the species-specific level of the human, that is, at the level of mind.

We can proceed now to the next fundamental question. How does this self-organizing whole conduct its negotiations in the dialectic with the environment? In other words, what motivates us in the great card game of life?

PART TWO:

HUMAN MOTIVATION

6

What Causes Alcoholism?

In one of his songs, country-western singer Hank Williams, Jr., sings that all his friends keep asking him, "Hank, why do you drink?" and Williams answers, "I'm just carrying on an ol' family tradition." Indeed he was, but it's not so simple as when it comes to self-destructive drinking. The books in the self-help aisles and the papers written in the universities have offered many reasons why we drink self-destructively, but nobody's hit on the correct answer.

In Part One of this book I spoke of human *organization*. In Part Two we are going to discuss human *motivation*. Why do we act, why do we make decisions? In answering, let's stick to the controlling image of the human as an organism-in-environment. So the question is, What motivates the human organism-in-environment to take action, to make decisions?

To begin with, we must clear up the confusion about causality in alcoholism. Every book I have read about alcoholism has a chapter headed, "The Causes of Alcoholism" or "Causality in Alcoholism." Again, when we ask, What causes alcoholism? we are not asking the right question. The appropriate question about alcoholism or any human behavior is not what causes it, but why people do it.

The conventions about causality that prevail in alcoholism studies emerge directly from the fundamental worldview of Descartes and Newton, the rationalism of the Enlightenment, the psychological mechanics of Freud in psychoanalysis, the behaviorism of Watson and Skinner, the mechanics of modern medicine, and the biological and cultural determinism of the biogeneticists.

As ultimate explanations of the behavior of the organic whole, however, these views are unacceptable. Cartesian-Newtonian mechanics, the basis for modern conventions about causality, has yielded to the richer implications of quantum mechanics and nonlocality. So let's try to make clear the notion of cause in the behavior of a self-organizing whole in an environment.

Keep in mind that species-specific human behavior, even in a causal environment, is *not* determined behavior. We saw something of this in the analogy of the poker player. The causes of an alcoholic's drinking do not determine that he drink. He is never billiard ball B reacting to billiard ball A. The causes of an alcoholic's drinking, however, are true causes. They cause change or movement; they may limit his environment. They cause movement in the dialectic, *but the change or movement is always made by the alcoholic, not by the cause!* If you put a bottle of whiskey in front of an alcoholic, you cause him to act—but *not* to drink. He must say yes or no.

Let's put that another way: the causes of an alcoholic's drinking determine the conditions to which he must respond (like the poker player), but they do not determine the response. Even if his biology provides extraordinary rewards or pleasures in drinking, or if powerful multifactorial conditions exist, these causal conditions do not determine the response. Thus we can say that if the conditions do not determine the response, then the alcoholic *chooses* to drink under causal conditions. This is the correct understanding of cause in alcoholism—and in all addiction.

Clearly, however, certain addicts are overwhelmed by conditions; they appear to have no choice whatever. True, but the inquiry must be framed this way: *Why have the individual's response mechanisms failed so that as a result he is overwhelmed?* We must keep our eye on *response*, not on determination.

In subsequent chapters we will explore the nature of human choice. The alcoholic's choice to drink is not the choice between vanilla and chocolate. It is the choice between life and death.

HUMAN MOTIVATION

Armed with the appropriate understanding of causality in specific human behavior, we can look at what it is that motivates the human to act. (Specifically human action is not eating, or going to bed, or scratching our heads.) The question to be asked is, How does the human being conduct himself or herself in the dialectic? This is the age-old question of human motivation, dressed up in twenty-first century language.

First of all, every organism has to *know* its environment. As Kenneth Boulding remarks, "even the amoeba has to *know.*" At the basic level of organismic life, the organism must ingest, metabolize, and excrete other matter. To do this, it must know the objects around it. At our level of organismic life, our knowledge is much more complex; it transcends sensory data and stimuli. We have a sense of ourselves responding rather then reacting.

PERCEPTION

We know our environment through perception. Perception generally refers to information received through the eyes, but it can also refer to sounds, smells, and touch. Alcoholism is located at the level of the individual's perceptions. Nothing forces the human to act in its species-specific modes of behavior. It is the *meanings* we experience in perception that govern our behavior. *This is the cardinal principle of human motivation.*

When we describe what happens at the perceiving level of human organization we are describing the conditions under which alcoholism occurs. To be understood, alcoholism must be discussed at this level.

(You may have noted by now that I use the term *describe* quite a bit, instead of define or analyze. The reason for that goes back to the notion of the whole and the part. You recall Capra saying that in a whole there are ultimately no parts at all: "What we call a part is merely a pattern in a web of relationships." Because we are talking about the activities of a whole, we cannot offer a mechanical analysis of parts. We can only describe aspects of the behavior of the whole. Thus we saw physicists referring to levels of description when talking about the mind-body question. Further, since quantum mechanics, we no longer speak of objective truth, but rather of approximations.)

Debated theories about perception have been proliferating and intensifying among intellectuals during the past forty years. We can break the dispute down into two camps—those putting emphasis on the *outside*, and those putting emphasis on the *inside*. What does that mean?

To know something outside myself, I have to represent the outside to my own inside. I have the outside in my head in some way or other, so something takes place between me and the outside. If I were a camera, the light rays coming from outside would impinge the photographic plate inside my head. I would go around looking at that photograph in my mind, but that is not what happens. As with a camera, light rays do impinge themselves upon my retina. But unlike the camera, these impressions are transformed into signals that travel along the optic nerve to the brain. No photograph results. A re-presentation does occur, however. I have an image in my head. I can describe what I saw many years later in great detail by recalling the image. The nature of the image cannot be understood as physical in our present understanding of that word. In other words, neuroscience cannot tell from the most sophisticated probing, scanning, and analysis of brain activity whether I have re-presented an image of a cat or a tree—even while scanning my brain at the very same time I am imaging the cat. The precise nature of the image is not known. It can only be described as experienced. We can be comfortable with this because we are now comfortable with the physicists' descriptions of nonmaterial levels in wholes.

The debate between those emphasizing the outside and those emphasizing the inside can be explained thus: One school of thought believes the outside object forms the image upon the brain's receptors, and the second school believes the inside forms the image from the light waves coming from the objects. Since neither position can prove, or demonstrate their side conclusively, strong feelings can divide these camps. I lean toward the inside school, for a number of reasons. The outside school, taken literally, would mean images are imprinted, allowing for no variation in perception among individuals. The outside view leaves unexplained our symbolic capacity, or power of abstraction. It cannot explain the phenomenon of Helen Keller who was deaf, dumb, and blind, but who produced universal concepts from touch alone.

The outside school criticizes the inside school for postulating some sort of mysterious nonmaterial process. This mysterious process takes undifferentiated light and sound waves and makes them into images. The outside school maintains that pre-packaged forms of light and sound are being *received* by the inside. In other words, we have inside our heads receptors, not transformers. The outside position is more congenial to mechanical determinism. The inside position is more congenial to our notions of self-regulating wholes.

A middle road, however, is more interesting in this debate. The old scholastics used to speak of *species impressa* and *species expressa*. They believed there was actual form outside the objects, which impressed itself as form upon the mind. But this *impression* had to be *expressed*. In other words, there was no image resulting from the outside impression until the mind expressed that image to itself. I find this a satisfying compromise between the either/or positions of the inside-outside schools. This view provides a strong role for the formative processes inside the organism, while also recognizing the prepackaged aspects of light and sound waves or outside forms.

The old scholastic view makes sense when applied to the varying levels of organic life. The same light and sound waves impinge upon plants, animals, and humans; their impressions are all identical. They are apprehending the same form. But each organic whole expresses for itself a different image from the same impression—an image tailored for its specific organic needs.

(For an easily accessible description of the inside-outside debate, I recommend *Cognition and Reality,* by Ulric Neisser, professor of Psychology at Cornell University. For a more general overview of both schools, see Howard Gardner, *The Mind's New Science.*)

We can also argue for the inside view, or what I call the expressive view, from the implications of modern physics. Heisenberg believed in abstract, nonmaterial forms as the ultimate reality. We have an innate capacity to abstract forms from material reality and re-present them in nonmaterial form in our heads. This process would seem to take place at the deepest level of our being, perhaps at the point where matter and life merge at the border of quantum reality. As Peat says, when examining a whole field, it is more natural to think of events unfolding out of a continuous background rather than built up in a piecewise fashion out of distinct elements. The relationship between our innate formative processes (abstraction) and the forms of our environment may actually be taking place at quantum levels of activity. I find support for this conjecture in Zohar's *The Quantum Self.*

Because the image is at the core of alcoholic behavior, let's spend more time talking about the new role of the image in twentieth-century thought.

7

The Image

Human behavior depends upon the image.

—Kenneth Boulding

Kenneth Boulding starts his book about the image with a simple description of the images he gets looking out his window over the campus where he is writing. We can all identify with that experience of the image, but what constitutes the image is another story. For the purposes of this book I will concentrate on the common experience of imagery. The image is the operative component in all addiction. The human organism is not motivated toward human acts by internal or external causalities; it is motivated by its images (or its "expressions" to itself) of those causalities.

There was considerable interest in the beginning of this century in the key issues of mental life. I want to go into that briefly. General views about alcoholism pay no attention to the existence of mental life. The image is ignored.

Because of the successes of the physical sciences and mathematical descriptions in the early years of the twentieth century, introspective data purporting to support mental constructs or processes were no longer acceptable. Behavioral psychologists in particular vehemently denied the validity of all internal experience. The behaviorist insisted upon two conditions for valid research: first, public methods of observation that could be quantified and verified; second, the requirement that all research focus strictly on behavior. No attention whatsoever was to be given to mind, thinking, planning, intention; and no value was to be placed on mental constructs like symbols, ideas, images, or schemas. A major principle was that the individual was a passive reactor and reflector of forces in the environment. The individual had no verifiable cognitive apparatus to react intentionally with the environment. The famous names associated with this viewpoint are Pavlov, Thorndike, and Watson. These men believed, as Gardner says, that "just as mechanics had explained the laws of the physical world, mechanistic models built on the reflex arc could explain human activity."

The major breakthrough from this behavioristic (mechanical) viewpoint occurred in 1948 at the Hixon Symposium. At this conference, a psychologist named Lashley told his colleagues that any theory of human activity had to account for complexly organized behaviors, like playing tennis, or playing a musical instrument. The reflex arc, Lashley insisted, could not account for all the complex, simultaneous activity in returning a tennis serve. It became clear to all in attendance that "the behaviorist answer to questions of the human mind was no answer at all."

(Simultaneously with the rejection of behaviorism, considerable discomfort arose with the unverifiable assertions of psychoanalysis about the human mind. Built entirely on metaphorical models, and mixing biological drives with psychological defenses, psychoanalysis did not win the confidence of the emerging cognitive science.)

The key insights attending the birth of cognitive science came from mathematics and computation, particularly in the field of logic. These insights were associated with the electronic computer; the computer seemed to mimic the human mind. The electronic structure of the computer, with its simple logical chains, suggests a connected neuronal logic among brain cells with their simple "on-off" operations of firing and not firing. This neuronal logic was soon seen as not simply stimulated by the senses, and reacting. The nature of brain response suggested the existence of some sort of pre-form or pattern for perceiving and acting. The pattern would be something like the software in a computer. This consideration of an internal, formative capacity is the most crucial departure from behaviorism. *An internal formative process is fundamental to the understanding of alcoholism.*

Clearly, the renaissance of cognition set the stage for a renewed interest in the image—the internal representation of the outside world. We can see the importance of the work of cognitive science for our thesis. Let's listen to Gardner:

> Rather than behavior being consequent upon environmental promptings, central brain processes actually precede and dictate the ways in which an organism carries out complex behavior; or, to put it simply, Lashley concluded that the form precedes and determines specific behavior; rather than being imposed from without, organization emanates from within the organism.

Gardner sums up the first principle of cognitive science this way:

> First of all, there is the belief that, in talking about human cognitive activities, it is necessary to speak about mental representations and to posit a level of analysis wholly separate from the biological or neurological, on the one hand, and the sociological or cultural, on the other.

And so we can say that the image, or internal representation, has been restored to its rightful place in the study of human action. The literature is intensive, scholarly, and growing. Controversy, of course, continues about the nature or constitutive elements of the image. That has not distracted from the usefulness of the image as the core of human action and behavior.

QUANTUM MECHANICS AND THE IMAGE

It is awe-inspiring to realize that through the images we form, we become participators rather than observers in the universe. As a result of quantum mechanics, Princeton physicist Wheeler is able to say:

> We had this old idea, that there was a universe out there, and here is man, the observer, safely protected from the universe by a six inch slab of plate glass. Now we have to learn from the quantum world that even to observe so minuscule an object as an electron we have to shatter that plate glass; we have to reach in there. . . . So the old word *observer* simply has to be crossed off the books, and we must put in the new word, *participator*. In this way we've come to realize the universe is a participatory universe.

Can we call cognition, then, participation? Is the abstract level of our symbols the level of linkages to the symmetries that comprise the order of the universe? I believe so. What quantum physicists—Heisenberg, Peat, Wheeler, Bohm, Davies, Capra—are writing may seem incomprehensibly sophisticated, but it may turn out to be quite primitive, once we shift from a causative mentality to a participatory mentality. All of this bodes well for mental constructs of image processing and formative symbolic processes. It bodes well, too, for a twenty-first-century understanding of the addictions of the human organism.

Life itself is mysterious, but some of the mystery can be illuminated when we realize the interconnectedness of life and the nonmaterial ways in which we link up through cognitive processes. It is most likely at bottom an acausal world—one of emerging and combining patterns and symmetries all the way up from the atom, to matter, to life, to society—a world unfolding out of a common ground. It is easier to envision our dialectical linkups in a world ultimately of symmetries and patterns than in a world of causal connections—the notion which currently mesmerizes us.

Perhaps it is the correspondence between our innate expressive experience and the outside form that brings us vitality. It is the experience of form that is vitality. We experience form as life, chaos as death. We can say that vitality is the felt participation of wholes within wholes. This participation can be described at a high level of abstraction. Perhaps this was what Rollo May was intimating when he said in the revised edition of *The Meaning of Anxiety* that he hoped that eventually a definition of anxiety would be fashioned at the highest level of abstraction. (See his Preface to the revised edition.)

With the image established as the central activity of the human organism, we are getting closer than ever to the demon in his lair. In the next chapter we take up the most important feature of the self—our feelings.

8

The Feeling Complex

The thesis I hope to substantiate here is that the entire psychological field—including human conception, responsible action, rationality, knowledge—is a vast and branching development of feeling.

—Susanne Langer

By this point in our narrative, some of you are undoubtedly getting curious about where feelings fit into all this. I have left feeling to this point because I wanted first to draw the mechanisms, so to speak, of the process of perception. Cognition, or perception, cannot in reality be separated from feelings. When we describe perception without simultaneously describing feelings we are following the rules of our minds—what the physicists call classical logic—and separating what cannot be separated. However, such logical separating is valid—we are describing aspects of a whole, not real parts of a whole.

It has long been the intellectual tradition to think of ourselves as rational beings first and as feeling beings second. Only recently, in this century, it has been suggested that we are phylogenetically and ontogenetically feeling beings. Phylogenetically means that feelings occurred first in our development in evolution as a species, to be followed by rational characteristics emerging from the feeling capacities. Ontogenetically means that in each individual's personal evolution—growth and development—feelings are also primary, to be followed by an increasing rational capability to organize primordial feelings as we get older.

Susanne Langer, in her classic *Mind: An Essay on Human Feeling,* wrote, "[T]he thesis I hope to substantiate here is that the entire psychological field—including human conception, responsible action, rationality, knowledge—is a vast and branching development of feeling." This was the beginning (along with Cassirer's work) of the focus upon symbol and meaning (feeling) that has gradually replaced the Cartesian-Newtonian focus upon our rationality.

Langer requires a substratum of "pre-conscious processes" that are not always felt, but do supply a "feeling-tone" that is always with us. Feeling tones, under arousal, build up into specific experiences of feeling. The human organism is at all times anticipating meanings in its perceptions. It is these meanings that arouse the feeling-tone into feelings.

We must not mistake feelings for mere signals. Feelings are the closest experience of the self available to us. We identify with our feelings and with our feeling state—that of well-being, or of discomfort. Nothing is more important to us than our feelings. I define feelings as *the personal experience of meanings in the stream of images in my mind*. These are the experiences from my encounters with my memories and with the images I have of my environment.

Feelings are experiences of wholes. They are not physical entities, they are not products of nerve functions. As Langer suggests, feelings are felt phases of neural activity. She compares feelings to the redness of iron when it is heated. The redness is a phase of the state of iron; the redness is not a thing in itself, nor a product.

It is interesting that philosophers like Langer and Cassirer were reaching conclusions quite congenial to the implications of quantum physics, systems theory, and dialectical biology. It appears as if some sort of universal awareness were unfolding in the twentieth century.

(Keep in mind, again, that these apparently irrelevant discussions always have a direct bearing upon the description we are developing of alcoholism. If feelings are phylogenetically and ontogenetically primary, then they will be so in alcoholism.)

Getting back to what we have said about the image and cognitive science, a careful reader of our brief report on cognitive science may have noticed that cognitive science has us leaping from perception to action. Behavior depends upon the image as Boulding says, but that leaves unanswered the question, *Why does an image make the organism move?* In other words, what about feelings and emotion? Cognitive science has deliberately set aside this question, concentrating upon the functional aspects of mental representations of the outside world. It sees the essential human activity as internally organized reception of information, not mere reaction to stimuli. For the cognitive scientist, action follows upon organized reception of information. Cognitive science, in effect, makes a leap here. It does not attempt to include motivation for behavior, even while recognizing the role of emotion.

Another branch of psychological research, originating about the same time as cognitive science (all of this enterprise came about as a revolution against behaviorism), has been working on the place of affects, or feelings, in human activity. A June 1991 cover article in *U.S. News and World Report,* titled "Where Emotions Come From," seems to have been prompted by the recent death of Silvan Tomkins, who is referred to as the father of affect theory. (Tomkins lists nine primary affects: interest, enjoyment, surprise, distress, fear, anger, shame, dissmell, and disgust. I comment more fully on affect theory in Appendix B.) Tomkins insisted that "affects are the primary motives of man" (1964). He believed the primary affects had been relegated to obscurity because Freud dealt only with the affects of aggression and anxiety. "Freud's failure to appreciate the primacy of the affects over drives made it more difficult to discover the missing affects, and a great deal of psychotherapy today is handicapped by insufficient sensitivity to the full spectrum of the primary affects." (1980). Tomkin's comments are quite up-to-date, but I believe that most psychotherapists, if not all psychiatrists, are working with feelings rather than drives. This is important. Feelings result from apprehension of meanings in relations with others and the environment. Drives are pure mechanisms of biological needs. We know now that as organisms our needs occur as those of a whole—in our case the needs of a symbolic-affective organism negotiating with its environment.

Today, as the *U.S. News and World Report* article points out, "in disciplines ranging from psychology to neuroscience, from semiotics to genetics and anthropology, emotions have moved to center stage. . . . " Throughout the history of intellectual pursuit, feelings have been an ignored stepchild. There is no question that humankind has been preoccupied with the idea of knowledge and reasoning. What has not come into general awareness is that all intellectual pursuit is always at the service of the feelings. Aristotle never would have completed a syllogism if it had not delivered a feeling of satisfaction. Knowledge, exploration, reasoning, and discovery always deliver states of psychic well-being, if not joy—and that is, after all, the goal of all activity.

IMAGE-FEELING

We have arrived at that feature of the human organism where alcoholism is located. Or put another way, we are coming to that description of the specifically human feature wherein we also describe alcoholism. I call this feature "the feeling complex" because it comprises the two aspects of the inseparable: the image and the feelings. All our mental activity is simultaneous with, and monitored by, the pre-conscious processes of feeling-tone and feelings. Not at all separable in reality, the image and the feelings can be discussed separately. It is within the feeling complex that we will find waiting for us the etiology (origins) of alcoholism and addiction. The image-feeling is actually the basic depth-psychological process of the human. Every internal expression made out of a sense impression is felt or experienced simultaneously by the feelings, a phase of central nervous system involvement.

Perhaps we can see now that the most intimate life of the self is the world of the internal image-feelings—the closest experience we can have of self. That is the way we experience our very identity, the way we feel about things. We do not enjoy things; we enjoy our internal experiences of things. Our interior life, the life of the self, our identity, is bound up with the constant collapse and re-creation of symbolic image-feelings. Understanding the feeling complex as the central human activity opens the door at last to the understanding of addiction.

THE FEELING COMPLEX AND ANTICIPATION

We are creeping up, step by step, to a description of the demon alcoholism. This methodical, linear investigation may be frustrating to those who want a quick definition of alcoholism. As I mentioned in the Introduction, however, I found that I understood the affliction of alcoholism by approaching it from a ground-up examination—beginning with subatomic reality, moving right up through atoms and molecules, and organisms, and finally arriving at the "top." There I found the organizing principles that make collections of atoms into behaving organisms.

We reached the top when we spoke of the feeling complex. Now let's take a look at what the feeling complex is all about. How does it fit into the picture of a self-organizing whole in a dialectic with its environment? The next notion we will consider is *anticipation*.

The idea of anticipation is commonplace. Our bodies anticipate food and drink, we are programmed to anticipate sex, we anticipate warmth and cold, we anticipate communication with one another. Anticipation has become an increasingly interesting concept in cognitive science; it seems almost a corollary to the innate expressive process; representation is actually expecting something to represent. William C. Dennett says, "[A]ll brains are, in essence, anticipation machines." *If you anticipate something, then you must be programmed beforehand to expect it.*

It will be indispensable to grasp at this point that preconscious feeling processes are anticipatory. They await expected excitations, expected meanings. Feelings partake of the formative aspects we require of imagery, and they react predictably with imagery. The actual smile of the child is not making me feel happy. I have transformed the impression of a smile into an internal image-feeling of happiness through my expectant formative process. I am programmed to react to the smile of a child. This notion of an innate expectant feeling process is key to our understanding of human motivation. A good example of the innate expectant, or anticipatory process in the organism is the suckling action of the newborn infant. It does not know mother, it does not know milk, it does not know the breast, yet it will purse its mouth and cry for the breast. Now we ask ourselves another crucial question: What does the human organism anticipate? What is the process of image-feeling expecting? That question seems easy to answer for the simplest organisms. Most of them, we would say, anticipate food to ingest, as an energy exchange. As we move up higher in the complexity of organizations, to plants and animals, we see them anticipating sunlight, rain, mating, and so on. We believe they anticipate these things, because their organic life develops appropriately by their reactions to these expectancies.

What about the anticipation of the human organism? It surely anticipates everything that the lower organisms do, but there is a difference. Lower animals appear to anticipate *direct* meanings only; we anticipate not only direct meanings, but *symbolic* meanings as well. A gravestone to a cat has only one meaning; it is an object in its path. A gravestone to a human being has several meanings. The back of a mother walking away means one thing to the family cat, another to the toddler.

When we talk about meanings for an organism, we ask ourselves what is meaningful for the human organism? We can conclude that all meanings for the human organism must be meanings of life and death. Although all the lower organisms anticipate the things they need to survive, only the human organism knows that that is why it needs them—*to survive!* Only the human organism is aware that it is vulnerable to annihilation.

MORTALITY AND THE HUMAN

It is time in our narrative to dwell on the idea of death in human motivation. The idea of death is never introduced into discussions about the definition of humankind, and it is universally left out of psychological structures and processes. This neglect is a significant part of the reason why attempts to describe alcoholism have all failed. We stand mystified at the power of addiction, at the power of denial. We have ignored "the skull grinning in at the banquet."

Only human beings are aware that they are going to die. Oddly enough, this characteristic of humankind is never used to describe humankind, or to define the human organism. Human beings are distinguished by their awareness of death; as organisms they live in an organic tension between survival and annihilation—and they know it. Life cannot even be understood as a concept without simultaneously understanding the meaning of death. Connection, integration, and movement are meaningless terms unless we simultaneously understand separation, disintegration, and stasis.

Rollo May first introduced to the wider public the specter lurking in our backgrounds with his work on anxiety. May defined anxiety (1977) as "the experience of being affirming itself against non-being." Interestingly enough, books and papers about anxiety were almost nonexistent before May; then in the several years following publication of *The Meaning of Anxiety*, May could count more than six thousand books and papers appearing on the subject! A nerve had been touched.

In 1973, Ernest Becker wrote his Pulitzer prize-winning *The Denial of Death,* a book so compelling that the *New York Times* took two consecutive days to review it. Becker convinced a wide audience that death is a mighty influence in everything we do. He inveighed against any form of therapy that sent a client out the door without some understanding that death was the constant shadow in all human discomfort and unease. Becker was an apparent dualist; he saw humankind as angels with their gaze on the starry heavens, but also as terrified animals with feet mired in muck. He reminded us that the smiling teeth of a beautiful woman exist only to grind and mash other organisms into a pulp for the acids in her stomach.

Becker offered a kind of resignation, or acceptance of reality (not unlike Freud's stoicism) as a way out for the neurotic whose problem was that he saw reality for what it is. There was no way Becker could see to integrate death and life into one unitary tension. Robert Jay Lifton, on the other hand, rejects Becker's dualism, and finds in death an animating principle, actually an animating tension in the organism, out of which life proceeds. The human organism's specific activity, therefore, is organized around this life-death polarity. We live by various modes of symbolic immortality or continuity of life. (We will discuss that at greater length later.) Keeping this in mind, we can take another look at Cassirer's definition of the human as *animal symbolicum*. I suggest a fuller definition of the human being is *animal symbolicum moriturum* (on the point of dying, or going to die).

For most of Western history, philosophers have defined humankind by its rational characteristic. Our ability to organize, make consistent, and communicate our mental images was thought to distinguish us from the lower organisms—but that has changed. Ernst Cassirer appears to have been the first to suggest convincingly that the human being should no longer be called *animal rationale*, the rational animal, but should instead be called *animal symbolicum*. He observes that the higher levels of animals have intelligence, and even pragmatic imagination, but we differ from them in what he calls our symbolic imagination. Let's try to explain what that means.

Human beings have the power of abstraction. (From the Latin, *abstrahere*, to draw or drag out of.) We can therefore name things. We draw out from a person the idea of person and that idea becomes a universal for us. The power of our language depends upon the power of abstraction, so that words then become symbols for abstract ideas about things. The animals, it is said, do not have a symbolic language, only an emotive language. We say that the animals do not have the power of abstraction. Therefore, they cannot make symbols. That is why we have the power of propositional language and they have the power only of emotive language. We are fundamentally distinguished from the animals by our *propositional* language. In order to make propositions we must communicate in symbolic language.

Cassirer comes upon his suggestion that we should be called *animal symbolicum* by pointing to our principal achievements. They all depend upon our abstractive-symbolic imagination—our music, our philosophy, our religions, our sense of our history, our art and architecture, our literature and poetry, our sciences, and our cultures.

None of these distinguishing characteristics is primarily rational; all flow instead from primary images and are subsequently organized and made rationally consistent. This observation would seem to affirm that the "inside" process of perception is innately formative (expressive) and not receptive. We cannot picture our creativity and our cultures being stamped upon us by outside forms alone.

It is time to add to Cassirer's proposition and call the human being *animal symbolicum moriturum*. The human being is the only organism that knows it is going to die. This presence of death to humankind has the most profound influence on art, music, and culture. The presence of death is animating; it is responsible for the enjoyment of vitality. On the other hand, the presence of death is also the key to the power of addiction.

9

Death and the Continuity of Life

> Much more elusive is the psychological relationship between the
> phenomenon of death and the flow of life. Psychological theory has
> tended either to neglect death or render it a kind of foreign body, to
> separate death from the general motivation of life.
>
> —Robert Jay Lifton

Two of the most important books written in the twentieth century are *The Denial of Death* by Ernest Becker, a cultural anthropologist, and *The Broken Connection* by Robert Jay Lifton, a psychiatrist. As we shall see, it is Lifton's work that at last enables us to construct a model of alcoholism.

Becker introduced to a wide public the most important factor in human behavior—the organism's brief cycle of coming into existence, replacing itself, and dying. Remarkably, neither Freud nor the psychologists gave our mortality cycle a central place in the study of humankind. The human's life cycle and *our awareness of it* would seem the obvious master model for an in-depth inquiry into human behavior. Other psychological models, including Freud's, are subparadigmatic. I use the life cycle as the principal model for inquiry into the nature of the human dynamic.

Becker's book won the Pulitzer Prize in 1974. The *New York Times* took two days to review the book, and Anatole Broyard, the reviewer, hailed *The Denial of Death* as one of the most significant books of the decade; but I suggest it is a key contribution to twentieth century thought. Becker's book is now comfortably ensconced, some twenty years later, in paperback editions in the bookstores of this country. (Becker is credited with renewing interest in the work of Otto Rank—Freud's first confidant, and the first in Freud's circle to break away from the sexual motif and return the human will to front and center.)

Becker is of immense importance to my project of illuminating the nature of alcoholism and addiction. I was sitting in my office high above Forty-Second Street twenty years ago when a friend called to tell me to go out at lunchtime and pick up a book called *The Denial of Death*. That was one of the most important calls I have ever received. I had been consulting psychiatrists and psychologists for many years. Becker helped me understand for the first time the nature of the anxiety that my counselors were unable to uncover for me. Becker did not displace the therapeutics being administered; he simply gave it all a foundation.

Lifton's book, *The Broken Connection*, also takes mortality as the centerpiece of human motivation. Lifton, however, differs significantly from Becker in his conception of the role of mortality in specific human behavior. Becker regards life and death from the dualistic perspective; he views the human as an organism with feet in the muck and head in the stars. Death is the enemy to be resigned to and compensated for. The life-and-death cycle does not fit into a unitary tension for Becker. For Lifton, on the other hand, life and death cannot be truly separated in the organism's species-specific activity. The organism seeks the continuity of life precisely within the organic life-death cycle. Although the human is going to die, it feels itself part of the on-going life on the planet. Where Becker sees the human as consumed by the terrors of creation, Lifton sees the human as pursuing symbolic enterprises around the continuity of both self and the species. Were it not for the thin veil of repression, says Becker, the human animal would shortly go insane from the impact of the real; for example, without repression (Becker might say) we would see the prized features of a beautiful smile—immaculate, straight, white teeth—as instruments for grinding, mashing, and reducing to pulp other organisms as the first step toward ingestion and eventual defecation. That is the reality, of course. But something more than repression is at work here. Lifton would prefer to see symbolic life equivalent meanings, which the organism innately produces, for instance, in rituals of candlelit dining.

Both Becker and Lifton have made an enormous contribution to a widely accessible poise toward mortality. I can only hope to give you the flavor of their work in this little book, but certain key notions of both men help to explain the philosophical underpinnings of Alcoholics Anonymous. Not only did Becker arouse a wide public to the significance of mortality in human behavior, but he also initiated a penetrating discussion about the nature of illusion. We shall get into that when we take up the principles of Alcoholics Anonymous.

DEATH AND SYMBOLIC IMMORTALITY

As the only organism aware of death, the human anticipates meanings of life and death. At all times, while negotiating in the dialectic, the human is negotiating to establish actual and symbolic life—or as Lifton would put it, the continuity of life. In negotiating with the environment, the individual perceives everything in terms of life and death, but symbolically of course, in terms of life and death *equivalents*. What are life and death equivalents for the human organism? Lifton explains:

> If we accept the natural unity of death and life, then we must assume that death does not suddenly appear out of nowhere but is present for us in some way at all times. If that is so, how does the experience of death begin for the individual? And how does it, over the course of life, relate to life? Images of life begin to form at birth and continue to exist throughout the life cycle. Much of that imagery consists of "death equivalents"—image-feelinqs of separation, disintegration, and stasis. [Stasis is frozen movement.]

Lifton's thought coincides with the attachment phenomenon of the young child for the mother, a subject well explored by Margaret Mahler (*The Psychological Birth of the Human Infant,* 1975), and John Bowlby (*Separation,* 1973).

At first the attachment—and separation—is experienced directly and physically. In later development it occurs symbolically, in words, glances, movements away, and so on. Nothing is more important to the developing human than various forms of attachments to primary caregivers. This early fundamental need for connection is never truly diminished throughout life. Instead, it becomes more symbolized, with powerful feelings always accompanying the symbols. In the adult, symbolic connections begin to take on different modes of realization. The fundamental need underlying connection is, of course, the underlying need for the continuity of life. Continuity of life is sought by the human organism in symbolic modes. Lifton details these modes as culture, religion, mythology, creativity of artistic expression, family life, and unity with nature.

Lifton believes (along with Boulding) that an "inchoate image" is present from the very beginning. This image "includes an interpretive anticipation of interaction with the environment." In the course of development there is a sequence. The image is first a kind of push, then pictures in the usual sense, and finally more abstract symbolization.

These innate images anticipate engagements with environment. They are always poised against danger in these engagements. This is understandable in terms of the organism's central task of staying in existence as what it is. Lifton says that the "elaboration of the inner idea of death from earliest childhood" can be understood first of all in the polarity between connection and separation. (Bowlby refers to attachment behavior around sucking, clinging, crying, and following.) As the young human develops, the attachment or connection shifts from the physical to symbolized relationships. These relationships begin with the mother, then with the larger interconnections of society and living in the world as a historical organism.

The major polarity experienced by the human organism we call connection/separation, but we can also describe another polarity, somewhat overlapping with connection/separation. When something goes awry (separation) with symbolized self-world relations, inner forms and images of self-in-the-world are felt as inadequate representations of the self (we shall call this shame). The result is a distinct sense of self-disintegration, of falling apart. We hear this quite commonly expressed as "I just went to pieces" or "I'm trying to get my act together." This secondary polarity we call integration/disintegration.

A third polarity that exists around death imagery in the organism is called movement/stasis. We are all familiar with the expressions "I just froze!" or "I was totally immobilized!" or "I couldn't move!" Lifton points to the vivid experience most of us have had with the extreme discomfort of a baby held too tightly. The infant has a powerful reaction to this restriction. Later in life, restriction becomes symbolically represented in the need for growth, progress, change. We hear the expression "She needed her space." Stasis is a deathlike experience.

Once we understand these formulations about the infant and its development, we can appreciate Lifton's enormously important shift of the depth psychological paradigm. Lifton replaced the traditional drive and defense with the deeper, richer model of death and the continuity of life.

There is nothing more important to the self-organizing human than the continuity of life.

As the human organism matures and goes through the developmental stages, its connective symbolism becomes more complex, but life and death are always the ultimate meaning behind the vast array of images and symbols. We settle into symbolic modes to organize this sense of immortality or continuity. Thus we can say that the *ultimate* meaning for the human organism is life and death. Within this ultimate meaning we find our *proximate* meanings of connection, integration, and movement. These proximate meanings we call life and death *equivalents*. If life and death are the ultimate meanings for the human organism, *then those two meanings must somehow be included in anything meaningful!*

In the first mode of continuity—the biological—the individual has a sense of living on through children and grandchildren. The proximate meanings, the life equivalents, will be the house, the backyard, the green lawn, the dog, the car. All these are symbolic of life and will be felt as life equivalents. We see grandparents looking into the faces of grandchildren, looking for likenesses of themselves. No other animals do this.

A second mode of continuity is the religious mode. We can describe this generally as a sense of power over death, meaning that "one is in harmony with a principle extending beyond the limited biological life span." Immortality is the ultimate meaning of religion. St. Paul said, "If Christ be not risen, our faith is in vain." The proximate meanings of religion—the life equivalents—are found in cathedrals, music, ritual, rules, congregations, temples, synagogues, and so forth.

A third mode is the mode of creativity, the "achievement of enduring human impact." We live on through our works. The proximate meanings in this mode would be from the paintings created, the businesses built, books written, the houses left behind, and so on.

A fourth mode can be described as the sense of union with nature. We love to look at vast panoramas and sense their having been here before us and continuing on forever. The proximate meanings of continuity would be in the sight of the mountain ranges, the plains, the herds of cattle, the mighty rivers. These proximate meanings lie behind our urge to protect our wilderness parks as places of renewal and refreshment.

The fifth mode of continuity we call the mode of experiential transcendence. This is the mode that interests us most in our study of alcoholism and addiction. The essential quality of this state is the muting of time and death in an overwhelming experience of unity and harmony. The word transcendence means going beyond while including. In the experience of transcendence, the dialectics and polarities of organismic existence collapse into an intense realization that the dialectic has been transcended; all is one.

Let's pause on the fifth mode—that of transcendence. We might just spot the demon alcoholism lurking here in the shadows. As Lifton explains, our sense of awareness of larger connection is the sense of transcendence. Transcendence is the most powerful of all the modes of symbolic continuity. To be truly vital it must be grounded in various combinations of the other modes. In other words, we cannot have a truly authentic experience of transcendence unless it includes organically sound symbolic connections—connections arising out of the needs of the organism.

Here we can put our finger on a core aspect of the problem of addiction. For many of us, the first experience with drugs or alcohol may be the first experience with transcendence. *A problem arises if individuals comes to this experience with inauthentic connections in their personal history.* These will be people heavily defended in their relationships as a result of developmental shaming or abuse. For many, after a drug or alcohol experience, "one never returns to exactly the same inner structures of the self. Having once broken old forms, one senses they can be broken again, or at least extended beyond earlier limitations." (Lifton). Here is where addiction begins. "In addition, an important memory remains, a still active image-feeling of intense inner unity." (Lifton). But rather than benefiting from this experience of transcendence, rather than a reordering of symbolic connections, or a psychic change toward enhanced image-feelings of connection, the addict comes out of these transcendent experiences, back to a preponderance of the old image feelings of separation, disintegration, and stasis. Truly organic experiences of transcendence can lead to conversion, a reordering of images. Chemically induced experiences do not. This essentially describes the bind of the alcoholic.

The task of the human organism is to provide for the continuity of life. Unlike the other animals, the human must perceive life equivalents in order to experience well-being. We are aware that we will not live as we are forever, but we are also aware of a sense of immortality that actually provides feelings of *vitality*. We have found that for the organism the source of vitality is in the proximate meanings of connection, integration, and movement—and ultimately in a sense of symbolic immortality. To realize this sense of ongoingness we develop modes of connection such as the image-feelings organized around family, religion, nature, and creativity. When these connections permit, we may experience moments of transcendence, sharp experiences of the ultimate unity of life and death.

Transcendence, however, must be grounded in healthy modes of symbolic continuity, such as connection in family, religion, and creativity. People often use alcohol to get to transcendence without being grounded. Because there are no grounded images to fall back upon, the alcohol-based experience demands repetition. This progresses from a need for transcendence to, finally, a need for numbing. The chemically induced image system does not work.

Now that we have described the goal of the human organism—symbolic immortality through various modes of continuity—we have to ask ourselves about the act of choosing those image-feelings of more life. We have not offered a complete description of human action until we discuss the notion of free will and choice. In the next chapter we review the question of free will and make some propositions from our controlling image of organism-in-environment.

Do we really have free will?

10

Free Will and Choice

Freud has remained identified with the destructive overwhelming aspects of environmental influences . . . and has put such creative energy into an effort to save the individual victims of life forces by means of a therapy of adaptation and adjustment that he has influenced the psychology of a whole world. Rank, with no minimizing of the environmental, has chosen instead . . . to assign to the individual his full share in the dynamic.

—Jessie Taft, translator of *Will Therapy* by Otto Rank

Probably no idea is more closely associated with alcoholism and the other addictions than the idea of the will. We are free agents, we choose to behave this way or that, we make decisions. Then why can we not just say no to our bad habits? A sizable number of people still believe alcoholism is a moral failure. It is basically a matter of will power, they insist, but a growing public has been educated to accept the thinking that the alcoholic is not so much weak willed as he or she is *sick*. Reluctantly, many now acknowledge that will power is not the remedy. In order to understand the nature of alcoholism, however, we do have to understand the will—and choice. We all have the experience of free will. We believe we make choices every day. We make elaborate decisions frequently. And yet the alcoholic seems unable to decide to stop and stay stopped even when being destroyed by the habit. What is wrong with the alcoholic's will?

The title of this book is *Alcoholism: A Matter of Choice*. The *will* is a primary matter for discussion. Understanding the notion of will is a keystone for the correct understanding of addiction. The will is the principal agent in both the addictive process and in the processes of recovery from addiction. As we have lamented elsewhere, this is not appreciated in the prevailing views about alcoholism.

(I remind the reader here that I have not forgotten I am speaking about an organic whole. Notions of will and ego are mental constructs only. They are descriptions of aspects of an inseparable whole. As we know from physics it is okay to describe those aspects while understanding that they arise from the activities of a whole. The will as such does not exist, but there is an aspect of organic human activity that we call *willing*.)

There are reasons why the will is ignored in alcoholism studies—for example, the general belief today that addiction is not simply a matter of will power; we have instead the prevailing viewpoints of biological and cultural determinism. Moreover, the will has been discarded in psychoanalytic theory, as well as in behavioral psychology and sociology.

As far as Freud was concerned, the will was irrelevant to his business. In his model of id, ego, and superego, the ego was a "plaything" between id and superego. Freud called the ego "the clown in the circus" trying to make itself heard. For Freud, will manifested itself mainly in resistance to the therapeutic process. Otto Rank, perhaps Freud's brightest protégé along with Jung, restored the will to analysis. Rank's appreciation of self-determination has only recently been resurrected into a place of prominence.

Rollo May, influenced by Rank, wrote important books on the will. *Love and Will* was published in 1969. May was called a phenomenologist—a psychologist who can coherently explain behavior but cannot empirically verify his theories. Many thinkers did not go along with May's ideas about the will. There was simply no way its existence could be demonstrated to be independent of ordinary cause and effect.

What *is* the will? The dictionary describes the will as the power to direct one's own actions. Rollo May calls the will the capacity to organize oneself for action in a certain direction. A great contemporary theologian, Karl Rahner, says will belongs to the primordial data of experience whereby man possesses himself, and that will can be described only by oblique descriptive reference to this experience. Otto Rank described will as an "autonomous organizing force in the individual . . . ."

Clearly, it is hard to define the will, so we have to ask again, what is it? If we examine a human brain on a laboratory table we will see an unattractive three-pound mass of tissue that we know is made up of billions of cells. Poke around in there all we want, we will not come up with a will, nor will we locate the cells that make up a will.

The will is not a faculty, nor an organ, nor a collection of cells. It is not a function of the brain. It is an activity of the organism that must be described at a level of organization different from the neurological level. It has to be described much as we described the symphony. To paraphrase the physicist Paul Davies, mind or will can no more be explained by brain than life can be explained by a collection of atoms. So even though we are talking about the will, there is no such thing as the will. There is a strong tendency among philosophers and psychologists to reify concepts like will. (Reify comes from the Latin *res*, or thing.) In the middle ages philosophers called the will a faculty, a designation that seemed to straddle an immaterial and material nature.

Now that we have a new model of the human as a self-organizing whole in an environment, we can be more comfortable in describing the will. We have lately become accustomed to the abstract aspects of human organization; we can posit such notions with confidence. We know that organisms recognize, or know their environments. We understand that organisms recognize what they need and then act upon that recognition. The human organism recognizes its needs through image-feelings. These are principally symbolic representations of life and death equivalents. So how do we experience the action of willing? We can sum up the willing operation in the human organism with two words: *owns* and *moves*. The mind owns or affirms its interior expression of meaning in the environment, and then moves on that meaning. The willing function can be broken down into stages. First, we affirm or own the image of the object. Second, we affirm the meaning of the object (how we feel about it). Third, we deliberate about the relative meaning of the object versus alternative objects and meanings. Fourth, we move upon the object, or make a decision.

The willing function can be described as that aspect of human organization that moves upon meanings in the environment. Willing can be seen as a corollary to the innate anticipation by the formative processes in human cognition. If we are expecting something, we will move on it when we recognize it.

CHOICE

Choice is the word we use to describe our experience of willing. We *do* make choices, that is, we review alternatives. The capacity to choose is bound up with our power to abstract and express symbolic meanings from impressions. These various meanings are always available in memory. We have the ability to review these meanings as alternatives.

Willing activity cannot be reduced to the complex firing of neurons. We do not have a *part* that chooses. Life, wholes, and mind are unexplainable. We can only describe them. A lot of folks get lost at this point; we are being asked to take a strange trip to another level of experience beyond flesh and blood. If this makes you uncomfortable, think of the stunned physicists who developed quantum theory. As Neils Bohr, one of the creators of quantum theory, remarked, "Anyone who is not shocked by quantum theory does not understand it." From the struggle to understand the physical nature of light, science has inexorably come up against the reality of an abstract world. Thanks to quantum theory, we can plunge ahead into abstract models of mind, including the function of willing.

We humans have startled ourselves with the discoveries of modern physics, but as Zukav has put it so beautifully,

> As one system of human experience winds down and another, more advanced system emerges, the older system may appear by comparison to be lacking, but from the perspective of the Universe, the language of comparison is not the language of lesser and better, but of limitation and opportunity.

Thus as we move from the limitations of a mechanical world, a world of biological and cultural determinism, into the abstract world of the whole, we are freeing ourselves to move from one level of experience to another in exploring the nature of alcoholism. The investigation into the question of alcoholism has been obstructed by our failure to engage the higher levels of description.

FREE WILL

We have defined will as that aspect of human organization that moves upon meanings in the environment. With this definition established, we come now to two important questions, both of which are essential to an understanding of the alcoholic. First, we must discuss *free will*, and second, *responsibility*.

Book shelves in libraries around the world groan under the weight of tomes written about free will. Certainly the question of free will has been one of the grand questions of philosophy and psychology. To this day there is no universal consensus on the nature of the experience of free will.

In the prevailing Cartesian mode of thought every effect must have a preceding cause in a direct linear relationship. Therefore the action of the will must be determined by a preceding event that causes the will to move. This approach, however, raised another difficulty back in the days when the will was thought of as immaterial. The question was how can the material and immaterial affect one another? Descartes solved this by having the immaterial mind connected to the body by the pineal gland and transmitting its orders to the body. The problem was solved in psychology by the behaviorists—who simply ignored the idea of will. They worked only with physical causality.

For centuries powerful thinkers argued about the freedom of the will. The classical question could be put like this: Are all human acts of will causally produced by antecedent conditions, or are at least some volitional actions exempt from causal determination? The problem with this question is the assumption about causality. As we have already seen, human acts are caused but not determined by the cause. What is caused is a response, not a reaction.

Debates about free will turn out to be logical debates, about the rules of the mind, and not debates about reality or experience. They do not take into consideration the experience of an organism-in-environment. As Zukav says, paraphrasing Finklestein, "Experience itself is not bound by these rules. Experience follows a much more permissive set of rules (quantum logic). Quantum logic is not only more exciting than classical logic, it is more real. It is based not on the way we think of things, but the way we *experience* them." Physicists have published papers demonstrating mathematically that it is impossible to describe experience with classical logic.

We know now that we cannot talk about the experience of free will by imposing systems of logic upon the operations of an organism-in-environment. This is another good reason for setting up a controlling image of the subject. No one has talked about the will in terms of an organic action in an environment.

Physicist Paul Davies discusses free will in his book *God and the New Physics*. While with Newton's laws of mechanics human beings were seen as nothing more than cogs in a giant universal machine, when scientists began to puzzle over the nature of light at the turn of the century, the new physics with quantum theory had to be explored. As Davies says, "The whole issue of freedom of choice and determinism went back into the melting pot." According to Davies, relativity and quantum theory did not explain free will, but enriched the problem. After a careful investigation of the implications of the new physics on free will, Davies remarks, "The new physics undoubtedly gives a new slant to the long standing enigma of free will and determinism, but it does not solve it."

Research in the new physics, Davies concludes, has turned up much positive thinking about the highest levels of human organization. "The existence of mind, for example, as an abstract, holistic, organizational pattern, capable even of disembodiment, refutes the reductionist philosophy that we are all nothing but moving mounds of atoms."

Now we can tackle the question of free will knowing that as we move into abstract levels beyond brain, we are on safe ground. We are organisms-in-environment that conduct our business with the environment through our minds, not our brains.

Perhaps we can resolve the problem of free will by simply stating that the question of free will is a meaningless question. We do not have a free will, we do not need it, and we do not want it. We have already seen that the ultimate meanings to the human organism are life and death, and that the proximate meanings are life and death equivalents. The organism is not the least interested in being free. It is interested in being alive. It is interested in experiencing vitality. The human organism is interested in connection, not freedom. (Freedom from constraint is a different matter. This country, as exemplified by the Statue of Liberty, was founded because freedom from unjust constraint was felt as a life equivalent for the organism. The great joy of the earlier immigrants was the feeling of vitality at being able to pursue the anticipations of the organism.)

In the Middle Ages, philosophers were principally concerned about the existence of an immortal soul that succeeded the body. The soul was in a very real sense free of the body. It was an *a priori* necessity that the will be free or we could not commit sin, or earn heaven. That the will was an organism's movement on meanings was beyond the pale of the greatest thinkers before the twentieth century. We know now that the will, or willing, cannot be understood outside its action as the organism's interaction with the environment; thus free will is a meaningless term for the human organism.

How, then, do we account for the feelings of free will that we experience? The answer is that we are not experiencing freedom. We mistake the feeling of vitality for freedom. An organism cannot rejoice in freedom, only in vitality. We describe the feeling of vitality as one of freedom because we can move on alternatives representing more life. What we think of as free choice is actually our ability to call up constellations of associated image-feelings of life and death equivalents.

Decision making among presented alternatives is not always instantaneous. We can actually see someone making a decision by watching that person's face. Decisions occur in time because the mental process of choice is supported by the physical processes of the brain. These must work in sequence of electrochemical activity. The reason we take time to make decisions, for the will to move, is that all alternatives have some life and death equivalent meanings for us. The meanings, or image-feelings in inventory associated with the alternatives, are called up and re-experienced. This is an enormously complex process, but the decision to move, or decide, will always be made at the time in favor of the image-feelings of more life. In this sense, human organisms are determined; we cannot choose less life.

In the argument about free will and determinism there is no simple clear-cut dichotomy. We *do* have the capacity to choose, but we are also determined to choose what we interpret as life. This is actually quite a positive and advantageous situation for the human organism. We can take as much time as we wish to process the alternatives. Through time we increase the possibility that we will come up with the alternative that has the strongest associations with image-feelings of more life.

Understanding free will in the way we have just outlined sheds a strong light directly on the nature of alcoholism. The key notion here is that the human organism is determined to choose image-feelings of more life. The terrible conflict of the alcoholic is centered around the image-feelings of life and death. As long as alcohol provides image feelings of more life, the alcoholic is determined to move on those images.

Alcoholics Anonymous never directly confronts the will to drink. It suggests instead a change to a different system of images.

RESPONSIBILITY

The question that immediately comes to mind after a discussion about choice is a question about responsibility. This question, too, evades simple and clear-cut definitions. The question of responsibility is even more difficult when we talk about the responsibility of the alcoholic; for example, our society's attitude toward responsibility in alcoholism is ambiguous. In theory, an alcoholic sitting on death row for rape and murder while drunk is also eligible for insurance coverage to treat the medical disease of alcoholism. He is sufficiently responsible for his actions to be killed for them, but he is also pictured as suffering from a disease that caused him to murder.

To talk about responsibility, once again we go back to our controlling image of the human as an organism-in-environment. Recall that humans negotiate their survival and vitality through image-feelings of connection, both immediate and symbolic. The human is participating in a dialectic, which begins with primary caregivers. From the very beginning, the human must be taught his responsibility within the dialectic. A sense of responsibility cannot be taught in lectures, or learned through reading about it. All throughout the developmental stages of bonding, separation, and individuation in childhood, the dialectic with caregivers must result in image-feelings of connection. This is how the human learns *boundaries*. This is an enormously important task for the adult caregivers—for which most of us are unprepared. Teaching boundaries—respecting the child's boundaries and teaching the child to respect our boundaries without shaming or alienating the child—requires an all-too-rare grasp of parenting. This process, however, is the beginning of the sense of responsibility. When the child learns that the connections in his environment are dependent upon his acknowledging the boundaries of others, he is learning to be responsive in his environment. When the child violates boundaries, he must be taught that he is jeopardizing his connections with others.

In many cultures, values are taught as moral issues—that is, as rational constructs. Values are better taught, instead, as primary relationships of response at the organic level of connection.

There is no easy answer for society in adopting a stance on society's response to alcoholic misbehavior. Society must hold all members accountable. Society must impose consequences. Such consequences as penalties for criminal behavior set the conditions of the dialectic. Public consequences are a teaching tool. Visible consequences set up symbolic meanings in certain types of behavior. These conditions must be in place for everyone to see. They must become part of the environment of the alcoholic so that they become part of the meanings he or she must deal with.

ALCOHOLISM AND CHOICE

It is precisely in the organic imperative to move upon connection that we find the terrible bind of the alcoholic. In the early stages of regular alcohol use, the chemical works wonders without significant ill effects. Alcoholics report feeling that they belonged, they could talk, they could dance, they literally found themselves. As use and dependency increased, however, connections began to decay.

The tragedy of the alcoholic is that he has come to see more life in what is actually less life. He is neither biologically nor socioculturally determined to drink. He is as an organism, however, determined to say yes to life. As long as alcohol is experienced as more life, he must choose to drink.

In the next section, we will take up the *basic fault*, a term borrowed from Michael Balint and Morris Berman. We will be looking at a description of the natural history of alcoholism.

11

The Basic Fault

> The person who is truly grounded in him or herself as a biological organism may espouse a cause, but they do not need it in order to feel that their existence is validated. God and country, feminism and sexism, Judaism and anti-Semitism, the religious fundamentalism of Bible belt Baptists and the self-conscious intellectualism ofthe *New York Review of Books* —any ism you care to name, really—are all attempts to create meaning for human beings who, if they had not suffered some primary loss early on, would not need it.
>
> —Morris Berman, *Coming to Our Senses*

Something can go wrong for the human organism-in-environment—not floods, earthquakes, pestilence, automobile accidents, and invasions of microbes that kill us—but something far more serious. Something can go wrong for the human organism in its fundamental dialect with its environment. Something can go awry in the organism's pursuit of the continuity of life.

As we know, the human conducts itself through innately formed image-feelings of connection; we are programmed to anticipate connection both directly and symbolically. Now the very word connection implies at least two terminals of connection. For connection to mean anything, at least two things must be connected; the connection depends upon two things relating somehow or other.

For the young human, connection consists of physical nurture, modeling, mirroring, manifestations of love, a sense of security. The human organism *anticipates* these connections. If this anticipation is not fulfilled, something goes wrong for the organism. The basic fault is that the primary caregivers can break the connection both directly and symbolically—what historian of science Morris Berman refers to as a basic disharmony between the caregiver and the child. Berman, among many others, finds this to be the root of all our ills.

The basic fault can be described in one word—shame. We are going to discuss shame in depth—and show how it is the principal occasion of alcoholism and other addictions.

A keynote quote for this part of our narrative could be taken from psychiatrist Donald Nathanson (*The Many Faces of Shame*). "Psychotherapy is like the automobile industry that has a major defect in its product. We ought to recall our product and re-tool in the name of shame."

In an article in the February 1992 *Atlantic* "Shame," by Robert Karen, Nathanson says he is on a personal "jihad" (mission) to "change the whole culture of psychiatry." According to the article, Nathanson is convinced that everyone now practicing therapy should be retrained; they must adapt to the fact that shame is now known to be the principal cause of all emotional distress. Nathanson is not alone. Shame is definitely the rediscovered emotion. The *Atlantic* article says shame is "the hottest of hot topics."

The first person, perhaps, to truly popularize the role of shame is John Bradshaw, the peripatetic lecturer and TV missionary to millions of "shame-based" folks across the country. Bradshaw has the message—no question. Many of us have been converted by Bradshaw's series on the family. I would most likely not have written this book if Bradshaw had not aroused my curiosity about family systems. And in this same vein of gratitude, I mention Gershen Kaufman, whose book *Shame: The Power of Caring*, enriched the notion of shame. Kaufman enabled me to see shame in the work of Robert W. Firestone (*The Fantasy Bond*), and most especially in the ideas of Robert Jay Lifton (*The Broken Connection*). That shame is a family affliction is thoroughly illuminated by Fossum and Mason in *Facing Shame*.

We are all familiar with several different shame experiences. We may be shy when meeting others; we feel embarrassed when we spill the soup; we can feel ashamed of our backgrounds. We note one common characteristic about all these feelings—they are all directed at the self, not at others. They all include a common feeling of deficiency in the self. This feeling is internally originated—not necessarily by the actions of others.

Shame is a fundamental feeling, the root of shyness and embarrassment. The feeling of shame is always social, or interpersonal. We can be walking alone in the mountains and suddenly feel ashamed at a memory, but the original shaming incident was interpersonal.

What I hope to add to the literature on shame is an understanding of shame's power base. What is not yet clear in writings about shame is the reason for the enormous power it has in human behavior; the current definitions of shame are somewhat anemic. When psychiatry and psychology walked away from Freudian drives, they developed no other power base for human motivation. Lifton has supplied that power base. Shame is generally defined as unbearable exposure of the self to both the self and others, but the dynamics are never dealt with. Why is exposure so debilitating?

The answers developed here are meant to explain the etiology of alcoholism. What makes the human organism unique is that it is aware of both terminals in the connection—itself and the environment. Other animals do not appear to be aware of a self. The human, aware of death, is therefore aware of the self in its connections. This is an important factor in considering the basic fault, or broken connection. The most significant image-feelings occur around other human organisms. The other human organism provides the most important realization of connection—probably because it is tied up with a number of organic features, principally that we cannot reproduce our kind without others, we cannot survive and develop without others, and we cannot identify ourselves without others. We learn about and experience ourselves through others—thus the abiding interest in theater, magazines, and novels.

Recently we are seeing an increasing recognition of the importance of connection. The notion of participation, that we are all essentially participants—connected—comes up front and center in such theories as the Gaia interpretation of life on the planet, and quite dramatically in the relationship between the observer and the behavior of subatomic matter in quantum mechanics. It comes up also in dialectical biology, which tells us the organism cannot be fully understood outside of its connections with its environment. There is, in addition, the growing consensus in the physical sciences that more important than reductionistic analysis, is the *holistic* viewpoint of relations. The subtleties of vast interweavings and interdependencies in the universe and in the growth of life on the planet are now inevitable considerations.

The only organism that is aware of itself in these connections, as far as we know, is the human organism—the only organism that knows that broken connections to the environment and to other humans mean death and annihilation. This awareness can be experienced globally in the increasing concern, even anxiety, about our gradual destruction of our environment. It can be experienced locally in the shock and grief over a divorce.

SHAME AND GUILT

There is a crucial difference in the way broken connection can be experienced. In one way, we experience guilt; in the other, we experience shame. The distinction is a fundamentally important one—one that was not made in the past by psychologists. I was cued to this difference several years ago when a friend in a Twelve Step program was elated to find the difference between his feelings of guilt and his feelings of shame. He said, "Guilt means I made a mistake; shame means I *am* a mistake!" In other words, in guilt it is *my* behavior that breaks connection; in shame it is the behavior of a primary caregiver who breaks connection with me. The image-feelings most important to the human organism are organized around caregivers from the beginning. If they break connection through abuse, abandonment, or neglect, we are being shamed.

Let's take a deeper look into shame, beginning with some of the current descriptions. Gershen Kaufman, who has written a most important book on shame, describes it this way:

> To feel shame is to feel seen in a painfully diminished sense. The self feels exposed both to itself and to anyone else present. It is this sudden unexpected feeling of exposure and accompanying self-consciousness that characterizes the essential nature of the affect of shame.

Fossum and Mason, writing about shame in family interaction, describe shame this way:

> Shame is an inner sense of being completely diminished or insufficient as a person. It is the self judging the self. A moment of shame may be humiliation so painful or an indignity so profound that one feels one has been robbed of her or his dignity or exposed as basically inadequate, bad, or worthy of rejection. A pervasive sense of shame is the ongoing premise that one is fundamentally bad, inadequate, unworthy, or not fully valid as a human being.

Willard Gaylin says, "Shame inevitably involves (if only in our imagination) exposure, but, unlike guilty fear, what we dread is not the results of the shame, but the exposure itself." Most authors (but not every author) emphasize the aspect of exposure. Ernest Kurz, for instance, disagrees: "The sense of shame comes before the sense of being seen—before, then, any advertence to 'other.' " If the core experience of shame is not exposure as such, we have to dig a little deeper, to find the dynamics below the experience of exposure.

We should emphasize here that shame is a judgment of the self about the self. Shame does not require that others see us as unworthy or inadequate, only that we see ourselves that way as a result of others breaking connection with us through abandonment, abuse, or neglect. We must remember this as we probe the origins of the feeling of shame.

Feelings of guilt are not about my identity, my sense of personal centering or grounding, but in shame I am disintegrated and uprooted. Guilt is felt as reparable; shame is felt as irreparable. Guilt can be as painful as shame. In many instances, the pain is an intermingling of guilt and shame, but what we have to keep in mind is that guilt can flow in a grounded and centered ego state. Shame flows in a confused, diminished, shattered ego state.

PARADOXICAL DEFENSE

We come now to the core of the shaming process. We negotiate in this process in one degree of intensity or another from the moment of birth. Our capacity to be shamed rests on our fundamental rejection of death. During the developmental years, it is not possible for the young human to accept death. Later, the adult can process mortality with tolerance, acceptance, or resignation—and even embrace the inevitable. Since the young human cannot accept death, or process the feelings about mortality, he or she cannot accept the death equivalents in separation from caregivers. It is not possible for the child to resign itself to separation and loss, or to undertake a grieving process. Connection with caregivers is essential.

Separation *does* occur for the young, however, and when it is experienced, a death equivalent feeling is evoked. In shaming, the feelings of broken connection are provoked by various forms of abandonment or abuse (emotional and physical), on the part of primary caregivers, but the young human cannot accept that the caregiver has broken the connection. Broken connection is a most powerful death equivalent over which the young human has no control. Therefore, *the child assigns the breaking of the connection to himself.* He thereby keeps *control.* He preserves the connection. This occurs in many different circumstances familiar to all of us; for example, a child may feel responsible for the father's leaving the family, or a child feels like the "dirty one" in an act of incest.

Robert Karen tells of an experiment conducted by Michael Lewis in which the faces of mothers voicing prohibitions to their youngsters were videotaped. Lewis found that thirty to forty percent of mothers' prohibitions were accompanied by facial expressions of disgust. What the child is picking up is not just a negative reaction to its behavior, but a negative reaction to the child's whole being. Abuse need not be physical. A caregiver can abuse with words, looks, even glances. Neglect need not be physical neglect. A caregiver may neglect the emotional needs of a child while feeding her a balanced diet.

This assignment of broken connection to the self is actually a deep defensive mechanism—a paradoxical defense. To defend himself against the death equivalent of separation, the child paradoxically attacks the self rather than the offending caregiver. Firestone calls these connections preserved by paradoxical defense, *fantasy bonds,* and has written a book by that name.

✓Shame can be described, therefore, as the attribution of abuse, abandonment, and neglect (or the perception thereof) on the part of caregivers to a deficit in the self rather than a deficit in the caregiver, in an effort to preserve the sense of connection.

I immediately add here that abuse, abandonment, and neglect are not necessarily overt or intentional acts of caregivers. Much depends upon the subjective perceptions of the child. We each enter the world with an enormously complex perceptive mechanism. It is not possible to exactly understand why individuals respond differently to the same caregiving.

When the shaming process is intense and repetitive, the feelings of worthlessness are internalized. They become part of the person's inventory of image-feelings by which future associations are contaminated. (Ever wonder why some people always see the glass as half empty, and others see it as half full?) A great deal of anger can build up during shaming—usually misdirected against the self. It can cause depression in later years, or it can be acted out in sociopathic behavior. (I am reminded here of Gregory

Bateson's theory of *double-bind* as a source of schizophrenia. Double-bind describes the terrible and painful confusion caused by mixed messages from caregivers.)

Internalized shame results in an enduring shame-based state characterized by (1) distrust, (2) self-dependence, and (3) painful confusion. To survive the onslaught of paradoxical defense, the young person will stop trusting the offending caregiver; she will live out a fantasy bond of connection to the offending caregiver.

Trust is essential for the successful completion of the developmental stages. Without it, the mutuality that is so critical in establishing responsibility and respect for boundaries may be permanently destroyed. Distrust makes it almost impossible to create healthy relationships.

Internalized shame also breeds self-dependence, the illusion of self-sufficiency. The self cannot trust others to supply nurturing, so it takes on the job of self-nurture. As Firestone says, "A self-nourishing life style emerges that shuts off personal feelings and is primarily defensive and self-protective."

Ernest Becker (*The Denial of Death*) has written powerfully about the *causa sui* (cause of oneself) project. The causa sui project, or total self-dependence, says Becker, is destined for failure in terms of a neurotic, possibly psychotic existence. Becker sees the shamed person as becoming a "little god" unto himself. "What else is he to do?" asks Becker. Since he can no longer trust—even while maintaining a fantasy bond—he must set up his own defensive system and provide self-nurture. How many of us know the angry, raging family whose members cannot go their separate ways? They are bonded and angry at the same time. All of this results in a life of painful confusion in relationships and self-evaluation. As Firestone says, all problems of relationships are caused by deep defenses.

DESCRIPTION OF SHAME

The first shaming events result in what we can call *primary shame*. Internalized primary shame is a permanent psychic condition. It originates in early life (the basic fault) because of broken connections by necessary others. If the adult breaks connection through abuse, abandonment, or neglect, systematic image-feelings of death equivalents are the results for the child. These broken connections are felt as caused by the self, and the child takes control through paradoxical defense. Throughout life, the constant stream of collapsing and recreated image-feelings can be tainted by a shame-based inventory of primary feelings.

Secondary shame is the painful experience of death equivalents evoked when exposure penetrates the defenses we have elaborately constructed from childhood. Exposure is not the core experience of shame. Exposure evokes the associated image-feelings from earlier, primary events. Secondary shaming events in later life receive their power from the internalized primary events.

Let's try to illustrate the difference between guilt and shame and primary and secondary shame. Let's suppose that Jack grew up in a supportive family where he was exposed to only minor, infrequent shaming events. He has learned to trust for the most part, and he is not overly self-dependent. Jack goes to a cocktail party in the neighborhood one night and there he is introduced to someone he cheated when he was delivering newspapers as a young man. Jack's predominant feeling meeting this person will be guilt. He may even try to figure out some way to remind the person of what he did and try to make amends. He will weigh what he should do in terms of his guilt. But now let's say Jack grew up in a nonsupportive family where he was frequently intensely shamed. He has learned to distrust, to be fiercely self-dependent, and he is carrying a load of subterranean anger. Jack goes to the cocktail party and meets someone he cheated years ago. Jack's predominant feelings at meeting this person will be shame, and probably some guilt as well. His shame will be secondary shame. No one is shaming him at the moment, but the shame receives its intensity from the primary experience of shame in early childhood. This Jack is what Bradshaw calls "a shame-based person." He will try to get away from the other person as quickly as possible. Ideas of amends do not come up. Which Jack at the cocktail party is more likely to scramble off to the bar for another drink?

Shame is the single most powerful and profound death equivalent. It is the principal contributor to all later neuroses and psychoses. The enormous power of shame need no longer be a mystery. It is a power flowing directly from the organism's fear of death. The core experience of shame is not exposure, as many authors maintain, but that of disintegration and dying.

In discussing shame as a condition caused by others in an early disharmony, I am not proposing a type of environmental determinism here. I am not suggesting that all humans who are exposed to shaming situations are inevitably shamed—and to the same degree. There may well be a question of innate temperaments involved. The work of Stella Chess and Alexander Thomas points to a given difference in temperaments among young babies that would probably result in different responses to the same shaming situations. And some psychoanalysts of the object relations school would argue for innate psychostructural deficits that would also explain varying reactions to the same shaming situations. We must never forget that each individual's reactions to the environment are vastly complex and cannot be well understood; however, shaming environments are powerful causative situations to which the human organism must respond in one way or another. In addition, the range of responses available to a young human is severely limited—particularly in the early years when separation and individuation are taking place and the identity is being formed. Identity formation occurs largely through parent idealization and mirroring.

People who have internalized shame may consistently form image-feelings on the dark side of the polarities. In other words, they may form meanings of separation, disintegration, and stasis in their impressions as the result of tainted associations with earlier shame-based image-feelings. They have learned, in their stream of symbolizing activity, to form death equivalent image-feelings. They habitually counter these death equivalents with fantasy connections, or with inwardly turned anger (depression), or with the controlling behaviors of self-dependence. What is lacking is authentic organismic connection and interdependence. For a substantial number of these shamed individuals—who may also be physiologically predisposed—the chemical alcohol works wonders.

We get some idea of the wonders alcohol performs if we reflect that image-feelings of the continuity of life are species-specific activities of the human organism (remember Lifton's modes of symbolic immortality—family, religion, patriotism, nature, creative work, and transcendence). Some shame-based persons, perhaps those at risk from neurochemical mood changing experiences, do actually experience sharp feelings of transcendence with alcohol. These people, perhaps habitually in a psychic state on the dark side of the polarities, may experience with alcohol an ecstasy, a standing outside themselves. Lifton describes such experiences this way:

> The self feels uniquely alive—connected, in movement, integrated—which is why we can say that this state provides at least a temporary sense of eliminating time and death. What it eliminates is the destructive side of the death symbol—proximate imagery of separa-

tion, stasis, and disintegration, as well as ultimate imagery of meaninglessness and impaired symbolic immortality.

Lifton here sums up perfectly the power of addiction to alcohol. The attraction to alcohol is the attraction to life itself. Why does the alcoholic yearn to drink again? After an experience of transcendence, "one never returns to exactly the same inner structure of the self. Having once broken old forms, one senses they can be broken again, or at least extended beyond earlier limitations. In addition, an important memory remains, a still active image-feeling of intense inner unity." The memory prompts the craving, long after alcohol has left the system. As we can see, craving must be described at a higher level of the organization than the neurochemical.

The human response to the effects of alcohol is a hugely complex affair. We know for a fact that only a small portion of the population—about seventeen million people—are drawn to abuse alcohol. Does that mean they are the only ones who have been shamed? Not at all. Alcohol is not the only source of connection, or numbing of separation. I have met dozens of recovering people whose symptoms were the same as mine, but they were overeaters, gamblers, codependents, credit card abusers, debtors, sex addicts. We accepted one another, shared our stories, and used the same principles together to recover.

Broken connections are death equivalents. Survivors will create controlling, fulfilling, self-dependent, self-nurturing behaviors to compensate. All too often these self-dependent survival compensations take the form of addictions. All addictions, no matter what, *are methods of control*.

Does this mean that someone who has not been shamed cannot become an alcoholic? Or become addicted in some other way? I cannot answer that with precision, of course. But what I can suggest with confidence is that addictions are struggles for control. The need to control, to be self-nurturing and self-dependent, springs from disharmonious primary relationships—the basic fault. The most basic obstacle to connection is shaming. The most basic responses to shaming are fantasy connection and self-dependence. It does not seem likely that people who do not have a basic deficit in symbolic connections will become problematically addicted.

Human life is a life of connections. In the twentieth century, physical scientists have been stunned by the complexity of connection of everything in the universe. It is not surprising to find the demons of addiction lurking in the species-specific processes of human connections in the environment.

ADDICTION

We are ready now to attempt a definition of addiction. Addiction has already been defined, of course, in dictionaries and hundreds of books and papers. Previous definitions, however, emerged from Cartesian views of cause-effect, and determinism. The role of the self has been traditionally side-stepped with disclaimers like vulnerabilities, predispositions, and the like.

The definition we propose for a twenty-first-century model of addiction is based on the new worldviews of the whole, the self-organizing organism-in-environment. In studying the nature of the human organism and its relationship to the environment we have seen that addiction must be cast in terms appropriate to species-specific characteristics of the whole. We have described "the basic fault" in terms of shame or disharmony in early bonding.

Addictions can be described as self-nurturing attachments. They restore image feelings of connection, integration, and freedom where there has been distrust, self-dependence, and painful confusion. Addictions are self-destructive because they are not authentic connections. They provide substitute image-feelings that are impermanent and transient. Addictions provoke severe conflict in the organism between authentic and inauthentic connections. The organism's innate formative process of interpreting meanings in the environment is interfered with and aborted. Further, chemical addictions are destructive of the metabolic and neuronal processes in the organism.

The feeling complex—the most important feature of human life—is centered from birth around bonding. (Note the close similarity between bonding and addiction; addiction is almost a natural state.) Bonding provides the human being with her or his image feelings of connection, integration, and freedom. If the bonding is impaired, maladaptations will take place during the developmental stages. Instead of bonding, the child will develop fantasy bonds. Addictions may be set up to take the place of authentic bonding. The human organism cannot survive without bonding. Take away appropriate bonding and the organism will bond inappropriately.

The instructions in the human organism to bond are manifest from birth. We cannot even know ourselves without mirroring, from the first moments of life onward. Even monks—who never talk to one another—pray together, work together, and eat together; they are highly bonded. They need to see who they are, and understand what they are doing by seeing themselves mirrored in other monks. Addictions are self-destructive because they are inappropriate bonds. Addictions are destructive because they permit fantasy bonds; they cannot establish an authentic dialectic in the environment. They cannot, therefore, lead us to truth.

ADDICTION: A MATTER OF CHOICE

We have seen in our discussion that choosing to drink self-destructively is not the choice between vanilla and chocolate; it is the choice between life and death. The feelings in alcoholism are the most powerful known to humankind. We can understand the impenetrable denial of the alcoholic. Drinking is a choice made by the highly defended individual who savors for the moment a taste of connection, perhaps even of transcendence. These are experiences he has denied himself since he formed his fantasy bonds years before.

Before we go on to our examination of the principles of Alcoholics Anonymous, we'll examine in the following chapter the prevailing views about alcoholism, and their failure to describe the affliction.

PART THREE:

THE PREVAILING VIEWS

12

The Failure of the Prevailing Views

The first effect of intoxication is invariably the establishment of a feeling that all is now well between them and their environment. In my experience, the yearning for this "feeling of harmony" is the most important cause of alcoholism, or for that matter, any form of addiction.

—Michael Balint

The literature available on the affliction called alcoholism comprises thousands of papers from laboratory research, thousands of articles, and hundreds of books. In the last ten years, several important books have appeared in the bookstores. The work has been done by many different kinds of specialists. One scientist tells us that seventeen scientific disciplines are doing research into alcoholism. The failure to face up to the volitional characteristic of alcoholism, however, has resulted in a vast literature that cannot put its finger on the core of the problem. Until we shift our efforts to an investigation of choice, we will continue to see alcoholism through a glass, darkly.

Understanding the difference between the two questions—what causes behavior, and why do people behave that way—is essential to understanding alcoholism. Not recognizing the difference is blocking the search for the origins of alcoholism. Is there an explanation for this? Yes. We have inherited the Cartesian-Newtonian habit of mind. We prefer the question— what *causes* alcoholism? It permits tangible, scientific, technological research. It permits common sense thinking about cause and effect. It lends itself to rational, convincing applications for grants and government support.

We squirm with the question—*why* do people become alcoholic? It takes us back to notions of will and choice. Such notions, we are told, are unverifiable, illusory, highly subjective, and so on. Academic psychologists eye volition like wary tourists beholding snake meat.

The predominant views about alcoholism are Cartesian. For researchers, the idea of examining volition is simply outside the conventions of their community. Instead, they insist, an "alcogene" will be discovered some day. Or a neuroscientist will tap into the right collection of neurons. Some day a psychiatrist will describe the right psychostructural deficit. Or a pharmacologist will develop the "magic bullet." Some day a nutritionist will come up with the right diet. And so on.

The fundamental problem with alcoholism research today is the failure to see the alcoholic as a self-organizing whole. The experts do not understand that the different disciplines they pursue are essentially fragmentary; that their subject matter is an aspect of a whole; that these aspects must be subsumed under a controlling view of the species-specific behavior of the whole; and that we must acknowledge the nature of human response to causes in the environment. The problem of chronic, self-destructive alcohol abuse desperately needs a powerful synthesis, not a continuing analysis.

HISTORY OF THE PREVAILING VIEWS

Efforts to confront alcoholism intensified and organized during the 1930s. Alcoholics Anonymous (AA) was founded in 1935. The nonprofessional, nonscientific fellowship would grow into a beacon of hope for millions of the hopeless. Scientific research into alcoholism in those days was confined to recording and analyzing psychological and sociological variables. The chemical effects of alcohol on body chemistry constituted the limit of laboratory work. There was not much interest in expanding laboratory work among biological scientists. The widespread attitude then was that alcoholism was a psychological, moral, or social problem.

A major step was taken with the founding of the Yale Center of Alcohol Studies in 1942 by Dr. E.M. Jellinek. In 1960, Jellinek published *The Disease Concept of Alcoholism,* which galvanized scientific interest in the malady. Before Jellinek's book, there was little research into neurological, endocrinological, metabolic, and genetic causes of alcoholism. Following his book, laboratory tests multiplied and animals were specially bred for testing.

Jellinek is remembered by workers in the field for his introduction of the multiple-factor concept into the causality of alcoholism. He proposed (1) biochemical vulnerability, (2) psychological factors, and (3) culturally acceptable habits.

√ Jellinek's book and the subsequent scientific interest laid the foundation for the widespread view of alcoholism's causalities as determinative. The timing for this was right. America was in love with science and technology. Psychological behaviorism had trampled all over subjective experience. Reductive science had scored stunning successes with atomic theories and molecular biology. And psychoanalysis took little interest in the alcoholic. (Psychiatry concluded that alcoholism was a pre-oedipal affliction. Others said there were no premorbid psychic conditions explaining alcoholism.)

THE DISEASE CONCEPT

The question of whether alcoholism should be described as a disease still raises hackles in some quarters. Our notions of disease are, for the most part, determinative and have nothing to do with choice. Disease does not ordinarily denote or connote a role for the organism as agent. The common notion of disease implies that alcoholism is something you *get*, not something you *do*. On the other hand, some authors are explaining the disease concept of alcoholism by reference to hypertension and atherosclerosis—both diseases that depend to some degree on the lifestyle and choices of the individual. The literature on the disease concept invariably refers to the "causes" of alcoholism in such a way that the specific human response is ignored. As we have been learning here, alcoholism is a most powerful disorder at the highest level of human organization and √ requires all the help—and more—that society would grant to a disease.

The idea that alcoholism is a disease took hold with hardly any opposition at a time when there were no clear ideas of any kind about the nature of the affliction. Physicians felt obliged to take on the problem, understandably. References to alcoholism as disease began as early as 1933, and gradually coalesced into the formal statements of the American Medical Association (AMA) during the years from 1956 to 1966. As the medical model became entrenched, however, a debate began that still rages here and there in fiery pockets of resistance to the disease concept.

It is important to recognize in assessing the arguments about the disease concept that neither side in the controversy has reference to the specific processes of the human organism—volition—in dealing with the causative factors. The medical model, as well as the behavioristic model, suffers from a distinct determinative viewpoint—or, at best, a distinct failure to illuminate the role of the subject. Nor do the views opposing the medical model understand choice in addiction. The human being has been left out. Alcoholism is still not understood.

In this vein, we must point out a major flaw in descriptions of alcoholism. The general tendency is to define alcoholism by the phenomena of powerlessness and craving, but the mistake here is attempting to define specific behavior when a toxin is present in the system, upsetting the species-specific balance of behavior.

Alcoholism must be described as the behavior of an individual who chooses to drink repeatedly (1) in spite of consequences, (2) when there is no alcohol in the bloodstream, and (3) when the symptoms of withdrawal have subsided. This is not to say that the signs of powerlessness after the first drink, or the feelings of craving during withdrawal, are not the signs of alcoholism. They most probably are. We cannot, however, define alcoholism when toxins have impaired species-specific behavior.

This position is supported by the phenomena of the other addictions. These other addictions are defined without the presence of chemicals in the bloodstream. Friends in other Twelve Step groups—gamblers, overeaters, codependents, debtors, sex addicts—report that their condition is exactly the same as mine. We used our addiction of choice for the same reasons, and we employ the same principles to recover.

Probably no question about human behavior has been more hotly debated recently than the question of whether alcoholism should be regarded as a disease, a bad habit, a failure of character, or what. Perhaps it will be helpful to select authors representing the strongest views and discuss their basic thinking at this point.

The disease concept of alcoholism has been generally accepted by American society. The AMA has endorsed the notion; insurance companies pay for its treatment. I drank alcoholically for twenty-two years. When I finally stopped, lying near death in the emergency room of a county hospital, everyone told me I had a disease. I was not comfortable with that diagnosis because I thought of disease as invading microbes, runaway cells, and malfunctioning organs that we fix with surgery and drugs. And there was the other kind of disease—that of the severely emotionally disturbed, the schizophrenic, and the psychotic. I did not identify with those afflictions either. I had a deep sense that I had, for some reason, done this to myself. I pictured myself having a fine, healthy body that I had come close to destroying.

I came to prefer the word *disorder*—which dictionaries use interchangeably with disease—because that word seemed to allow for my mental capacities as somehow out of order. What scared me was that my highest faculties were involved in my drinking. I chose to drink, just as I am choosing now not to drink. I chose to deny my problem for years, just as I choose now to admit it. If I had an affliction that originated at the level of choice, then it seemed to me I had a disorder more serious than the usual ideas of disease. Eventually, I was able to describe alcoholism as a disorder of the feeling complex.

THE PHYSIOLOGICAL MODEL

Let's take a look now at various interpretations of the disease model. We will begin with a book by Kenneth Blum, Ph.D., *Alcohol and the Addictive Brain*. Blum has been studying alcoholism for more than twenty-five years in biogenetic research. He has traveled the world to discuss alcoholism with dozens of scientists.

Blum talks of alcoholism this way:

> . . . [T]he growing weight of laboratory and clinical findings leaves no doubt in my mind that alcoholism is a *physiological disease process* [Blum's emphasis], largely genetic in origin, that can be triggered or complicated by psychological or sociological influences . . . . [I]t is an inescapable fact that *alcoholism remains a largely unsolved medical problem* [Blum's emphasis].

We can see that Blum is a relentless biogenetic determinist who believes, in his own words, that someday a silver bullet will be discovered to relieve alcoholism altogether. We have to look carefully at the logical sequence of events in Blum's idea of process. The question arises, how do psychological factors or sociological factors bring about a physiological disease process? We can understand how psychological factors (stress, worry) influence the body's overproduction of acids that can cause ulcers, or lead to heart disease. But Blum's process leaves out a step: Psychological factors actually *influence a decision* to use alcohol, and then the alcohol in turn acts upon the physiology. When acid attacks my stomach because of stress, I do not add the acid myself, but in alcoholism I add the chemical myself.

The foundation for disagreement with Blum is that there may be (but are not necessarily) metabolic, endocrinological, or electrochemical abnormalities present that are activated in the presence of alcohol. When a physiological event takes place with alcohol, it results in heightened feelings more pronounced than if there were no abnormalities present. When the alcohol is gone from the system, the physiological event is over and the feelings have subsided. The physiologial event induced by alcohol does not call for another physiological event, in the sense that an appetite such as for food and water, has been set up. The feeling event, however, is remembered—particularly if it is abnormally pronounced—and can be re-felt even without the reintroduction of alcohol. Recalling the feeling may even have a physical effect. It is imperative to recognize the sequence here. It is the feeling recalled from memory that may call for another event. There is no physical appetite to repeat the event unless the memory calls it up.

If the physiological event is repeated continuously, habituation and adaptation may take place, which is normal. When adaptation sets in, the body may call for relief of the discomfort for a limited time. The condition of habituation and adaptation is always a reaction of the body to repeated events. Adaptation is not the cause of itself. If the repetition of events is stopped, the adapted need will subside and homeostasis will return. Alcoholism is not a "physiological disease process." When there is no alcohol present, the physiological process will stop spontaneously—and that means it is not a process. We are dealing simply with adaptation to repeated events. What remains when adaptation has subsided and physiological events are not repeated is the memory of the feelings. There is no process at the physiological level.

Neural adaptation to a chemical is not a disease process. It is quite normal if one takes in alcohol repeatedly. *What is not normal is the need to repeat the feelings.* The need to repeat the feelings is not physiologically driven.

When there is no alcohol present, precisely how do nonphysical factors start another physical event? The memory of the feelings may lead to the choice to use alcohol to repeat the feelings. Certain appetites such as those for food, or water, or sex do not need a memory of feelings to activate them, but the appetite for alcohol requires a memory of the experience.

Blum is not a member of the multifactorial school. He is, rather, an outright determinist of the biological view. He pauses here and there to tip his hat to the psychologists and sociologists, but not long enough to entertain their notions. Blum is not alone. There are other popular books advocating the biological viewpoint such as James Milam's *Under the Influence.* Another recent book proposes poor nutrition as the cause of alcoholism.

ADAPTATION

Biological determinism leads us to consider the facts of adaptation. One of the strongest arguments for the biological determination of alcoholism is the neurological. A great deal is made of withdrawal. Some advocates maintain that withdrawal discomfort keeps its hold for many months or longer, and thus can "cause" a relapse.

No discussion of addiction can be complete without some review of the neurological components of addiction. We can start out by saying that all the complex systems in the brain are organized around one central effort: to provide balance and coordination among all the cellular systems. It works to provide a sense of well-being. It works at every moment to provide "normalcy." Normalcy is a key notion in addiction; the addict is attempting to feel normal.

As we have seen, images are evaluated by the organism for life and death meanings of connection and separation. An awareness of connection is indispensable for normal functioning. When life equivalents of connection are perceived as unavailable the organism will adapt. It will ceaselessly attempt to achieve normalcy, or balance, through control, self-dependence, and self-nurture. The goal of all addictive behavior is to achieve balance, normalcy—to feel good. Because feeling good is the most important feature of human life, we may even go so far as to commit suicide to feel better.

The brain responds to all information through enormously complex cellular systems, the basic component of which is the neuron. Scientists tell us that the brain contains about one hundred billion neurons(!), and that each one may have as many as several thousand connections. The principal activity of the brain is transmitting and receiving information among these billions of neurons, through chemical transmitters. Addictive patterns are established in the following stages: feedback, habituation, and adaptation. It is the adaptive stage that underpins attachment, or addiction. We are told that adaptive (addictive) cellular patterns are also established for nonsubstance addictions such as sex, work, shopping. So let's go through the cellular stages of addiction.

Much information is available about the cellular stages of addiction. For the following description of cellular involvement in addiction, I am indebted to Gerald May, a Washington-based psychiatrist.

Feedback: When a shaming event occurs, that is, when necessary connections are perceived as broken, the cells receiving this information send out chemical transmitters to other cells, raising the alarm, and death equivalent feelings phase in. But the receiving cells, while accepting the message, will send back inhibitory messages to the excited cells to calm down, so that the entire system is not thrown out of balance. This feedback is the body's first defensive reaction to stress of any kind. It can occur as *inhibitory* feedback to the overactive cells in the system; or it can occur as a *stimulating* feedback to cells not acting sufficiently; or it can occur as *facilitating* feedback to cells that are reacting appropriately. In the case of messages of life coming from reactions to alcohol, the feedback will be positive and facilitating.

Habituation: Remember, the whole system is always striving for balance, for normalcy. That is why even heightened experiences do not retain the high. Alcohol is either a stimulant or a depressant. When feedback does not calm down the initiating cells, or normalize the reaction, the receiving cells will gradually habituate. Habituate does not mean get into a habit; it describes the process in which the cells become less sensitive and responsive to stimuli. Cells receiving repetitive stimuli over time will begin both to suppress the conduction of the messages from the other cells and to inhibit their own receptors. Thus normalcy is achieved. When neither feedback nor habituation can prevent an assault upon the entire system, however, then a new approach is employed by the cells to regain stability and balance.

This last approach is called *adaptation*. Countless systems of cells will adjust their functions to achieve a new normalcy in place of the old one. The cells will make physical changes in themselves, increasing or destroying transmitters, even destroying receptor sites. Once this new pattern is established, a new normalcy is achieved. When this is accomplished, it requires more alcohol, or more of the addictive behavior, to get the feelings desired.

Adaptation is the enemy of the alcoholic. Gradually, to continue the image-feelings of connection, he must consume more alcohol more often, thus establishing ever new levels of adaptation. What a couple of drinks did for him twenty years ago now takes a quart of liquor a day, washed down with beer. Many authors believe that adaptation calls for more alcohol. On the contrary, it is the need to repeat the feelings that adaptation is blunting, that calls for more alcohol.

What should be plain to see is the secondary role of the neurological system in alcoholism. *Neurological adaptation does not drive the addiction; rather, it interferes with the addiction.* The organism is addicted to the feelings of connection—the life equivalents provided by alcohol. As adaptation cuts down on the heightened feelings, the alcoholic must use more and more, to the point where she is destroying her body. The nervous system is not demanding more; her feeling complex is. This is not to say that an adapted state does not neurologically demand maintenance. After many years of moving into ever more adapted stages of alcoholism, who knows how deeply and pervasively the entire system has been involved? The agony of withdrawal is proof of that. The discomfort of stopping even fingernail biting is plainly experienced. Until the nervous system has re-adapted to the state without the addictive substance or behavior, it will play a strong role in the motivation to continue. The nervous system is not the originator of addiction; it does not demand increasing use. The addictions of the human organism cannot be defined in neurological terms. The nervous system *reacts* at its level to the *responses* of the feeling complex. It does not demand addictions.

(The literature abounds with words like "trigger" and "cues." These are strictly Pavlovian notions. Even Skinner had to walk away from them when he developed operant conditioning. Specifically human behavior is never triggered or cued.)

The biological viewpoint is not the most popular among authors and clinicians. The predominant view seems to be the multifactorial view first proposed by Jellinek in 1960. Within the multifactorial view, however, is a leaning toward the physiological as the strongest of the three factors. This is to be expected. The terrible power of alcoholism does not seem to lurk in psychological and cultural factors. Because of our Cartesian view of cause and effect, we are more comfortable attributing such power over us to physical forces. As a result, we often see alcoholism described, erroneously, as a physiologically based disease influenced by psychological and cultural factors.

The Alcoholic Gene

Blum is not alone in his belief that alcoholism is largely determined by the genes. Most people, whether they are struggling with addiction or not, have the idea that alcoholism is genetic in origin. Books, newspapers, talk shows, and magazines have conveyed this message. (For an enlightening discussion on the publicity about genes, see Stanton Peele, *The Truth About Addiction and Recovery*, 1991.)

Genetic causality is identified with the "billiard ball B" mindset. Wherever we see billiard ball B moving, we immediately look for billiard ball A, which caused it to move. We know today, however, that the human organism is not billiard ball B, nor is the nature of human interaction in environment anything like a game of billiards.

Any book that trumpets the genetic factor in alcoholism is promising the hopeful reader more on its cover than he or she will get from the pages within. Such a book can only tell the curious reader that he may have a vulnerability, but that is it. Precisely why she chooses to drink when she knows it is not good for her is not explained.

The notion of genetic causality beckons so relentlessly because we have no place else to look to explain our behaviors. Neither our hard nor soft sciences have developed a model of specifically human behavior, thanks to the Cartesian revolution in the hard sciences, and its influence upon the soft (social) sciences. Because psychology, sociology, and psychoanalysis craved the same objective validity that physics and mathematics provided to the hard sciences, we have no model today for the human phenomenon of choice.

The idea that human behavior is genetically driven was given a powerful impetus by E.O. Wilson's best selling *Sociobiology: The New Synthesis* (1975), a widely discussed book at the time. The human mind was nowhere to be found in Wilson's pages, a major mistake for which he was robustly taken to task in various books by Gould, Lewontin, and Flanagan. (See particularly *The Science of the Mind* by Owen Flanagan). Ashley Montagu refers to the work of Lewontin, Rose, and Kamin (*Not in Our Genes*) as a "rip-roaring dismantling of the recent rise of biologistic interpretations of why we behave as we do."

When Wilson's book appeared in the 1970s, it caused an uproar among social scientists. Wilson had violated the sacred canons of the "standard social science model" (SSSM). This model postulated that (1) the human individual is completely plastic, entirely malleable, as if it anticipated nothing; and (2) therefore human behavior is controlled or determined by the culture.

Wilson attempted to make the opposite case, that genes control and destine human behavior, but he also gave the genes extraordinary status. He said that the "individual organism is only their (the genes') vehicle." Another sociobiologist, Richard Dawkins, pictured "the higher levels of biological organization, the mind, the organism, or the person, as more or less incidental features of reality, as copying machines for the genes." Dawkins is known for his notion of "the selfish gene."

Some authors applaud Wilson for restoring a role to the organism in contrast to the human blob offered by the SSSM, but Wilson did so rather perversely. He (and Dawkins) focused upon the gene to the point of giving it ascendancy even over the individual whole. The gene, however, is a subordinate aspect of the organization of the whole. Wholes (humans) we know now have a hierarchy of organization (referred to as levels of description by physicists). Wilson and Dawkins describe the physiological level as superior to the mental level.

While it is not within the scope of this book to explain the workings of DNA in the human whole, I will offer brief summary views of experts whose work is easily available.

Stephen Jay Gould points out (*Ever Since Darwin*) that our genes contribute the capacities but not the behavior of the organism. He says that we cannot imply that "our patterns of behavior or social arrangements are in any way directly determined by our genes. Potential and determination are different concepts." Saying the same thing as Gould, Owen Flanagan, in *The Science of the Mind*, stresses: "This difference in genetic allowance or capacity, on the one hand, and genetic promotion or predisposition on the other, is crucial." Flanagan makes the point that "our genes have provided an exceedingly flexible cognitive system." As we have seen, addiction must be described at the cognitive level of human organization.

Sydney Cohen (*The Chemical Brain*) emphasizes that "genetics is not destiny." He adds, "Those who have no genetic loading whatsoever cannot be assured that they are immune to becoming alcoholic. It may be that a majority of alcoholics have no inherited vulnerability." Benjamin Pierce (*The Family Genetic Sourcebook*) writes, "In spite of evidence for a strong hereditary component to alcoholism, anyone with an alcoholic relative should keep in mind certain facts: the majority of individuals with a genetic predisposition to alcoholism never become alcoholics. . . ." Pierce's conclusion parallels an observation by Herbert Fingarette (*Heavy Drinking*), commenting on Goodwin's study of heredity. Fingarette points out that Goodwin's work shows that 18 percent of sons who had an alcoholic parent became alcoholic. This compares with only 5 percent who did not have an alcoholic parent—granted, a statistically significant difference. But what does it also indicate? Fingarette observes this also means that 82 percent of the sons of alcoholic parents did not become alcoholic!

Edgar P. Nace, M.D. (*The Treatment of Alcoholism*), points out from a 1979 study, that 45 percent to 80 percent of alcoholics did not have an alcoholic relative. In another study—Sweden 1981— 60 percent of the males, regardless of the severity of the alcoholism, did not have a family history of alcoholism. Nace concludes, ". . . [A]s important as genetic factors may eventually prove to be, such factors do not seem to be necessary, nor are they sufficient, for the development of alcoholism in most patients."

GENOTYPE AND PHENOTYPE

Some readers may come across the terms *genotype* and *phenotype* with regard to notions of human behavior. These terms have to do with a distinction between genetic instructions and the phenotypical (observable) behavior of the organism in environment. Genotype indicates basic genetic instructions for the development of human features—which interact with environment. Phenotype describes observable human behavior in the environment, resulting from interaction of genotype and the environment. Neither genotype nor phenotype illuminates specifically human action, processes, or dynamics. The reader should be aware that alcoholism cannot be described either as genotypical or as phenotypical; the person is left out. Human action must be described in terms of genotype-*choice*-phenotype.

Alcoholism, nonetheless, is most often described in the limited terms of phenotypical behavior, for example in the diagnoses proposed in the Diagnostic and Statistical Manual (DSM-IV most recently). The dynamics, or nature, of alcoholism must be described, however, in terms of the symbolic-affective apprehension of life and death meanings in the environment, as was explained in earlier chapters. Genotype and phenotype do not in any way describe human motivation around meanings.

The distinction between the genome and phenotypical behavior is described by Nobel laureate Gerald M. Edelman (*Neural Darwinism*). Edelman states that it is mathematically inconceivable that the human genome specifies the entire wiring diagram of the brain. The genome, powerful as it is, contains too few instructions by several orders of magnitude to build a fully functional brain. The synaptic connections that evolve in a brain over time are the complex causal outcome of (1) genotypic instructions, (2) endogenous biochemical processes, and (3) vast amounts of individual unique organism-environment interaction. Here we see the development of the brain being described in terms of the genotypical instruction and phenotypical behavior. We see the genome instructing the development of the organism's specific human features and the organism's capacity to act in specifically human fashion. Alcoholism is not a fundamental human characteristic or feature, and it seems hardly likely that it is the role of the genes to specifically provide for it. One might argue that if the genes are responsible for alcoholic drinking behavior, then there must also be a gene to stop such behavior! The way we behave, or the choices we make, are not caused by our genes. Our genes provide our species-specific features of reaction and response, but they do not cause or determine the response. Even if a gene were found—or some combination of DNA factors—directly associated with alcoholism, that gene cannot determine alcoholic behavior. It can determine only a susceptibility, which might render the felt effects of alcohol abnormally attractive to the individual.

What is the appeal of the genetic factor for the general public (and for many scientists)? First of all, the vast majority of us still view the world and the human organism as a Cartesian machine; it is almost impossible for us to look for nonmechanical causes of anything. It takes time to become comfortable realizing that the abstract, or immaterial world is just as real as the material world, as Heisenberg and others have discovered. The insistence upon genetic causes of behavior is typical of classical epistemology and classical logic—which cannot deliver the ultimate understanding of nature. (This shocking conclusion was first presented to the world in 1927, when a convention of the world's top physicists decided that ultimate reality was not amenable to classical descriptions; thus, Neils Bohr could say that anyone who was not profoundly shocked by quantum mechanics did not understand it.)

Second, it is much more palatable to put a behavioral problem into a medical or physiological perspective. Third, we like predictability. The genetic theory gives us that. If Dad and Granddad tippled themselves into the grave, then perhaps I had better cut down—a very sensible idea. And further, many people feel relieved of guilt and shame when they read that their problems are genetically determined. They can as easily be relieved of guilt and shame when they understand the true nature of addiction.

Alcoholism, addiction, criminality—what have you—is something more than genetic coding and a billion firing neurons. In this book, the explanation of that statement is set down.

THE EIGHTH SPECIAL REPORT TO THE UNITED STATES CONGRESS (1993)

The Special Report to the Congress from the Secretary of Health and Human Services is an important document, surveying the national problem of alcoholism. In a very real sense, it is the official position of the United

States government on alcoholism. I include the Report under the physiological heading because it holds out hope for progress within the disciplines of genetic research and neuroscience. The National Institute on Alcohol and Alcohol Abuse is in an unenviable position. They are working within a strictly Cartesian viewpoint, which cannot deliver an accurate description of alcoholism, and yet every few years, they must turn out a progress report when there is no progress to report. Issued periodically, it has yet to report substantive results, and is largely a reshuffling of the material in earlier reports. It is based on the assumption that science will eventually uncover the causes of alcoholism if we just keep probing deeper into biochemical and neurological levels of human organization. Lately, genetics and neuroscience are the darlings of the Report. As we have seen, both of these areas may yield more information about the composition of the whole, but they will never describe the specific activity of the whole. Let me comment upon a few summary findings in the Report.

> Alcohol dependence, often called alcoholism, refers to a disease characterized by abnormal alcohol-seeking behavior that leads to impaired control over drinking. Although alcoholics and alcohol abusers experience many of the same harmful effects of drinking, the critical difference between the two is the physical dependence displayed by alcoholics and their impaired ability to regulate their consumption of alcohol.

The Special Report, in error, attempts to define alcoholism in terms of physical dependence. The human organism is physically dependent upon food, water, and air. The physical dependence in alcoholism is simply cellular adaptation. The dependence is transient, itself depending upon whether the individual chooses to drink. It cannot describe the essence of the affliction. After withdrawal, physical dependence subsides dramatically, and in time disappears altogether. Physical dependence—adaptation—does not characterize alcoholism; it is a sign. Instead, the choice to drink again in spite of consequences, after alcohol is gone from the system, characterizes alcoholism. Individuals can choose not to drink during the height of withdrawal agony—demonstrating that adaptation does not determine the choice to drink.

In the words of the Report, alcoholism is a "disease characterized by abnormal alcohol-seeking behavior." It is the "alcohol-seeking" that requires illumination. The "dependence," or adaptation, flows quite naturally from that behavior. Keep in mind that adaptation to the continued ingestion of alcohol is not a physical disease process but a normal reaction of the body. Why some individuals are more likely to be alcohol-seeking than other individuals cannot be answered by describing the physical levels of human action. Even though alcohol delivers more neurological "reward cascades" for some individuals, that does not make drinking inevitable. Another observation must be made about alcohol dependence. The severe physical dependency the drinking alcoholic shows is certainly a sign of the alcoholic, but it does not reveal the nature of alcoholism. As long as alcohol is continually in the system and as long as adaptation persists, there will be signs of physical dependence. Alcoholism can be diagnosed from a variety of signs, but it cannot be understood from the symptoms. The question still remains: Why does the individual choose to drink again in spite of the known consequences, when there is no alcohol in the system? The answer to this question will describe the nature of alcoholism.

> Findings from family, adoption, and twin studies have shown that vulnerability to alcoholism is determined by a complex interplay of genetic and environmental factors. This information has stimulated much research aimed at identifying the specific genetic, psychological, and social determinants that underlie the development of the disease.

It is important to examine carefully the wording: ". . . studies have shown that vulnerability to alcoholism is determined by a complex interplay of genetic and environmental factors." Two key attitudes emerge from this quotation. First of all, the word *vulnerability*. This acknowledges that the genes do not cause or determine alcoholism. We have seen why not in the section on genetics. Second, the statement calls for an interplay between genetic and environmental factors. We have here what I call the case of the missing person. Note that in the Report the "interplay" takes place between genetic factors and environmental factors. The person is nowhere to be found! Remember, there is a step between the genetic instructions and the influence of the environment; that step is called *perception*. Environmental information has to be processed through our formative capacities where choices and decisions are made. Our genes determine the potential to do this; they do not determine the choices and decisions! Those choices will be determined by the meanings the individual perceives in the environment.

Advances in neuroscience have provided much knowledge of alcohol's acute and chronic actions on the central and peripheral nervous systems. These advances have been facilitated by the developments of such sophisticated new research tools as electrophysiologial, imaging, and molecular biology techniques, which are enabling neuroscience researchers to analyze alcohol's effects on systems and regions in the brain. Through these research efforts we are gaining insight into the chemical and physiological processes that underlie alcohol addiction.

Note the absence of the basic question: Why was alcohol introduced into the system? Neuroscience has become the principal hope of the mechanistic view of alcoholism. Neuroscience is fundamentally reductive. What can we hope to learn from insights into the chemical and physiological processes? As we have seen, the most thoroughgoing research on the brain is not going to illuminate the nature of specific human action. We took up this point in the chapter on the mind–brain controversy. At some point we will have to admit that human action must be described at a different level of human organization.

A promising area of study that addresses gene-environment interactions examines the possible link between the genetically based phenomenon of personality and genetic susceptibility for alcohol use disorders. These studies potentially can provide insight into why some genetically vulnerable persons never develop alcohol problems whereas others shift to problem drinking.

The promise of such studies will never be realized until we properly examine the interaction itself between susceptibility and social processes. (We have already seen noted scientists comment that interaction is "only the beginning of wisdom.") Notice the expression "gene-environment interactions." The expression should read "gene-*person*-environment interactions." When we look for the reasons that some people become full-fledged alcoholics and others do not, we will have to take into account human perceptions of meaning as they occur in the feeling complex.

We can sum up the basic flaw in the Report simply by noting that it is a Cartesian project working from the mechanistic view of the human organism in its environment. The Report is not in the least self-conscious about its perspective. It attempts no controlling image of the human organism.

The practical impact of the Report could well be continued funding for research into blind alleys. Intensified research for the "causes" of alcoholism in genetics and neuroscience will be of very limited use in the treatment of what is a specifically human problem—a problem of the organism as a whole. A focus upon the question of why some individuals (the majority) resist their predisposition to alcoholism would be a step in the right direction.

THE MULTIFACTORIAL VIEW

The pure biological viewpoint is not the most popular among authors and clinicians. The predominant view seems to be the multifactorial view first proposed by Jellinek in 1960. Within the multifactorial view is a leaning toward the physiological as the strongest of the three factors. This is to be expected, as the terrible power of alcoholism does not seem to lurk in the psychological and cultural factors. Because of our Cartesian, mechanical view of cause and effect, we are more comfortable attributing such power over us to physical forces.

The multifactorial view appears to dominate the clinical literature. Jellinek proposed that true alcoholism generally had three causative factors: physiological, psychological, and sociological. He proposed (1) biochemical vulnerability, (2) psychological factors, and (3) culturally acceptable habits. Jellinek believed, as Vaillant reports, that what was needed was not an argument that one or another factor is the most important cause of alcoholism, but an effort to understand the relative etiological contribution of each variable to the total clinical picture.

At first glance the multifactorial view would seem to fly in the face of Cartesian medicine. Some authors even welcomed it as holistic, but it cannot be holistic without the inclusion of the role of the subject. When carefully examined, the multifactorial viewpoint simply assigns multiple causes to the disorder. You take a dash of the biological, a splash of the psychological, and a snippet of the sociological, mix them up, and presto! you have an alcoholic. It is additive rather than holistic. Jellinek's pioneering efforts were solidly within the Cartesian-Newtonian worldview.

There is without doubt multifactorial causality in the etiology of alcoholism. Where the multifactorial position falls short is in its failure to consider the nature of causality in human behavior. We have already seen how causality works in the behavior of the human organism-in-environment. The multifactorial position fails to distinguish between causality and determination.

Highly regarded authors insist that alcoholism is a multifactorial disease, but in doing so do not touch upon the role of the organism. As these authors employ the term, it is descriptive of factors viewed deterministically and additively. The idea that there are several distinct causative factors at work in the alcoholic's repeated choice to drink is certainly a well-documented observation, but the alcoholic is never billiard ball D being struck by billiard balls A, B, and C. Recall that multifactorial conditions are true causes to which the organism must respond—but they do not determine the organism's response; the organism does. As simple as this sounds, it is nevertheless a key source of confusion in much of the literature.

In *Not In Our Genes,* Lewontin, Rose, and Kamin tell us that human life may be deterministic, but it is so within an enormously complex organization of intersecting causes and occasions, and includes interpenetrations of cognitive, physical, and social factors. Recall that basically the organism is determined and limited within its species-specific behavior. It must do what it must do as an organism. In other words, it is determined in its organic assignments. In human life, however, this determination happens in such a way that the entire human situation gives rise to experiences of choice and responsibility. At no time within its organic limitations is the human organism determined by circumstances when acting as a human.

What is lacking in the multifactorial viewpoint proposed by Jellinek is a controlling image (model) of the human being, as has been explained previously in this book. Nobody ever explains precisely what it (the subject) is that these factors are influencing.

Another author supporting the disease concept is Edgar Nace, M.D. Nace wrote an excellent book for physicians, *The Treatment of Alcoholism,* believing that most doctors know little or nothing about alcoholism. He is an associate professor of clinical psychiatry at Southwestern Medical School in Texas. Nace has one of the most carefully thought out positions available in the literature.

Nace defines alcoholism as follows:

> To understand the alcoholic we must try to imagine a condition few of us have experienced: psychological dependence on a chemical. This form of dependence is not the state of physical dependence characterized by tolerance to alcohol and emergence of withdrawal symptoms when alcohol is discontinued. Psychological dependence precedes physical dependence by at least five years. . . . Psychological dependence is the essence of the disease and is the central organizing experience of the alcoholic.

Nace's attitude is sharply opposed to Blum's; both men describe alcoholism as a disease, but one as a physiologically based disease, the other as a psychologically based disease. Let me talk first about psychological dependence, and then discuss Nace's defense of the disease concept.

Nace describes psychological dependence as the evolving priority of alcohol in the individual's life. It also involves self-doubt, the sense that one cannot cope without alcohol, and a sense of loss if no alcohol is available. Revolving around his primary construct of psychological dependence Nace finds craving, loss of control, personality regression, denial, and conflicted behavior.

Missing in Nace's description of psychological dependence is the unasked question: Why does psychological dependence develop? Saying that psychological dependence is an increasing priority of alcohol is rather tautological. I can be psychologically dependent upon the love of my children, upon my social security check every month, upon my health insurance, and so on. To understand psychological dependence upon alcohol we have to dig deeper.

Dependence upon alcohol is needing image-feelings of connection provided by alcohol. Alcohol provides connections the individual does not experience without the chemical. Alcohol is very powerful because it directly affects the specific human awareness of life equivalents. Or it numbs the death equivalent of separation.

LOSS OF CONTROL

The ubiquitous question about loss of control makes a prominent appearance in Nace's book. Lately, loss of control has become the central interest of many researchers. In an article in the *New England Journal of Medicine* (August 26, 1993), two psychiatrists write: "The concept of alcohol dependence has broadened beyond one of simple tolerance and physiologic dependence and has shifted to focus on an impairment in the ability to control one's use of alcohol."

As it is presented, their idea of loss of control is incorrect and confused. Nace quotes Keller, writing in the *British Journal of Addiction*: "Why one loses control is not known, but it is the pathognomonic sign of alcoholism. If we understood the cause of loss of control, the etiology of alcoholism might be explained." Keller is right that we do not understand loss of control; we are still groping toward an understanding of alcoholism. Understanding loss of control can be the road to the hideout of the demon.

Loss of control appears under two distinct aspects. They must be understood as distinct.

(1) The loss of control that occurs after the alcoholic takes alcohol into the system is obvious and is *not of concern* in searching for the etiology of the addiction. Unfortunately, this appears to be the loss of control about which

Keller is writing. A toxin is present in the system and we cannot describe species-specific behavior under that condition.

(2) The so-called loss of control that occurs when there is no alcohol in the system must be the focus of attention, but describing the alcoholic's choice to drink when there is no alcohol in the system as loss of control is a fundamental error. Loss of control is the *appearance* only. The decision to drink again is *actually taking control!* It is an attempt to feel better, or numb out. Alcohol per se has nothing to do with the decision to drink, but the memory of alcohol-induced feelings offers a form of control not available without it. At that moment there is no control to lose, and a form of control can be gained by using alcohol. The memory of alcohol presents a way of controlling that offers more life (or numbing) than does the existing state. Taking the drink is assuming control, not losing it—a critically important distinction to understand. The human organism is a self-organizing whole. It does not "lose control" in its specific behavior, but it can attempt to control inappropriately. This is the key notion behind the success of Alcoholics Anonymous (AA). AA recognizes that as a means of control alcohol does not work.

We may mistake the alcoholic's decision to control as a loss of control because of the loathing, self-disgust, and hopelessness that go along with the decision to drink again. The loathing and self-disgust arise from the sense of failure that he has once again chosen the inappropriate control. The sense of failure arises from a conflict of symbol systems. The alcoholic knows there is a better life in not drinking. He knows that he should be managing his life without attempting to control it with alcohol, *but he does not have a sufficiently developed symbol system to provide more image-feelings of life in not drinking.* His control of his feelings (self-nurture) through alcohol is more familiar and reliable. Let me give an example. In the early stages of recovery, an invitation to a recovering alcoholic to go out to an elegant restaurant for a steak and lobster dinner causes a panic. All the alcoholic's image-feelings in memory about that restaurant are bound up with the great drinks they serve. She was in the habit of controlling her feelings, her moods, with alcohol. She is being expected now to control her feelings with nothing but good food, companionship, and ambiance. Later, after many years into recovery, she has been to that restaurant a dozen times without using alcohol. She has built up a brand-new inventory of image-feelings about dining there without alcohol. She can now control her mood there without alcohol. Her former "loss of control," and taking a drink under those circumstances, was thought of purely as loss of control. She now understands that she did not lose control formerly; she was attempting to control in the absence of another more appropriate system of image-feelings.

(At AA meetings it is common to hear the expression "I could not stop" or "I no longer *wanted* to drink; I *had* to." When alcohol is constantly in the system, the decision to drink repeatedly is generally not specifically human behavior. We can refer to this phase of drinking as out of control.)

Understanding loss of control as instead the *attempt to control* is the fundamental insight on which the program of Alcoholics Anonymous is built. Scientific and academic communities have not yet grasped AA's notion of powerlessness, or fundamental limitation.

Nace defends the psychological disease concept this way: "The concepts that justify considering alcoholism as a disease, even in the light of our limited understanding of pathology, are derived from the altered psychological and behavioral experience of the alcoholic patient . . ." I agree with Nace as far as he goes, but he still does not probe the nature of that experience. In another place, Nace says, "The cause of alcoholism is unknown, but is best thought of as multi-determined." Here we have the flavor of determinism again.

We have to examine carefully Nace's use of the term disease on the basis of "changes in the structure of cognitive functioning." Instead of structure I prefer the word *process*. Thanks to the notion of wholes emerging after quantum mechanics, it is better to forego the Cartesian view of structures in wholes in favor of processes. Alcoholism does not depend on changes in the psychological structure. *Alcoholism depends on the interpretation of meanings apprehended by the formative process.* The formative process can be skewed by "the basic fault"—the disharmony in primary connections beginning possibly even before birth.

Another author who accepts the disease concept of alcoholism is George Vaillant, M.D. Vaillant, a psychiatrist, is author of *The Natural History of Alcoholism,* a long awaited and widely acclaimed interpretation of the findings of the Harvard study. The Harvard study tracked six hundred volunteers for forty years, resulting in the most impressive sociological study done for alcoholism. Vaillant's interpretations are characterized by a welcome objectivity and honesty. Vaillant is not an enthusiast about the disease concept. He does believe, however, that the affliction is deadly and deserves the attention that any disease requires.

Vaillant talks about alcoholism this way:

> Uncontrolled, maladaptive ingestion of alcohol is not a disease in
> the sense of biological disorder; rather, alcoholism is a disorder of
> behavior . . . there is no more reason to subsume alcohol abuse under
> the medical model than to include compulsive fingernail biting,
> gambling, or child molesting in textbooks of medicine.

Vaillant represents a view differing from both that of Blum, a
physiological determinist, and Nace, who sees psychological dependence
as the essence of alcoholism. When Vaillant speaks of disorder of behavior,
he does not attempt to describe the dynamic of behavior. Vaillant leans
toward a sociological determinism. His focal point of interest in the problem
lies in sociological prospective behavioral studies. It is a characteristic of
sociologists, I am told, to equate behavior with human action—a tendency
that leads the reader to believe they are defining human dynamics when in
fact they make no attempt whatsoever to deal with individual variables and
choices. Thus prospective studies, like the Harvard study, make excellent
surveys of the conditions under which alcoholism occurs, but they offer no
explanations for individual response to those conditions.

The sociological approach as explanation has been criticized by many
authors (Jantsch, for one) because it regards people in groups, classes, and
clusters. Berman says, "The argument here . . . is that the life of the body,
and the emotions, and the subjective experience of how the mind and body
interact, constitute the real events of our lives." These real individual events
are not taken into consideration in sociology.

Vaillant sees no harm in calling alcoholism a disease. "Alcoholism can reflect
both a conditioned habit and a disease; and the disease of alcoholism can be as
well defined by a sociological model as by a medical model. Thus, alcoholism
is a construct of a higher order of complexity than, say pregnancy or measles."
This total elimination of the "ego" is most surprising coming from a
psychiatrist! Vaillant accepts the notion of alcoholism as conditioned habit as
well as a determining disease. Vaillant remains within the mechanical model.
In another place, he says:

> But I must concede at the outset that however dexterously alcohol-
> ism may be shoehorned into a medical model, both its etiology and
> treatment are largely social. Indeed, in modern medicine there may
> be no other instance of sociology's contributing so much to our
> understanding of a so-called disease.

This is a bit confused; sociology has nothing to do with the etiology of
species-specific human response. Sociology describes the behavior of

collections and groups and classes; it never describes the motivations of the individual. A rigorous survey of the conditions to which individuals respond is helpful. A knowledge of the patterns and complexities of the human in her or his environment can assist in forecasting, preventing, and removing conditions that may evoke the alcoholic response. It gives direction to both research and treatment.

I have briefly given you my views of three of the strongest voices who promote the disease concept, or at least are friendly to it.

HABIT

The concept of habit in addiction is not as popular as the disease viewpoint, and authors who subscribe to the habit school of thought do not endorse the disease concept. The habit viewpoint is predominant among academic psychologists and sociologists. It is the view of many dedicated and influential authors and workers in the field of addiction studies. Proponents of the habit notion of addiction must be reckoned with in any attempt to establish the nature of addictive behaviors.

Two prominent authors regard alcoholism as fundamentally a bad habit; G. Alan Marlatt and Stanton Peele have become strong voices—Marlatt in the field, Peele in the popular arena. Let's begin with Marlatt. His most recent work is *Relapse Prevention*. Marlatt says:

> From a social-learning perspective, addictive behaviors represent a category of "bad habits," including such behaviors as problem drinking. . . . Addictive behaviors are viewed as overlearned *habits* that can be modified and analyzed in the same manner as other habits . . . .Those who subscribe to the addictive behavior model are particularly interested in studying the *determinants* of addictive habits, including situational and environmental antecedents, beliefs and expectations, and the individual's family history and prior learning experience with the substance or activity. In addition there is an equal interest in discovering the *consequences* of these behaviors, so as to better understand . . . the reinforcing effects that may contribute to increased use. (Marlatt's emphases)

In the following discussions, I explain a fundamental difference between Marlatt's position and my own. Marlatt says, "One of the central underlying assumptions of this approach is that addictive behaviors consist of overlearned, maladaptive habit patterns." I disagree. The habitual aspect of alcoholism, or any addiction, is not its defining characteristic. It is a profound error to identify habit with the essential nature of alcoholism. Habit is not a species-specific characteristic of the human organism.

Marlatt's psychology is pure Skinner, and that means, in short, a psychology that is not adequate to explaining the specific human activity of addiction. For that reason, I will attempt to locate Skinner in this discussion for the reader, assuming that most people picking up this book are about as conversant with Skinner as I was when I began this study. I refer the reader to the commentaries of Finley Carpenter, *The Skinner Primer*, and Owen Flanagan, *The Science of the Mind*.

Two of the most important ideas in the history of behavioral studies have been stimulus response (Pavlov's dog), and operant conditioning, as developed by B.F. Skinner. Many authors consider Skinner the most important psychologist after Freud. Marlatt's ideas about the nature of alcoholism are based squarely on Skinner's propositions, but in order to grasp something of the nature of Skinner's contribution, I think we have to understand a bit about stimulus response first. Everyone has heard about the dog who salivated whenever Pavlov rang a bell. Shortly after the discovery of stimulus response became a milestone in behavioral psychology, its shortcomings as a complete explanation of human activity became apparent.

The classical stimulus response idea elaborated by Pavlov was at first believed to be an ultimate explanation for all organic behavior. Stimulus response proposed that all activity of an organism was preceded by stimuli in the environment that drew forth or actually caused a response from the organism. Stimulus response theory of human behavior is clearly a Cartesian outlook of pure mechanics. It had been most important to the pioneers in the development of American psychology that its methods ape as closely as possible the rational scientific successes of the physical sciences. We have seen, however, that the specific activity of the human organism, as a self-regulating whole in its environment, cannot be explained mechanically.

Stimulus response suggests that the organism is passive, is activated only by stimuli, and that the stimuli can always be identified. Skinner, however, saw that organisms are capable, in fact, of initiating action—that they are not always passive reactors to stimulants, and that stimuli or causes of human activity can not always be clearly identified. Skinner believed, too, that pure mechanics, and therefore stimulus response, could not ultimately explain human behavior. He was forced to this conclusion because the precise causes of every human action could not be scientifically isolated and identified. And here lies an important point to understand about Skinner's philosophy of psychology. Skinner was not in the least interested in the explanatory features of his psychology. His was a pure science based on observations of behavior and not on vague constructions about the workings of the mind. Commentators on Skinner point out his passion to avoid mental constructs of any kind as explanatory devices.

Skinner rescued behavioral psychology from the simpler mechanics of stimulus response with his basic hypothesis that the behavior of all organisms is determined by the consequences they experience from their own behavior. The sharp difference from stimulus response is apparent. In other words, instead of waiting to be moved by the bell, the organism is moved instead by the reinforcement it experiences in an action it has initiated. Oddly, as Flanagan has pointed out, Skinner is not interested in what first moved the organism. He is only interested in the subsequent pattern of reinforcement—that the organism will actively pursue those activities which it knows will reinforce the experiences it had previously. Skinner called this process operant conditioning.

At this point, Skinner must be confronted in his belief that operant conditioning can account for all human behavior. Skinner introduced the notions of reward and reinforcement into the motivation of behavior, but what is being rewarded and what is being reinforced? Skinner would answer that he does not care, simply because we cannot know that. Psychologists disagreeing with Skinner do not accept that; such a position denies important experiences of human behavior that should not be ignored or dismissed.

As we know from the work of dialectical biologists, as in *Not in Our Genes*, negotiations with our environment produce a certain amount of novelty in that relationship. Novelty cannot be explained solely by operant conditioning. In a dialectic, by definition, one is not always immediately rewarded and reinforced by his actions, but learns to compromise and create novelty in relationships.

I have already shown that the human organism has innate capacities to anticipate reward and reinforcement; the very idea of reward implies anticipation. The very idea of reinforcement implies that some process is being strengthened. Surely it is clear that a *tabula rasa* cannot anticipate and therefore cannot be rewarded and reinforced. A whole psychology must accept not only the idea of operant conditioning, but the descriptions of the innate processes that can result in operant conditioning. The principal flaw in Skinner's contribution is that he refuses to participate in descriptions of these innate processes.

We have seen that cognitive science, in its breakaway from behaviorism, has reinstated the notion of the image, or internal representation of the environment. The tendency has been away from operant conditioning as the sole description of human behavior. We have also seen that we can be more comfortable these days with abstract descriptions of human organization (which Skinner and behaviorists shun) because of the notions of the whole implied in quantum mechanics and nonlocality.

(Sociologists and psychologists of the Skinnerian school might profit from a weekend devoted to a discussion of level confusion. Modern physics has made an enormously important contribution to psychology, but the psychological community does not know that. It is perfectly okay these days to speak of and describe the abstract levels of organic wholes; in fact, it is inevitable.)

Marlatt's description of alcoholism relies exclusively on the idea of operant conditioning and learning. Addictions are nothing more than "overlearned habits"—a sorely restricted view of human activity. Human beings can be trained to change their behaviors, of course, and this is what Marlatt would like to do; he remains comfortably within the mechanistic world view. We have seen, however, that changing a behavior is not enough—that the human organism is moved by the meanings it perceives in a dialectic with its environment. It follows that before we attempt to change behavior we must change fundamental perceptions of meaning. That is what behaviorism fails to do.

A whole psychology of the human will treat, first of all, the specific human characteristic of anticipation of meanings in the environment, and then propose behavioristic techniques to strengthen and reinforce a new interpretation of meaning. Once the human has decided what is meaningful, she can then develop patterns of behavior around those meanings. The alcoholic's interpretation of what is meaningful has been skewed by distrust, self-dependence, and painful confusion. Behavioristic techniques may not resolve the internal conflicts resulting from earlier shaming.

An understanding of the nature of specifically human behavior is most important in developing appropriate remedies for Marlatt's maladaptive behavior. Habit is not specifically human behavior. If the problem is attacked simply as habit, it may not yield the changes needed at the level of specific human behavior. Habit is merely an aspect of human action. Of course addiction can be described as an overlearned habit, but what does the term habit tell us about addiction that we do not already know?

Relapse Prevention, in the Cartesian worldview, talks about *determinants* of addictive behavior rather than conditions; the subject is being left out. Marlatt also refers to the addict's beliefs and expectations. The question should be about the *nature* of these beliefs and expectations. What is being expected and why? In addiction, something has gone wrong in the inner processes of expectation and belief.

In Marlatt's description we have a tautological description of addictive behaviors. We get no explanation of reinforcement, why it occurs, what is being reinforced; we see the usual confusion between determinants and causality; and we are given no explanation of belief and expectation in the overlearning process. What precisely does the term overlearning mean? What does it explain? What is the nature of expectation? What precisely is being expected by the human organism?

Alcoholism is species-specific behavior (when it is properly defined as choices made without alcohol in the system). That is not to say that we do not develop many habits that contribute to the perpetuation of alcoholism. The human organism-in-environment is a creature of both species-specific behavior and the habits that flow from that behavior.

In dealing with alcoholism, behavioral techniques are effective once the alcoholic begins to change his defensive and controlling interpretations of meanings in his environment. If he is taught that his alcoholism is nothing more than a powerful habit, then he is not likely to understand why he has acquired this habit. He will not learn the nature of his choices. If he does not give up control, behavioristic techniques will be bandages over the wounds.

Another author who promotes the view that alcoholism is a bad habit is Stanton Peele. Peele has sunk his teeth into the disease concept like an enraged pit bull. His last two books are angry polemics against the addiction recovery "industry," and the program of AA. Peele authored *Love and Addiction*, *The Diseasing of America*, and *The Truth About Addiction and Recovery*.

Love and Addiction was an important contribution to the addiction field in 1975. Peele was probably the first to popularize the view that addiction was not limited to substance abuse, but could be applied to relationships, work, and other aspects of human existence. In *Love and Addiction*, Peele leans to specifically human responses to environment, such as fear of threats to security, lack of self-confidence, and generally negative views of the world and people. For example, Peele says: "Addiction is a complex and wide-ranging reaction." In another place he says: "[W]e need a concept of addiction that emphasizes the way people interpret and organize their experience." These are the activities of inner processes, not our mechanical habits. The following passage from *Love and Addiction* strongly suggests that addiction is more than a bad habit:

> Addiction is not a mysterious chemical process; it is the logical outgrowth of the way a drug makes a person feel . . . A person repeatedly seeks artificial infusions of a sensation, whether it be one of somnolence or vitality, that is not supplied by the organic balance of his life as a whole. Such infusions insulate him from the fact that the world he perceives psychologically is becoming farther and farther removed from the real state of his body or his life.

Later, in his polemical work, we find a shift in perspective: "An addiction is a habitual response and a source of gratification or security." He adds, "[I]t is important to place addictive habits in their proper context, as part of people's lives, their personalities, their relationships, their environments, their perspectives." Obviously, addictions are habitual responses. Obviously they deliver gratification and security. We know all that, but why does the human organism become addicted to these experiences of gratification and security? What is the process of addiction? Why does the human organism develop a habit that is so difficult to change? Here we see Peele skirting and surrounding the essential question but never raising it again.

Peele remains in the Skinnerian school here; a good description of behavior is all that is necessary. The processes of addiction need not be investigated. For example, the following is the principal definition of addiction found on the first page of *The Truth About Addiction and Recovery*:

> Addiction is an ingrained habit that undermines your health, your work, your relationships, your self-respect, but that you feel you cannot change. Addictions are hard to change because you have relied on them—in many cases for years or decades—as ways of getting through life, of gaining satisfaction, of spending time, and even of defining who you are.

Unfortunately, Peele is unable to improve on that definition as the book progresses. Because Peele prefers to develop a description of human behavior (habit) rather then a model of human action, his behavioristic model has the ring of an elaborate tautology. Habit describes human behavior, but adds nothing to our understanding of human action. It is a notion that leaves untouched the image-feeling process that characterizes human motivation and activity.

To rely upon notions of habit in talking of alcoholism—or any addiction—is to deeply impoverish the level of discourse about the subject.

It should be recognized at the outset that alcoholism is a bad habit so that we can get on with the investigation into the nature of the affliction.

Peele seems to jump from an earlier description of addiction as a matter of interior processes to behavioristic habit because he is not able to find a model of the human being. Even though recognizing that inner systems exist, he is reluctant to deal with them as such—in line with a Skinnerian philosophy that it is not possible to say anything meaningful about inner processes because they cannot be publicly observed or measured. Along with many psychologists and sociologists who follow a stimulus response, operant conditioning theory of human behavior, Peele, after all, is not able to recommend treatment that is not purely behaviorist. That, perhaps, is the reason for the shift in perspective from interior processes to habit.

Peele's view of AA is perhaps the weakest part of his work; he indulges in an arbitrary and misinformed deconstruction of the AA experience in order to reconstruct the experience to suit his own views. His clumsy dismissal of a significant movement is most surprising. I question the nature and extent of the supportive data for his conclusions. Having attended more than 1,500 meetings in this country and abroad, I do not recognize a single characteristic of AA offered by Peele.

(A book enjoying longevity in the bookstores is *Heavy Drinking* by Herbert Fingarette. Fingarette is a self-styled expert on alcoholism who has admittedly never treated a single alcoholic, but shows up anyway on television panels and testifies as an expert. In the second half of his book, Fingarette repeatedly defines addiction as *central activity*. I emphasize it because Fingarette does. Having Fingarette explain alcoholism to you is like going to a doctor who tells you that you feel sick precisely because you feel sick!)

PSYCHOANALYSIS

Psychoanalysis is the classic therapeutic technique developed by Freud. It is practiced by both psychiatrists and psychologists, although it was originally only in the hands of the medical community. Psychoanalysis is what it says it is: It analyzes or breaks down the human "psyche" or personality into three parts, the ego, the id, and the superego. The id, also called the unconscious, harbors the deep instinctual needs and drives constantly seeking expression. The only drives that Freud deals with are sexuality and aggression. The ego tries to accommodate these drives as well as it can in the environment in which it must negotiate its well-being. Freud's description of the ego as the "clown in the circus" indicates its nebulous state in between the id and the superego; questions of choice and will are not acknowledged in classical Freudian analysis. The superego comprises the large body of internalized parental and societal prohibitions. The life of the ego, the personality, is a lifelong struggle or balancing act between the demands of the id and the superego. Repressing the instinctual needs creates anxiety, as they are always demanding expression. We create all sorts of defenses against the id, but little leaks occur in the form of dreams, slips of the tongue, and joking.

To go along with this basic structure, Freud spelled out how it works through the developmental stages of the human. In other words the libido, or sexual urge, seeks its gratification in different ways corresponding to the developmental stage. Human psychic life begins with the oral stage, then goes through the anal, the phallic (the Oedipal stage), the latent, and finally the genital stage in puberty in which appropriate gratification is sought with the opposite sex.

The principal criticism of classical Freudianism is that it is too mechanical, presenting human life as a collection of bottled-up urges that can be relieved only by using other people as objects to achieve discharge. Important revisions have been made by Freud's followers and others. We have now an emphasis upon interpersonal relations, shifts to other needs besides sex and aggression, and a restoration of the willing aspect or personal responsibility for change.

Perhaps the most significant development within the psychoanalytic school has been the emphasis upon "object relations." Object relations shifts from the Freudian focus upon drives and defense to the ego's relations with its environment. The best description I have found of object relation occurs in Morris N. Eagle's book, *Recent Developments in Psychoanalysis*:

> [A]ll the evidence taken together indicates that an interest in objects
> as well as the development of affectional bonds is not simply a
> derivative or outgrowth of libidinal energies and aims or a conse-
> quence of gratification of other needs, but is a critical independent
> aspect of development which expresses inborn propensities to
> establish cognitive and affective links in the world.

Psychoanalysis does not have an illustrious history in dealing with alcoholism. It has neither defined it successfully within its own models nor treated it with confidence. The psychoanalytic community's attempts to confront alcoholism concentrated upon "psychostructural deficits." A psychostructure is an enduring arrangement of functional systems in the personality, for example, the self-concept, or the superego. A psychostructure is the posture from which one negotiates in the environment. Psychostructural deficits would be recognized, for instance, as a weak ego, or a fragile self. Psychoanalysis considered alcoholism a malady with pre-Oedipal origins. In other words, the alcoholic is fixated at the oral and anal stages of development. Since psychoanalysis made no commitment to treat the pre-oedipal character (Donovan, *American Journal of Psychiatry*, 1986), few efforts were made in behalf of the alcoholic. In the 1960s, however, according to Donovan, psychoanalysis decided that the pre-Oedipal character was treatable and therefore the alcoholic could also be managed. The leaders in this change were Balint, Kohut, and Kernberg. These analysts were working out of a shift from the strict Freudian model to what they called object relations, in which the focus included the subject's relationships in her environment.

Donovan quotes a passage from Balint that is worth presenting here: "The first effect of intoxication is invariably the establishment of a feeling that everything is now well between them and their environment. In my experience, the yearning for this 'feeling of harmony' is the most important cause of alcoholism, or for that matter, any form of addiction." There is not a better description of alcoholism available! The object relations school, however, does not pursue *the dynamics of psychostructural deficits*—and it is of great importance to understand how these deficits originate. Perhaps psychoanalysts do not want to get into this too deeply as it might take them too far from the classical model.

Moving beyond the Freudian model of drives and defense, and using a controlling image of an organism as a whole in environment, we have an easier time accounting for psychostructural deficits, as we have seen. The organism, through its formative processes, assigns meanings of life and death equivalents to its perceptions. We have seen that the fundamental meaning is always connection or separation; that the "basic fault" is the early disharmony, or shaming, that can result in distrust, self-dependence, and painful confusion.

The position of Balint, for example, is surely on target. He sees that the core of the malady is located at the appropriate level of human organization. The essence of the disorder centers around "feelings of harmony."

The psychoanalytic approach differs from the psychological approach in that the analytic approach concentrates on the inner processes of the individual. It depends upon metaphorical models, while the psychological approach is generally behavioristic. Inner processes are ignored in favor of reactions determined by circumstances. The analytic approach as it stands, however, has not kept up with the major paradigm shift suggested by Robert Jay Lifton.

Psychoanalysis seems to be losing ground among the psychiatrists themselves. Back in 1976, Robert Jay Lifton, the prominent psychiatrist and public philosopher, wrote:

> We are now in the relatively early phases of a momentous shift in the psychological paradigm—a shift away from both the classical psychoanalytic model of instinct and defense, and even from the approach and perspective inherent in the word "analysis" itself. The indications are everywhere around us: the deep uneasiness, bordering on despair, of large numbers of practitioners and investigators as they experience threats to the validity of the existing classical paradigm along with an absence of a new paradigm sufficiently powerful to replace it.

Lifton developed that powerful paradigm, but psychiatry has not moved in that direction. Instead, psychiatry has moved away from abstraction and metaphor, as they see it, to a more physically oriented approach. Many psychiatrists have begun to identify themselves as biopsychiatrists. Biopsychiatrist Mark Gold writes in *The Good News About Drugs and Alcohol*:

> [A] decade and a half or so ago, psychiatry had fallen into a state of near total disarray. Why? Basically because those who practiced psychiatry had forgotten, literally, where their heads were at. They ignored the neurobiological fact that their heads—and those of their patients, for that matter—were attached to bodies.... They set aside all their years of training in anatomy, biochemistry, and physiology ... and focused instead on the psychodynamic or "all in the head" aspects of mental illness.

Here we see a glaring example of the failure to work from a controlling image. Talking therapies did not work, so let's concentrate on the biological aspects. No one bothered to stop and ask, what is the nature of the subject we are talking about? What is this human being who has both a head and body? Should we change our model?

The shift from psychiatry to biopsychiatry has without question improved the medical profession's ability to treat the physical complexities of human well-being. So much of our sense of vitality is linked to chemical imbalances, dietary insufficiencies, or brain disease. There really is nothing to be hoped for in psychotherapy if the chemical-neurological base is impaired, but the shift to biopsychiatry has been an unfortunate one for understanding the nature of alcoholism and addiction. All addictions—

drugs, alcohol, gambling, sex, work—have the same origins. The switch to biopsychiatry would appear to have no significant bearing on addiction in general. This is not to say that the appropriate use of drugs in many forms of mental illness is not helpful; however, it is not the absence of these drugs that creates the problem of addiction. The point is that what has gone awry in human organization—addiction—is not a chemical failure (although what has gone awry can cause chemical failures). In most cases what has caused mental illness and addiction involves the species-specific level of human organization—*the basic need for appropriate connections as an organism-in-environment*. Drug therapy simply intervenes at the neurological level of organization, affecting the higher levels of organization where the problem is located. Because certain drugs alleviate symptoms, however, we cannot assume that we understand the problem.

Nor is Gold's definition of addiction acceptable. He says, "Addiction is a disease characterized by repetitive and destructive use of one or more mood-altering substances, and stems from a biological vulnerability exposed or induced by environmental forces." Earlier in this book we examined that definition. We see once again the "vulnerability" (which exasperates Lewontin, Rose, and Kamin in *Not in Our Genes*). The subject is nowhere to be found in the equation, but interestingly enough, Gold lends support to my contention that the deterministic type of approach is wrong. Gold says, "Any medical drug treatment program in 1991 that fails to include a Twelve Step strategy (AA) is not a serious program and simply will not work." The Twelve Step program is aimed at the species-specific behavior of the human organism. It works only with the innate formative processes of human organization. One wonders why scientists like Gold are not curious about *why* their drug programs cannot work without AA.

The feeling of failure among psychiatrists, as reported by Lifton and Gold, and the enthusiastic shift to biology as part of the problem, is typically American. We are so used to technological and scientific success, but we will never cure alcoholism. Nor will the world ever be a perfectly happy place. The specifically human problem is the fact of mortality and our awareness of it. The basic fault of the human organism centers around the attack upon our need of connection and integration from the very beginning. Connection is our number-one need, but separation seems to be wreaking havoc. Surely in the quantum mechanical age we need no longer doubt our essential interdependence. What Morris Berman has called the "disharmony" that is at work from the moment of birth if not before, is the core of the human problem. Until we accept that and turn our attention to it, psychiatrists will continue to doubt their role and turn more and more to biological and neuroscientific solutions—the American solutions. Psychiatry would be better served if psychiatrists examined their models and their controlling images instead of plunging headily into the "miracles" of drug interventions. While drug intervention may work, it does not explain the problem. It does not offer a solution. The healthier path was chosen by Lifton, who turned to a radical change in models rather than to drugs.

THE DIAGNOSTIC AND STATISTICAL MANUAL

The American Medical Association, through its psychiatric branch, has assumed the responsibility for publishing the official descriptions of mental disorders in the Diagnostic and Statistical Manual (DSM-IV). The handbook is widely available, widely consulted, and often sought out by people who want to find out what alcoholism is. This is the guide used by courts and insurance companies to establish whether a condition exists.

The DSM-IV describes the symptoms of alcohol abuse and alcohol dependence. If a person's behavior meets a certain number of behavioral conditions, that person can assume he or she has a problem with alcoholism. The manual is a diagnostic tool only; it does not attempt to explain or discuss the causality of alcoholism.

THE PSYCHOLOGICAL MODEL

Academic psychologists specializing in alcoholism claim to be coming on strong in the past decade. One of the best surveys of progress in these quarters comes from The Research Institute on Alcoholism in Buffalo, New York. Edited by Howard T. Blane and Kenneth E. Leonard, *Psychological Theories of Drinking and Alcoholism* contains brief articles by a number of experts.

These articles offer novel subparadigms that fail to refer to the master paradigm. They present such themes as social learning theory, opponent process theory, self-awareness approach, interaction theory, expectancy theory, and so on. These psychological inquiries, like the multifactorial and biological, do not offer a controlling image of the subject.

In the article on social learning theory, authors Abrams and Niaura reject explanations of human behavior based solely on classical and operant conditioning. They offer instead an interaction between personal factors and environment in such a way that behavior results from interlocking determinants. "Causality is, therefore, multidirectional among the factors." As Lewontin, Rose, and Kamin remark, "Interactionism is the beginning of wisdom"—but only the beginning. The notion of reciprocal determinism in this social learning theory is still mechanical. It places subject and object as distinct and separate from each other, knocking each other about. But the findings of quantum mechanics, nonlocality, and dialectical biology indicate instead a profound connection rather than mechanical separateness. If we proceed down the trail toward a quantum mechanical substratum of connection, we can answer more questions about the nature of interaction. When a theory of social action leaves out interdependence, the strongest notion behind motivation is obscured.

Abrams and Niaura recognize symbolizing capacity, forethought capability, vicarious capability, and self-regulatory capability. These all imply a rich inner capacity that is missing in behavioristic psychology. They see the organism as an active agent rather than a passive billiard ball, but they stop short of exploring the nature of human activity. Once again, we are left haunted by motivation, anticipation, feeling, and choice. Alcoholism is an attachment so powerful that it destroys human life. Where does this power come from? That question has been answered in this book.

Ultimately, to clarify the concepts about alcoholism, we must clarify the essentials of treatment. Some authors believe that treatment of alcoholism is not always necessary. They say there are maturation points in individuals' development where they stop drinking—that sudden conversions can occur as a result of marriage, the birth of a child, a new job, or the death of a loved one. These conversions may indeed occur, perhaps on an even greater scale than those conversions brought about by treatment; however, many individuals need intervention or assistance. Many of us choose to seek help to reorganize our lives.

Help has been available in the program of Alcoholics Anonymous (AA) for over sixty years. AA is the only approach that corresponds to the modern concepts of wholes emerging from quantum mechanics and nonlocality. So let's take a look.

Part Four:
The Remedy

13

The Philosophy of Alcoholics Anonymous

First of all, we had to quit playing God.

—Bill Wilson

Psychological science should enter the domain it has tended either
to ignore, further mystify, or else misrepresent by nervously and
reductively invoking its own clinical terms instead of examining the
phenomenology of man's experience of his larger connectedness.

—Robert Jay Lifton, *The Broken Connection*

When a shipwrecked man is pulled out of the sea into
a lifeboat he is not inclined to investigate how the lifeboat stays afloat, but
that is what I did from the moment I stumbled into an Alcoholics
Anonymous (AA) meeting, hospital bands still on my wrist. Weak,
emaciated, pale, and haggard, I sat in the crowded, smoky room and asked
myself, how does this work? It was not long before I heard the old adage
that if you ask the longtimers in AA how it works they will respond, "Very
well, thank you." Then someone else remarked, "We bury our intellectuals."
He was a lawyer. As time went by I noticed that my newfound friends—
a doctor, a president of a corporation, a financial analyst, a printing
salesperson—were not the least bit interested in the intellectual underpinnings,
if any, of the program. Eventually, a close woman friend became concerned
about my intense interest in the scientific basis of the fellowship. She told
me a joke about the recovering alcoholic who saw two signs, one pointing

directly to heaven, the other pointing to a lecture on heaven. Guess which sign I was following?

ALCOHOLICS ANONYMOUS AND THE QUANTUM AGE

Up to this point in the book, I have established the nature of alcoholism in the quantum age. We have seen that alcoholism is the repeated decision to control feelings of connection and separation, through a chemical, in spite of the consequences. It remains now to discover the remedy that is appropriate to this description.

What makes AA different from other approaches to recovery is its quantum-age perspective.

1. All other approaches to recovery from alcoholism see human behavior from the Cartesian viewpoint of control. AA's perspective abandons Cartesian control in favor of quantum-age *participation*.

2. In quantum-age systems theory, human inquiry is described at three levels that correspond perfectly to the first three Steps of AA.

3. AA transcends rational Cartesian inquiry into reality. In quantum-age levels of inquiry, the rational level is the lowest level; the rational-objective is subordinate to the subjective-connective and the unitive levels.

These points will be clear as we discuss the Steps below.

AA is the only program that addresses head-on the specific problem of alcoholism. By its Steps it places the individual squarely in the center of his reality. Through the first three Steps, he realizes he no longer needs to set up defenses and control his environment. He comes to understand that he is a participant. He becomes a respondent. In the final nine Steps, he actively reorganizes his stance as a participant and a respondent.

In the pages ahead we will take up the first three Steps of AA. These are the foundational Steps. They are also the subject of the most misunderstanding and controversy.

"YOU DON'T GET THIS, DO YOU?"

In those early years, I plunged into the business of working the program. I continued my reading and studying. Sometime during my sixth year in the fellowship, a woman friend said to me over coffee one night in a diner, "You don't get this at all, do you? I am amazed that a man with your gifts doesn't understand what is going on here!" I was stunned! I believed I understood just as much as anybody else. I was making coffee for meetings, chairing meetings, going out speaking at other meetings— but my conversation during those years was always about "getting my life under control," or "understanding how this works," and so on. In fact, I was not getting it.

That same year, one of my twin daughters got married and I collapsed. I subsequently discovered that her marriage opened up the vast well of feelings that I had buried for twenty-five years in alcohol. I went into psychotherapy. I worked with a professional who had for most of his adult life been a successful engineer and manufacturer. He turned to clinical psychology late in life. He remarked at the outset of our sessions that he found AA to be "the most profound philosophical experience of my life." At last—slowly—I began to understand what was going on.

Also in that same year, there was a turning point in my intellectual investigations. For years I had been reading in psychology and philosophy, trying to become comfortable with a commitment to the Twelve Steps. Then on an impulse one day, in Barnes & Noble in Manhattan, I wandered over to the science section. A book that caught my eye was called *God and the New Physics*. An Australian physicist, Paul Davies, introduced me to the radical shift from the mechanical world of Descartes and Newton to the universe of wholes and interdependencies.

Shortly after reading the physicists, I was introduced to the thoughts of the organicists, scientists like Whitehead, who were looking at the organic nature of the universe. That was my first exposure to the twentieth-century revolution in science. That was also the breakthrough I needed to understand the dynamics of AA and the Twelve Steps.

I have found AA the only remedy for addiction that is congruent with the model of the disorder as I have described it. We have seen in preceding chapters that the human, a symbolic-affective organism-in-environment, comes into this world poised in a life-death tension. This tension is unitary and animating, prodding the individual to realize its specific destiny in the larger system of things. We also know that the tension can be skewed toward the dualistic and deadening—the vulnerability we described in the basic fault. At the extreme ends of the life-death spectrum, we find the organism either defending and controlling in the environment, or participating and responding in the environment. Most of us blend degrees of these two postures throughout our lives.

Alcoholics find themselves at the extreme end of defending and controlling. By using alcohol, however, they discover the other end, a kind of ersatz participation and response—at least in the beginning. After a while, when alcohol can no longer deliver the life equivalents, they use it to numb the death equivalents.

Many authors believe AA is one of the most significant social events in history. Aldous Huxley considered Bill Wilson "the most important social architect of the century." M. Scott Peck calls AA the most successful community the world has ever known. The AA experience accounts for the widespread use of the support group for just about every emotional and physical ailment. The burgeoning belief in this country that we can help ourselves through personal change in groups derives from the experience of AA.

HISTORY

Shortly after the birth of Alcoholics Anonymous, alcoholism began to be seen as an enormous national problem in terms of health, family life, and economic drain. Scientists, academics, health professionals, and governments took an interest and developed a variety of diagnoses and remedies. Throughout it all, however, AA became a household word, and it appears even today to be the first place people think of when someone needs help with a drinking problem. Even though in recent years many psychologists, sociologists, and scientists have weighed in with differing approaches, the so-called treatment industry in the United States uses AA in its programs almost universally. Since 1935, the most apparently effective attack upon alcoholism did not arise from theoretical models, nor from laboratory research, nor clinical practices in medicine or psychology, but from the desperate experience of two reforming alcoholics.

Alcoholics Anonymous is a uniquely American phenomenon. It can be located in the context both of American history, and of religious ideas in America. Following Kurtz, I will attempt to locate my own model in the changing context of American intellectual and religious ideas. American character, shaped by individualism, rationalism, and capitalism, is ready for a quantum-age experience—the connection, participation, and responsibility of the Twelve Steps of AA.

Modern Western history began with the break away from absolute monarchy and, most especially, from ecclesiastical domination. This transformation had both its intuitive and its rational sides. We can see this in the great intuitive cry for "liberty, equality, and fraternity," and in Descartes' enthronement of the clear and distinct idea. The rationalist structure of our *Constitution* was certainly motivated by these intuitions. It was the intuitive ("self-evident" truths) that gave birth to the rational brilliance of the founding fathers. America is considered by most historians and sociologists to be the culmination and embodiment of Enlightenment ideas about individual and social progress.

Other nations looking at the United States remark on our individualism. It is seen as selfish, lacking community, and drifting in relative moral standards. But many foreigners see our individualism as a celebration of personal freedom, of personal autonomy, and of creativity. There are even moral consequences of American individualism; individuals have "sacred" rights—especially against the collective.

Modern American society is organized around three prominent features: individualism, rationalism, and capitalism. To understand AA in this context, we have to look at its members as individual organisms negotiating in this environment through intuition and rationality. Again, let me say I do not propose a duality in people. I do not find some people solely intuitive and others rational. We are all both, but for reasons associated with the basic fault, we tend to exhibit more of one than the other in our negotiations with our environment.

Individualism: Individualism is generally defined from two points of view. The first holds that individualism emphasizes the rights, liberties, and independence of the individual in society. The second holds that individualism means that the person favors and pursues personal interests instead of common or collective interests. Both descriptions can be applied to American individualism. Individualistic societies lean toward protecting the rights of the individual against the interests of the collective.

Individualism is not a reasonable state. That is to say, we do not reason to the idea that we should be free and autonomous. Individualism is an intuitive conclusion. We are first of all meaning-feeling organisms, and secondarily rational. As the *Declaration of Independence* states, "We hold these truths to be self-evident."

Rationalism: Our society is a rational society, as a result of the Enlightenment. America was the first experiment in rational Enlightenment theory coming out of France and England. Rationalism is the basis of individualism. Rationalism threw human beings back upon their own powers to think clearly and empirically; to trust nothing but their own capacity to organize and control reality in a productive and orderly manner. The framers of the *Constitution* were rationalists; they viewed God as the great clockmaker who started the universe and let it run off like a great machine. They constructed a rational architecture called the *Constitution* to provide for the smooth working of society.

Capitalism is the economic system of our society, usually referred to as free enterprise, entrepreneuralism, or free market economy. The engine of capitalism is self-interest—enlightened self-interest, it is hoped. Capitalism cannot exist without self-interested individualism.

The question is, can an individualistic, rational, capitalist society provide for the fundamental needs of a symbolic-affective human-in-environment? The answer is no. As Peter L. Berger points out (*The Capitalist Revolution*), because of the destructive side of capitalism, staunch Republicans—aware of the "cold side" of their vision—insist that capitalism can be conducted only against a background of strong family and religious ties. This leaves out a larger sense of community including all levels of society.

Built upon Cartesianism, the Enlightenment enthroned reason and control, but failed to adequately describe the individual, and left him separated from the environment. Zohar says that the use of the word *individual* instead of the word *person* suggests the estrangement of the human from its environment. The organism was looked upon as an independent collection of parts with a unified function, as against today's view of the organism as a whole in an environment.

One of the ways individuals, groups, and societies can be distinguished is by their emphasis on either intuition or rationalism. We get some intimations of rational leanings and intuitional leanings right from the beginnings of Western intellectual thought with the ideas of Plato and his pupil, Aristotle. Both were metaphysicians, but Plato was an idealist whereas Aristotle was a realist. Plato seemed to favor an intuitive awareness, while Aristotle became the master logician. Plato thought of reality as a kind of projection of independently existing forms in another dimension of reality, but Aristotle preferred to see these forms confined to objective reality itself. Plato, we might say, intuited a reality beyond the immediately observable, while Aristotle preferred to reason from the visible.

In speaking of intuition and rationalism, we are not proposing a dualism. Rationalists attempt to organize what they have first intuited, and intuitionists tend to rationalize, make coherent and logical, what they have intuited. (Intuition could be another term for what I have called image-feeling throughout this book. Intuition can be described as an aspect of *anticipation,* a crucial notion for the organism-in-environment.)

Preoccupation with a rationalist, individualistic perspective grows out of a distrust of intuition. Intuition can fail in shaming societies, such as dictatorships, patriarchies, aristocracies, or theocracies, just as it can fail in families. Rationalism can become the characteristic of the survivors of such societies because the individual, unable to participate intuitively in a shaming environment, finds it necessary to fall back on his own powers, to act upon his distrust, become self-dependent. He must assume control. The eventual price for a rationally oriented society, however, is painful uneasiness, alienation, and emptiness.

In this country, we own the finest constitutional system the world has ever known. America is the jewel of the Enlightenment, the triumph of reason. Our individuality is guaranteed by a perfectly rational architecture; yet, as Robert Bellah tells us, today we are alienated, uneasy, struggling with commitment, and fairly widely addicted. Because the Enlightenment and our *Constitution* have restricted us to a vocabulary of individualism and reason, we have "lost the language necessary to make moral and social sense of our lives." Christopher Lasch writes about our "culture of narcissism"— this in a nation reported to be the most church-going in the world! Our principal relationships with one another are contractual (rational) relationships. Take, for example, a core instrument in human relations— the contract. Contracts serve a desirable mutual participation, but their primary purpose is to secure a defense against each other at the same time!

What is the nature of the problem? Here we have the most sophisticated social experiment in history, and yet we have a society afflicted with pervasive inequality, injustice, crime at every level, and an ever-increasing mountain of litigation against each other.

As a mathematician might say, the problem to be solved is for an organism-in-environment burdened with a basic fault. In the individual developmental stages, each one of us discovers a way to deal with the basic fault. Depending upon the context of the family, the individual will lean toward defense and control, or toward response and participation—and this is true for the family itself in the context of society. Because of the gap between child and parent, as Berman describes the basic vulnerability, we move toward an early rationalism (control) instead of a more balanced mix of intuition and reason. These stances are given their motivation, or power, from the life-death equivalents of connection-separation.

All of human history has been played out by a symbolic-affective organism coming into its brief moment in the life cycle poised against a basic fault. The accomplishments and failures of every form of civilization can be described in terms of the basic fault. By fault here we do not mean a blameworthy deficiency on the part of the organism; we are using the term in the sense that scientists speak of a fault in the earth's crust. Humankind assumes some responsibility for it; somehow humankind has offended the gods. In the biblical tradition of the West, Adam and Eve disobeyed God, and forever after humankind has had to struggle against the debilitating effects of that original sin. Later, Freud would sharpen up our vision of the basic fault. He offered us a scheme of the fault as an internal conflict between an unconscious and conscious level of the human psyche, between natural drives and societal repression. After Freud, human history was regarded from a psychoanalytical point of view.

It was not until the mid-twentieth century that the basic fault was satisfactorily described, for instance, in Lifton's book, *The Broken Connection*. It is strikingly appropriate that this book should appear in the same part of the century that saw the revolution in physics from Cartesian mechanism to quantum mechanics. Lifton accomplished the shift from Freudian mechanics to a model of death awareness and the symbolic continuity of life. The human organism comes into its cycle in time anticipating its life in terms of connection and form. The basic fault is experienced in terms of separation and chaos. This is not a duality, a misperception common to most theories of good and bad, life and death, body and soul. Lifton provided psychology with a shift from dualism to unitary polarities—a shift that is consonant with the shift in physics from mechanical parts to indivisible wholes. What we have instead is a polarity within the same organism, and because of this polarity we are vulnerable to shaming— an evoking of the death pole when connections are broken.

The death side of the polarity is not necessarily intrinsically evil, as in a duality. Chaos and separation are aspects of the tension of wholes. Chaos and separation are felt as evil, but thereby become animating. We must live in a balance between form and connection and its opposite, chaos and separation.

This polarity allows for contradictory interests—altruism and selfishness—to exist within the individual himself, and not place him in total opposition to others. The world of humankind does not exist as a struggle among separate parts, but as a tension of polarities in a whole. Because of the outcomes of the basic fault, individuals in the whole will tend to separate into differing and opposing modes of symbolic immortality—warring religions and nations, for example. (In this regard, Joseph Campbell liked to say that the differing religions of the Middle East—Christianity, Judaism, and Islam—are fighting over different metaphors.) The individuals in the whole will pursue their interests from within a mingling of defenses and controls on the one hand, and participation and response on the other.

A danger right now in this country is the belief that we must return to basics, reclaim our heritage, restore traditional values, and re-enshrine the traditional family. None of this is possible, nor desirable. The only absolute we can honor today is the human anticipation of connection with one another and our environment. We must keep this ever before us as we confront the future and move into it. Our effort must be to acknowledge what we have learned from the past and apply that to the evolving circumstances of the present and future.

This is the struggle of the American experiment—to embed a fierce individualism in a greater community of common interests. There are two extremes yawning to swallow us up at either end: the first is the total alienation of individualism and the other is the loss of the individual in a rigid communitarianism. The first says I do not need others to actualize who I am; the other says we are nothing but parts of the whole.

Spurred on by the startling implication in quantum mechanics, we are beginning to see the individual differently. Danah Zohar writes in *The Quantum Society*, "Beyond the always shifting boundaries of the 'I', relational holism draws the unfixed aspects of the self into ever wider circles of creative relationship—the intimate partner, the family, the group, the nation, humanity itself."

The individual organism cannot be defined outside its environment. It comes into its environment programmed to respond and participate. The organism first intuits its environment (image-feeling), and then organizes those experiences rationally. If its connections are broken in any way by the environment (separation and chaos), it will take up a posture of defense and control. If the process of intuition is skewed by shaming (broken connections), the organism will organize its intuitions into rational defense and control instead of into response and participation. Because of broken connections, the organism will distrust its intuitions and become characteristically rational.

When intuition (connection) is completely lost to rationality (subject-object distancing), then we come to realize that in a totally rationalized world of self and environment, the self can become insatiable. It is looking for intuitive connections that have been broken, and inauthentic connections can arise in the form of addictions—substitutes for intuitional connection.

In a rational construct, such as our constitutional way of life, the needs of the organism-in-environment are not met. With the background of the Enlightenment and the *Constitution*, we are left to our own devices to nourish our fundamentally intuitive nature. The very concept of individualism militates against our fundamental need for intuited connection.

THE CULTURE OF MORE

Lifton's depth-psychological model of connection and separation is undergirded by Zohar's quantum model of relational holism. None of these new scientific discoveries can be grasped in mechanistic, controlling terms of the Enlightenment, or Cartesian-Newtonian views. Thus we see the unease with an unenlightened individualism, which by its very nature must become a culture of more. As the historian Kurtz has pointed out, a stark individualism inevitably becomes insatiable. There are no other symbol systems of connection available except those of accumulating, possessing, and attaining power.

The principal antidote to the controlling, mechanical notions of individuality is the realization and acceptance of limitation—not taking away autonomy, but instead properly describing the autonomy of an organism limited to its species-specific tasks, as required by its own wholeness, and by its relations to its environment. This poise of essential limitation must be struck before the realization of participation can take place. Limitation usually dawns in consciousness when the individualist is suddenly confronted with the consequences of insatiability. A new reality of the self must be organized.

ALCOHOLICS ANONYMOUS AS A RELIGIOUS IDEA

The events in American history immediately preceding the founding of Alcoholics Anonymous led up to the death struggle of *laissez-faire* capitalism in the 1929 crash of the financial markets. Since the turn of the century, the Progressives had been optimistically tinkering with the relationship between economic organizations and government in order "to 'rationalize' the tumultuous process of social and political change" (Bellah). But then American capitalism witnessed the impossible—idle industrial capacity simultaneous with thirty percent unemployment. With the advent of the Roosevelt Administration, the Second World War, and John Maynard Keynes' ideas, government took over the reins to stimulate the economy and put Americans back to work. At the same time, in another part of the world, basic human certainty about the nature of reality was tumbling with the discovery of quantum mechanics and the realization of vast interdependencies.

As fate would have it, Bill Wilson was working in the financial markets. We can safely guess that he was inordinately impressed with the failure of the markets, and between that and his hopeless struggle against alcohol, he was quite ready to accept the notion of personal and human limitation—the core idea of AA. The notion of limitation was impressed upon the White middle class males starting AA. They came out of the Great Depression. They were acquainted with opportunity, but saw themselves fail. It was easier for them to see limitation as an essential notion. A powerful and proud nation of individualists saw their government moving in to rescue them. This was surely surrender.

Today, with our new ecological consciousness and the new views of organicism and interdependencies from physics, we infuse this sense of limitation with a sense of participation—a crucial development. Although the core notion of AA is limitation, it flowers into the notion of participation—the program part of AA's Twelve Steps. Gradually, through the Twelve Steps, the recovering alcoholic is brought through limitation to participation. Participation cannot be experienced without the experience first of limitation. Limitation has long been a fundamental religious idea.

What the AA member is resisting about religion, Kurtz suggests, is the "churchy" connotations in the term religious. AA, however, bears little resemblance to American religions as such. Key differences are that AA is never concerned with a particular religious narrative, a charismatic founder, reward and punishment, or an afterlife. AA is resisting more than the churchy connotation of religion. AA is not religion; AA is an ultimate experience. Religions are proximate modes of the ultimate experience. AA's experience does not have to be realized in a religious format.

In 1934, Bill Wilson was a ruined alcoholic on the verge of his fourth hospitalization. The turning point came for Wilson when he entertained an old drinking friend in his kitchen one evening, Edwin Thatcher, who had stopped drinking, much to Wilson's dismay. Thatcher behaved like a missionary that night in Wilson's kitchen, bringing the message of sobriety and salvation. Thatcher had gotten the message himself from another "hopeless drunk" whom he had encountered in the Oxford Group. The Oxford Group was an intense collection of individuals who wanted to restore pietistic evangelism to the Christian world. This other drunk had been treated by Carl Jung, who had told him that only a spiritual conversion could save him. Kurtz tells us that from the Oxford Group, AA inherited "much of its tone, style, and practice."

Wilson kept drinking after Thatcher's visit, but his old drinking buddy's sober enthusiasm and hopefulness had made a profound impression. In the hospital again for his fourth detoxification, Wilson put together his doctor's declaration of his hopelessness with the thoughts crowding his mind about Thatcher, the Oxford Group principles, Jung's influence on the converted member of the Group, and what he had himself been reading in William James' *Varieties of Religious Experience*. All of this resulted in a dramatic spiritual experience for Wilson in that hospital room. Because it was a visit from a recovering alcoholic that had precipitated his own spiritual experience, Wilson believed he should share his experience with other alcoholics. This did not work immediately, but in 1935, on a failed business trip to Akron, Ohio, Wilson fought a powerful compulsion to drink again by frantically trying to find another drunk to work with. Through his connections with the Oxford Group, Wilson made contact with Dr. Robert Holbrook Smith, an Akron surgeon, whose own career and very life were disintegrating from alcoholism. Wilson told his story to a reluctant Dr. Bob, and a month later Alcoholics Anonymous came into being.

The unique dynamic in telling one's story seems to have come about spontaneously for Bill Wilson. Early in his own recovery, Wilson knew that his continued sobriety depended upon reaching out to other hopeless drunks. On the surface this does not seem so extraordinary, of course. Many people have tried to save others by reaching out to them. But what was extraordinary about Wilson's attitude was that he knew he had to do this to save himself! When he set about trying desperately to find a drunk to work with, he was totally absorbed in the process of his own sobriety. He had to tell his story to another alcoholic, whether invited to or not. It was his powerful conviction that drunks could help one another through sharing their experience. This was Wilson's gift to the world.

It took several years, Kurtz tells us, for the fledgling group to disengage itself from the Oxford Group. Recovering alcoholics found themselves uncomfortable with the particular religious atmosphere of the Oxford Group. Early AAs found the Oxford Group "too religious," too fixed upon perfection, too rigid in their practices.

Wilson and the early members were troubled in particular by the Four Absolutes of the Oxford Group. It was these ideals that caused AA's formal break from the Oxford Group. The Four Absolutes of the Oxford Group were: Absolute Honesty, Absolute Purity, Absolute Unselfishness, and Absolute Love. In a letter to critics, Wilson explained

> The ideals of purity, honesty, unselfishness, and love are as adhered to by members of Alcoholics Anonymous as by any other group of people, but we found that when you put the word "absolute" before them, alcoholics just couldn't stand the pace, and too many went out and got drunk again.

In AA's *Big Book,* Chapter 5 states, "We claim spiritual progress not spiritual perfection."

It never occurred to Wilson and the early AAs that they could save themselves by a mere act of self-control, or will power, or any rational techniques. They were impressed by Jung's statement about spiritual conversion, Wilson's own dramatic spiritual experience, and the writings of William James in *Varieties of Religious Experience.* They were also very fearful of alienating drunks who could not accept a religious format. They advised Wilson to tone down the tale of his own conversion. It was clear to them that not everyone they approached was going to have this kind of "divine" visitation.

AA is not a religion, but it subsists, from the beginning, on a religious worldview resembling evangelical pietism. As Kurtz relates, "Thus both its proximate origins and its historical context exposed Alcoholics Anonymous to the Evangelical Pietist style of religious insight." Kurtz goes on to point out that "the deep extent to which the Evangelical Pietist insight infuses and dominates the AA program hardly surprises." On the other hand, AA was also very American. From the beginning, AA members sought the thoughts of William James "whenever they self-consciously sought to understand themselves and their program in terms of intellectual context and content." Kurtz concludes that "the program from its very beginning was so totally immersed in and infused by the intellectual culture so well reflected by William James, that the fellowship readily found itself in this quintessentially American philosopher's thought."

If one scrutinizes AA's history for any sign of dogma, or absolutism, it would no doubt be AA insistence that no human being can be perfect. Wilson abhorred even the attempt to be perfect, seeing such efforts to be the self-destruction of the recovering alcoholic. "We claim spiritual progress, not spiritual perfection." Wilson counseled newcomers to the program to forget about results and concentrate on honesty and effort on a daily basis.

(One of the fundamental paradigm shifts emerging from modern science is the understanding of the world in terms of *process* rather than *structure*. An awareness of this kind was clearly at work in the minds of the early members. Absolutes are logical structures, or constructs, and as we know now, do not conform to reality. The relentless insistence in AA upon progress one day at a time [a process], is a spiritual view quite in step with the insights available from modern science.)

As Kurtz insists, the basic concept of AA is built upon a spirituality of imperfection. He says in one place: whereas the "vocabulary of religion is solid, the vocabulary of spirituality is fluid." We can add that Wilson and the others experienced the idea of absolutes as another aspect of the human attempt to control. The idea that human beings were in such control of their destinies that they could aspire to an absolute perfection was thoroughly unacceptable to Wilson. The early AAs shuddered at the notion of control—grasping right from the beginning the importance of accepting their limitations.

Perhaps the reader can see at this point why I find AA the ideal remedy for addiction. If we remember the analogy of the card game, which cannot be played without the voluntary acceptance of limitation on the part of each player; and that the human individual negotiates this "card game" of life not as an organism, but as an organism-in-environment, then AA's core notions of limitation and participation distinguish it from other approaches to behavioral change.

CONTROL: THE CORE NOTION OF ALCOHOLICS ANONYMOUS

AA defines itself as both fellowship and program. As we have learned from our treatment of wholes, aspects of things cannot always be separated in actuality—and that applies to fellowship and program in AA. The two aspects are legitimately separated and studied as aspects, but neither the peculiar fellowship of AA nor its peculiar program can exist without the other. In this book I am going to respond largely to the aspect of program, assuming that it is embedded in the fellowship. I am concentrating on program simply because the major intent of this book is to illuminate the nature of alcoholism and other addictions. The nature of alcoholism is revealed in an explanation of the nature of human choice. It follows that I should focus on the remedy that invokes a model of human choice. It is a logical next step to explain the program, or stages of choice in the program of AA. According to AA, recovering alcoholics never "arrive." They are choosing on a daily basis.

Let's start out with a couple of simple illustrations of how we use the word control. Often we see in the news a picture of a car wrapped around a tree, and a caption stating that the driver lost control on a winding road in the dark. In AA thinking, the driver did not lose control of the car. The steering column did not break; the tires did not burst. What actually happened was that the driver controlled the car beyond the limitations of driver-road-vehicle conditions. This is the core thinking of the Twelve Step movement.

Recently I went to a seminar with my daughter about the fear of flying, given by a 747 captain. A gifted teacher, the veteran pilot told us assembled worriers that our problem was a control issue. We all looked at one another. How could terror be translated into a control issue? He explained that there is a system in place larger than ourselves which manages the outcome of the flight. If we can "surrender" (his word) to the larger system, then we can read, relax, study, or sleep. He then spent the rest of the seminar trying to give us reasons to give up control and trust the system. Perhaps these simple illustrations of control notions offer a good introduction to the thinking of AA.

THE TWELVE STEPS OF ALCOHOLICS ANONYMOUS

Before I plunge into an examination of the Steps of Alcoholics Anonymous, I should point out that the Twelve Steps are not psychotherapy, and are not formally substitutes for therapeutic techniques. Therapies are usually designed, in one way or another, to bring to awareness unconscious or subconscious conflicts in the individual's mind. Psychotherapies are meant to untangle buried "issues" and bring to light the mental/emotional defenses, or controls we developed—for better or worse throughout the developmental stages.

The Twelve Steps are instead primitive and primordial. They are pre-therapeutic. They provide a change, or a conversion in the way of viewing oneself in the world. As Gregory Bateson says, the Twelve Steps bring about a change in epistemology, a new way of understanding the self in the environment. Anthropologist Carl E. Thune of Princeton, writing a phenomenological perspective of AA, suggests that "a treatment regimen directed at reconstitution and redefinition of self and world provides a better way to deal with alcoholism than a model holding it analogous to physical diseases. This is AA's claim; and I suggest that it lies at the heart of the success that AA has enjoyed."

As in my own case, psychotherapeutic techniques for unraveling defenses are enormously more effective when played out with individuals who are willing to redefine their place in the world and give up control.

I want to share with you now my realization of how the Twelve Steps of Alcoholics Anonymous work, although most people in AA do not care how AA works—only that it *does* work. AA's principles are built entirely upon experience, not theory or analysis (although as organismic experience it does yield to analytical description). AA's success lies precisely in its placing of experience over analysis—something that the movement shares with modern trends in scientific thought.

Anyone seeking to understand the Twelve Steps will not find an intellectual, academic, or scholarly body of material available from AA itself. There is no scholarly written tradition such as that supplied by theologians for the various religious denominations. Because AA does not "engage in any controversies," it has not developed any formal apologetics, nor has it sent spokespeople into the world to explain itself. This is not to say that several scholars have not attempted to place AA both as fellowship and as philosophy, into its proper context in the twentieth century. I have in mind, for example, Norman K. Denzin, professor of sociology at the University of Illinois, who has written a most penetrating view of AA; the anthropologist Gregory Bateson, who has discovered in AA a similarity between his own system of cybernetics and the epistemology of AA; Princeton anthropologist

Carl E. Thune, who has written about AA from a phenomenological approach; historian of science Morris Berman, who has followed up on Bateson with his own exposition of AA's first three Steps; and Ernest Kurtz, who has written about both the history and the philosophy of AA. There may well be others whose work I have not yet come across.

One more point before getting into the Steps—I am going to focus upon the first three Steps in this brief treatment. These first three are the foundational Steps—those bringing about the change in the individual to make the remaining nine Steps possible. The first three are also the controversial Steps—bringing the most criticism and the most praise. The Twelve Steps are:

1. We admitted we were powerless over alcohol; that our lives had become unmanageable.

2. Came to believe that a Power greater than ourselves could restore us to sanity.

3. Made a decision to turn our will and our lives over to the care of God, as we understood Him.

4. Made a searching and fearless moral inventory of ourselves.

5. Admitted to God, to ourselves, and to another human being the exact nature of our wrongs.

6. Were entirely ready to have God remove all these defects of character.

7. Humbly asked Him to remove our shortcomings.

8. Made a list of all persons we had harmed, and became willing to make amends to them all.

9. Made direct amends to such people wherever possible, except when to do so would injure them or others.

10. Continued to take personal inventory and when we were wrong promptly admitted it.

11. Sought through prayer and meditation to improve our conscious contact with God, as we understood Him, praying only for knowledge of His will for us, and the power to carry that out.

12. Having had a spiritual awakening as the result of these steps, we tried to carry this message to alcoholics, and to practice these principles in all our affairs.

STEP ONE: "WE ADMITTED WE WERE POWERLESS OVER ALCOHOL."

"We admitted we were powerless over alcohol. "While it appears as a rather innocuous declaration, of little profundity, and certainly more than obvious to the onlooker, Step One is an enormous stumbling block for an alarming number of alcoholics (and other addicts). Most clinical workers (and members of AA) believe that failure to deeply internalize this step is the major setup for relapse into addictive behavior. The story of the alcoholic is the repeated attempts to make alcohol work.

The insight that resulted in the formulation of Step One was the awareness of personal limitation. When Bill Wilson said, "First of all, we had to stop playing God," he presented the world with a most amazing juxtaposition of images. A hopeless drunk playing God? This is, of course, the signal genius of AA, placing the movement squarely within the major intellectual shifts in the twentieth century—not to say that Wilson and the others were acquainted with organicism or quantum theory. Wilson's insights occurred at the same time a shift in awarenesses emerged during the middle and later periods in some sectors of twentieth-century American intellectual life—in the failure of *laissez-faire* capitalism, in the organicism of Whitehead, and the shift from Cartesian mechanics. In the meanwhile, as we have seen, the various disciplines studying the phenomenon of alcoholism have been continuously trying to find the causes of alcoholism, while AA continues to place its emphasis on the choices of the individual.

Step One is also the fork in the road for the two major attitudes about recovery; this is where sides are taken about the notion of control. Step One is a major irritant to a growing number of academic psychologists and clinical workers who tend to bristle at the "negative" AA notion of powerlessness. They lean toward more reinforcing notions of self-reliance, self-empowerment, independence, personal autonomy, and the like. At work here in these criticisms of AA is a nearly invincible poise within the Cartesian view, the notion of control we have lived with for three hundred years—and will not soon see displaced.

As physicist Paul Davies says, we have been "hypnotized" by the Cartesian picture of the clockwork universe. What Wilson and the early members did for themselves was shatter the trance that holds Western humankind in its thrall. There is probably no stronger lesson that we cannot control-at-will than the lesson of addiction. Thus both the ideas of Bill Wilson and the commentary of Kurtz are set forth in the vocabulary of ego-deflation, conversion, and surrender. These words describe the central and triumphant experience of AA.

Kurtz's title for his book, *Not-God*, sums up his understanding of AA and the thinking of Bill Wilson and the earliest members. The notion of powerlessness is the core insight of Twelve Step philosophy, but I found it easier to grasp when Kurtz explained that powerlessness over alcohol introduces the alcoholic to his or her limitations. In *Not-God*, Kurtz says:

> [T]he fundamental and first message of Alcoholics Anonymous to its members is that they are not infinite, not absolute, not God. Every alcoholic's problem had first been, according to this insight, claiming God-like powers, especially that of control.

Wilson emphasized the alcoholic's pride, grandiosity, and immaturity; "we had to quit playing God." This notion of the pathetic addict's attempting to control was and is utterly foreign to American psychology. It remains the basic discomfort for many professionals who would like to be conversant with AA and Twelve Step programs. In the Cartesian world, in which mental health professionals have been trained, it is only the aspect of being in-or-out-of-control that is examined. The way out of addiction, they say, is to take back control.

It is a logical imperative to ask again: What are the defining characteristics of alcoholism that must be addressed in a coherent philosophy of recovery? We find that the defining characteristic of any addiction is the effort to control.

As was discussed in the chapter titled "The Basic Fault," the human comes into this world anticipating connection, and is almost immediately plunged into a dialectic to get its needs met. Depending upon the nurturing quality of its environment, the developing human will learn to secure its needs in the dialectic of connection either from a posture of control and defense, or from a posture of participation and responsibility, most generally, of course, from a mix of both postures.

As Becker and others have pointed out, the infant human is not a passive blob, but is ready to control as required to get its needs. If it were not, of course, there could be no dialectic. However, if the nurturing is appropriate, the controlling aspect of the developing human's role will be tempered by a sense of participation, and it will find that acting responsibly in the dialectic is a primary source of reinforced connection. Later in development, the young human will experience connection by doing some nurturing itself. In a shaming environment, the developing organism will resort to defenses and controls, even to the paradoxical defense of fantasy bonding, wherein the shamed individual blames himself or herself for the broken connections, being unable to accept the death equivalent in separation. The result is a life of almost unbearable repression and alienation. Along comes the chemical alcohol. Presto! All is well with the self in the world!

The defining characteristic of alcoholism is the repeated attempt to control (or numb) one's image-feelings of connection or separation through alcohol in spite of the consequences, so it is reasonable that the appropriate remedy should focus upon the individual's controlling attempts as well as upon the environmental conditions. This approach is virtually impossible to understand by a society looking to causalities, as in medicine, psychology, and sociology. As we have shown earlier, American psychology and sociology have no concept of, and no model for, specifically human action—and as a result will focus upon the causative aspects of behavior rather than upon the dialectical role of the organism. We can understand this now as the legacy from an exclusively Cartesian worldview.

Probably the most important insight we have established is that the human organism is responding *within an organization of overall complexity, not reacting within an order of control.* This is the key contribution of AA. The failure to grasp this notion is also the reason why the prevailing views are unable to describe the nature of alcoholism.

The basic task for a program of recovery from alcoholism is to help the individual change from a poise of defense and control to one of participation and responsibility. Human life is a mix of these tendencies. Because we are organisms tensed between life and death, we can say that all of us behave with a mix of those positions. The alcoholic, or any addict, is correcting the aridities in a life of defense and control.

The first personal issue I had to confront was AA's insistence upon powerlessness over alcohol. I felt no need to fight this attitude, but it made little sense. Wasn't I here, after all, to just break a bad habit and regain my self-control? My recent experience in the county hospital, along with the hallucinations and utter pain and confusion that preceded it, rendered me teachable, however, so I listened—for a long time!

(I enjoy the story of the young financial wizard who was delivered for the fifth time into the detox unit of a state hospital. He came to, shaking in his hospital bed, to see the same huge black counselor, his face scarred from the streets, glaring down at him for the fifth time in three years. The counselor said, "Well, man, we gonna do this your way again, or my way?" To which the young master of the world replied, "Your way, Sir!")

Kurtz tells us that the founders of AA and the early members sought some intellectual support for the notion of surrender from Carl Jung and from the writing of William James. Kurtz incorporates a quote from *The Varieties of Religious Experience* in another of his illuminating books called *The Spirituality of Imperfection*. (As you read the following, recall that James is regarded as the greatest American psychologist!)

> [T]he way to success, as vouched by innumerable authentic personal narrations, is . . . by . . . surrender. . . . Passivity, not activity; relaxation, not intentness, should be now the rule. Give up the feeling of responsibility, let go your hold, resign the care of your destiny to higher powers, be genuinely indifferent to what becomes of it all, and you will find not only that you gain a perfect inward relief, but often also, in addition, the particular goods you sincerely thought you were renouncing. . . . Something must give way, a native hardness must break down and liquefy; and this event . . . is frequently sudden and automatic, and leaves on the Subject an impression that he has been wrought upon by an external power . . . a form of regeneration by relaxing, by letting go. . . . It is but giving your little private convulsive self a rest, and finding that a greater Self is there.

Kurtz adds,

> Perhaps the greatest paradox in the story of spirituality is the mystical insight that we are able to experience release only if we ourselves let go. This is the paradox of surrender. Surrender begins with the acceptance that we are not in control of the matter at hand—in fact, we are not in absolute control of anything. Thus the experience of surrender involves the letting in of reality.

One of the first professional men to scrutinize the dynamics of AA was psychiatrist Harry M. Tiebout, writing in the *Quarterly Journal of Studies on Alcohol* during the years 1949 to 1954. He is especially well known among AA members for his two papers, "The act of surrender in the therapeutic process" (*Quarterly Journal of Studies on Alcoholism*, 1949), and "Surrender versus compliance in therapy" (*Quarterly Journal of Studies on Alcoholism*, 1953).

Tiebout believed that in therapy the act of surrender is essential, bringing about a state "in which defiance and grandiosity no longer raise havoc with adjustment, and serenity and the capacity to function as a human being are able to take over permanently." In the second paper, Tiebout discussed the difference between compliance and surrender—a most useful distinction for alcoholics. Many come into AA in a sincere compliance with the wishes of their families or their bosses. Tiebout points out, however, that compliance is not acceptance, and without acceptance (surrender), there can be no "conversion," or fundamental change in attitude.

Morris Berman explains, in *The Reenchantment of the World*, that it was the genius of the founders of AA which found "a surrender that conferred on the individual not maudlin impotence, but power. In other words, it rendered him active in the world."

In a chapter of *The Denial of Death*, titled "The Psychoanalyst Kierkegaard," we find Becker interpreting Kierkegaard: "The self must be destroyed, brought down to nothing, in order for self-transcendence to begin. Then the self can begin to relate itself to powers beyond itself." And then in another passage, Becker says:

> Once the person begins to look to his relationship to the Ultimate Power, to infinitude, and to refashion his links from those around him to that Ultimate Power, he opens up to himself the horizon of unlimited possibility, of real freedom. This is Kierkegaard's message.

The popular literature is talking about self-reliance, self-empowerment, self-control, resilience, taking charge, and so forth, but this is surely not the language of Kierkegaard, Becker, or AA. The language of AA is ego-deflation, conversion, surrender, and letting go!

Gregory Bateson (*Steps to an Ecology of Mind*), regarded as one of the great thinkers of this century (also husband of Margaret Mead and father of Mary Catherine Bateson), was attracted by the AA philosophy of not-in-control ("The Cybernetics of 'Self': A Theory of Alcoholism"), and was quite taken with the "genius" of Bill Wilson, cofounder of AA. Bateson believed the alcoholic's problem was a matter of "alcoholic pride." The alcoholic's pride, Bateson says, was not in his accomplishments, but *in his illusions of being in control*. He says about AA's Step One, "The myth of self-power is thereby broken by the demonstration of a greater power." Further explaining AA's not-in-control concept, Bateson says, "Philosophically viewed, this first step is not a surrender; it is simply a change in epistemology, a change in how to know about the personality in the world."

SYSTEMS THEORY

Bateson suggested, "[T]he non-alcoholic world has many lessons which it might learn from the epistemology of systems theory and the ways of AA." Bateson was the first to link up systems theory with the philosophy of AA. AA could be described as a perfect embodiment of systems theory. In AA we see the rational, subjective, and unitary levels of human inquiry into reality. As sociologist Denzin emphasizes, AA is lived experience. For AA, reality is a larger system than mind is able to comprehend; however, a member is responsible to rationally organize her or his participation and commitment to reality.

The first three Steps of Alcoholics Anonymous correspond to the three levels of inquiry in systems theory.

> Step One is a surrender—a rational decision based on acceptance of facts.

> Step Two is a subjective awareness of connections, of belonging to a system with different levels. Belonging to the group, belonging to the higher system, belonging to other individuals. Step Two brings a sense of sanity, of wholeness. The strain of individualism vanishes.

> Step Three is a commitment to the unity of life—acceptance that the overall system is in charge. We have only to participate. The system is responsible for the outcomes.

Recall that as Bateson says, the alcoholic, by Step One, has relocated himself in the world, has come up with a new epistemology of self in a system. Within that stance, new inquiries or levels of inquiry are relevant to the organism's specific conduct of itself in the environment. Simply put, if I am not in control, who or what is? Need anything be in control at all? To come to grips with this question, we examine our experience—now an acceptable procedure, thanks to modern science.

Is systems theory a fundamentally spiritual theory? Systems theory posits first of all that reality is a unified system of relationships and interdependencies. I describe spirituality as a quality of human participation in the system. When human participation is suffused with awareness, concern, and commitment, it is spiritual. Spirituality is a quality of human action. There is only a qualitative difference between human action and spiritual action.

AA's spirituality is fundamental, as is systems theory, but neither AA nor systems theory is religious. Religions are proximate, symbolic modes of connection. Systems theory and AA are ultimate modes of connection. To be effective, religions must ultimately be concerned with the spiritual quality of human participation. Many people in AA do return to traditional religions with a new, grounded perspective.

In the mechanistic conception of the world, we believe that the only mode of inquiry into our realities is the rational mode—subject-object distancing. In AA, we have come to recognize other levels of inquiry into reality—what I call somatic inquiry, which includes subject-object distancing but goes beyond it into the more fundamental inquiries initiated by the body through the meaning-feeling process. The nonrational levels of inquiry are well described by Eric Jantsch and Morris Berman (*Coming to our Senses* and *The Reenchantment of the World*). Quantum mechanics, quantum logic, and organicism suggest the radical implications that include these new, nonclassical inquiries into reality.

STEP TWO: "CAME TO BELIEVE THAT A POWER GREATER THAN OURSELVES . . ."

For the recovering alcoholic, intellectual inquiry into the nature of AA's program is unnecessary and is generally discouraged for newcomers especially. When we fall in love, for instance, it is not recommended that we inquire into the nature of the phenomenon. The dynamics of fellowship, and appreciation for a new approach to life in the world, constitute the attraction of the AA program. Any responsible inquiry into the nature of AA's program must, however, take into consideration the viewpoints of such powerful intellectuals as Gregory Bateson.

In *Steps to an Ecology of Mind*, Bateson included a chapter entitled "The Cybernetics of 'Self': A Theory of Alcoholism." Within that chapter he wrote a section headed "The Theology of Alcoholics Anonymous." The reader should be aware that Bateson is not a supernaturalist. In other places he makes it clear that he does not accept the traditional notions of the religions. His acceptance of God and prayer in AA's Twelve Step program is pleasantly mellow. Bateson did not see AA as nonrational, or pre-rational. Bateson saw before him in the Twelve Steps a perfectly rational and logical way of understanding the human's place in the system. A second look at AA's Twelve Steps quickly reveals that aspect that so intrigued the logician Bateson. He saw no religious aspect in AA that disturbed him. He allowed for prayer and the personalization of the Higher Power, because essentially it was the Higher Power as you understand Him. Prayer was an act of disposing oneself to take part in the system.

AA's Twelve Steps can be seen as cold-bloodedly logical, completely devoid of any religious dogma or feeling. This, we can guess, is why Bateson was able to be attracted to the relentless logic of AA.

Let me suggest what the logician Bateson saw when he was writing about the theology of AA: There is no dogma in the Twelve Steps. There is no formal body of teachings whatever. AA is a recommended procedure, developed from experience and not revelation, for establishing oneself within a correct epistemology of self-in-a-system. There is not the least suggestion throughout the Twelve Steps that we should worship the higher power. We simply maintain "conscious contact" with the higher power. There is no concept at all about seeking forgiveness. We simply make amends. There is no consideration whatever about a life hereafter. There is no thought about sin or offense against the higher power. Original sin and fallen human nature are seen as character defects. Nowhere is there the least thought about reward and punishment in the relationship with the higher power. (Bateson found that particularly important.) The idea of penance is instead a matter of making amends. There is suggestion of sorrow in making amends. In prayer, we do not ask for anything at all, simply the ability to carry out the plan of the system. The Twelve Steps are not embedded in any religious story about salvation and redemption. AA has no version of the beginnings or endings of this world. The Twelve Steps are utterly devoid of mythology, or powerful founding figures. AA deliberately shuns owning or building places to meet, unlike the churches and temples of religion. AA does not evangelize or preach. AA does not provide for instruction in its rules and beliefs. There is no hierarchy; there are no teachers. We listen to no sermons. AA has no system of moral theology, and takes no position in moral controversy. In effect, there are no grounds for thinking of AA as religious. AA is better thought of as a fellowship or community with a common set of convictions about the self in the world. AA itself, in its *Big Book*, sums up its position on religion and spirituality as follows:

> We find that no one need have difficulty with the spirituality of the program. *Willingness, honesty, and open mindedness are the essentials of recovery, but these are indispensable* (AA's emphasis).

In the *Big Book* there is an urgency about finding God, whatever you call Him. The first AAs were deeply impressed with their own conversions from hopeless drunks to self-respecting individuals. They are telling the world what they experienced. They had become intensely aware of a power greater than themselves, but they had absolutely no desire to set up a church, to form a hierarchy, to become an authoritative organization. On the contrary, when a well-known Jesuit theologian expressed his concern to Bill Wilson that AA could not survive without formal structure, Wilson promptly rejected the suggestion.

In speaking of AA's Step Two, "Came to believe . . ." and Step Three, "Made a decision to turn our will and our lives over . . ." Bateson emphasizes: *There is a power greater than the self.* Cybernetics would go one step further and recognize that the self, as ordinarily understood, is only a small part of a much larger trial-and-error system which does the thinking, acting, and deciding.

Bateson goes on: "The 'self' is a false reification of an improperly delimited part of this much larger field of interlocking processes." (This thought is identical to Kierkegaard's belief that the self must be destroyed to experience transcendence.) Bateson would suggest, I am sure, that before we listen to lectures about empowerment, self-esteem, independence, self-control, resilience, taking charge, and so on, we learn something first about the nature of our relationship to this world. Bateson sums up a lengthy discussion of AA's higher power concept with these words, "In sum, the relationship of each individual to the Power is best defined in the words *is part of.*"

Bateson's assessment of AA is couched in terms of formal systems theory. He is interested in the abstractions of form and symmetry, or mind in the universe, something that rational scientific philosophy had discarded before quantum mechanics and systems theory transcended the Cartesian world.

I am not altogether comfortable with Bateson's model of AA's dynamics. In his system, Bateson leaves unexplained the dynamics of the human organism. He does not consider that the human organism is a symbol-producing creature who lives by the meaning-feelings through which it interacts with the environment. It is not clear in Bateson what makes the human move within the system. The point is that Bateson shows that AA's powerlessness, or not-in-control, cannot be deconstructed as irrational by a rational scientific world; such an interpretation of AA's pre-rational steps is no longer acceptable in the age of organicism, wholes, and the implications from quantum physics.

I do not consider the first three steps purely rational, as Bateson appears to see them. First of all, we are not rational creatures. Any species-specific movement by the human organism is the movement of a whole, and in this case, the human whole moves upon anticipations of connections in the environment. These anticipations are not rational in their nature. Our rationality simply affirms and organizes our moves. Further, when we anticipate something, the anticipation is always accompanied by an experience (feeling) of the meaning (life or death) in the perception.

While we can talk with Bateson of changes in epistemology, what we must also talk about is the experience of authentic connection. That is actually the dynamic behind the change in epistemology. As Denzin says, AA must be looked at as lived experience. This kind of thinking is up-front in intellectual circles today because of the revolution against subject-object distancing in our inquiries into the nature of things.

Following on Bateson, historian Berman says:

> AA's second principle (the higher power) provides the basis for an alternative epistemology that is genuinely holistic . . . The individual ego (conscious will) leaves the field in favor of a more mature form of self . . . . Such a surrender is not a collapse, but a renewal. For the alcoholic who has finally "hit bottom," as AA calls it, the first two steps of the AA program in effect constitute Learning III and the alcoholic frequently experiences them as a religious (spiritual) conversion.

(I had originally intended to include here Bateson's theories of Learning I, II, and III, to which Berman refers, but because of their abstract nature, it is better to simply refer interested readers to Bateson's book, *Steps to an Ecology of Mind*.)

WHAT HAPPENS AFTER STEP ONE?

AA does not leave the matter of sobriety at the first step of surrender. The early AA members found that after they surrendered, they "came to believe" that a power greater than themselves could restore them to sanity. Once this belief had taken hold, they then relate that they "made a decision" to turn themselves over to the care of God, as each member understood God. Is this a natural progression?

Recall that living organisms *anticipate*. Anticipation is a definitive characteristic of organisms. A corollary of anticipation is inquiry. Once limitation is experienced, it is quite natural for the symbolic organism also to experience a new sense of *inquiry*. The sense of connectedness seems somehow more important even than the self. (Commentators who do not understand the dynamics refer to this sense of connectedness as "just another addiction.") Almost immediately, the recovering person begins to sense that the AA group transcends the self. Connection seems to imply for the connected individual an element of experience for which he or she is not the cause. The recovering alcoholic who successfully integrates the notion of limitation in Step One is now fully out of the Cartesian order of control and into an inchoate realization of interdependence. She senses participation in a larger web of relationships. Grasping the sense of connectedness leads quite naturally to a sense of something greater than self—and since we innately anticipate connection, there is a sense of organismic fulfillment at being connected to something larger.

One of the phenomena that can be observed in AA is the relief that many members find in being able to return to a fresh feeling about the faith they had abandoned. They have found that it does not require a specifically religious faith to take a new look at their traditional God. They are approaching their old religious format from their own experience of their newfound place in a system of things. Joseph Campbell reacted in this way when Bill Moyers asked him on television if he had "faith." Campbell mused for a while, then said he did not need faith. He had experience.

While many of us like to think that we reject higher powers as we mature rationally, I suggest that for some of us, at least, there is another way to look at this. Our problem with higher powers begins at birth, when life-death imagery moves from the inchoate quickly to formed image-feeling, and we actually anticipate the engagement with our environment—in which engagement we can lose out. If primordial trust is not established at that time, the ground is set for the *causa sui* lie and the rejection of all higher powers. The individual is also set up at that time for either/or referents to a God. If the parents inculcate a God system, basing it on shame and guilt, then the individual, attempting to survive the onslaught of shame, will often lose faith in that God system. Moreover, as Joseph Campbell points out, the overturned God will become a demon the individual must shake off his back. Thus the aversion to higher power notions often experienced by shame-tormented individuals. Further, the recovering addict has devoted most of his life to controlling, playing God, a product of his own *causa sui* lie from the beginning, driven by death equivalent image-feelings, pathetically trying to fit into this world. He has experienced no help from the beginning.

He was early turned over to a shaming God by his parents, a shaming system that promised relief on its terms only. In Christianity, for example, he is taught that death is a punishment for original sin, whereas the individual learns later that death is part of the life cycle, nature's program (or God's will) to increase the complexity and levels of living organisms. The very dialectic in which he is engaged as a symbolic-affective organism has been presented to him as a punishment for being what he is!

In a certain way, this echoes the feelings of Ernest Becker in *The Denial of Death*. For him, death is not so much part of the life cycle, but is actually the terror of creation for which we must compensate with creative illusions. As we have seen, Lifton, on the other hand, finds death part of the life cycle in his unitary vision of symbolic continuity. The question we must ask ourselves is: How is it possible that any system that emphasizes punishment, guilt, and shame can give birth to specifically human re-creations of life equivalents? And so the setup for the religious either/or referent; it is either the god of the parents or no god at all. This is what AA sought strenuously to avoid, and why AA insists that its collective symbolism is spiritual and not religious. Because of his history of shame, the recovering person is able to take only small doses of affirmation, of unconditional acceptance, which can whittle away at that shame base. His tattered will is still not ready to experience any higher power as trustworthy or even existing for her. He has been on his own too long.

ILLUSION OR REALITY?

To enter into a discussion about the higher power, we must also enter into an examination of the concept of a higher power. It means different things to different people. Gregory Bateson, for instance, was delighted with AA's notion of a higher power because it is a totally rational, nonsupernatural view of the self in the world. For Bateson, AA's first three steps are a razor-sharp assessment of the human condition. The higher power is the system of interlocking dependencies of which we are a part. The trick to being a whole person is to see one's reality from this point of view. Once this viewpoint is assimilated, the individual can then "surrender" to the system, accept it, live with it, cooperate with it.

Anthropologist Becker and psychoanalyst Rank have another idea about the higher power. (They make no distinction between religion and higher power, whereas AA does.) Religion and presumably higher powers are illusions necessary for sanity in a dualistic world. (Becker's favorite image of humankind is the angel looking upward with feet mired in muck.) What we have to do now is discover whether or not higher power, religion, and God, are all compensating illusions, or fundamental philosophy, or solid experience. The first notion we should tackle is the common belief that God and religion are illusions. This is usually the stance of the "thinking" or rational person, who dismisses religion. As we shall see, however, Becker and Rank did not consider illusion unacceptable.

(Strictly speaking, religions cannot be illusions. Illusions are filtered facts, but religion is not a fact, not a perceived reality. Religions are formative symbolic modes of continuity. What Rank and Becker were saying, equivalently, is that symbolic modes of continuity are necessary for sanity in what they saw as a dualistic world.)

In *The Denial of Death*, Becker introduced to a wide American audience what he called "the problem of illusion." He was attempting, as he tells us in his opening pages, to merge modern psychology with a mythico-religious perspective. This is an important discussion for us at this time because it bears upon the strong appeal of the Twelve Steps for people attempting to recover from addictions.

Our traditional attitude toward illusion is that it is self-deception, and as such is probably not a desirable habit of mind, but that attitude seems to be changing in some quarters. As a matter of fact, illusions can be seen to be a positive aspect of our specific feature as humans. In an interesting book called *Positive Illusion: Creative Self-Deception and the Healthy Mind,* Shelley Taylor tells us that delusions are false beliefs that persist despite the facts, but illusions, she says, accommodate the facts, "though perhaps reluctantly." Rank and Becker both believed that human beings needed illusions. Rank says, "With the truth, one cannot live. To be able to live, one needs illusions."

Today, we can amend that idea to suggest illusions are actually a part of our truth. They are part of our experience, and our experience is seen now as closer to our truth than conventional rationality and logic. Illusions are generally considered escapes from reality, and in a sense, of course, they are. Rank, Becker, and Taylor, however, are suggesting that our capacity to filter the facts is also a fundamental part of our reality. Remember that the beautiful teeth of a glamorous model have two realities. One is the impression we prefer—the lovely smile of straight white teeth. The other reality is that her teeth are tools for mashing and grinding other living organisms into pulp for the devastating acids in her stomach. We are not deluded by the impression of teeth as beautiful. We know what the teeth are, and their real purpose—which is not to brighten a smile, but we prefer the illusion while "accommodating the facts" about them. Becker, unfortunately I think, was quite distressed by the literal reality of things. While he spoke eloquently of creative illusions, the realities seemed too much with him. Our illusions about those realities, however, are just as real as the realities themselves. In other words, our formative symbolic processes, which deliver meanings of life equivalents to us, are a specific feature of our organic nature. It is perfectly okay to commit to these symbolic modes of illusion.

Take, for example, our notions about retirement. The reality is that the body is reaching the point of decay and breakdown preceding death in the life cycle. The illusion is that it is a time of greater freedom and personal opportunity. Both aspects are very real to us. The first aspect is likely to produce neurosis, whereas the second aspect produces health and enjoyment. Take your choice.

Rank and Becker took this thinking into the realm of religious illusions. Becker says, for instance, in *The Denial of Death*, "And so the question for the science of mental health must become an absolutely new and revolutionary one, yet one that reflects the essence of the human condition: On what level of illusion does one live?" Becker is probing into exactly the right field. (Lifton would respond that we live at the level of our symbolic modes of immortality.)

Becker seems to equate creative illusion with a Freudian-like notion of repression. In other words, we repress the idea that teeth are pulp mashers in favor of the more aesthetic impression, but I do not think that is precisely what is happening. We do not repress the actuality so that it is waiting for us like pus under a scab. Instead, our specific formative feature of anticipating life and death equivalents presents teeth to us as an attractive part of the human being; it is not necessary that a repressing mechanism be simultaneously at work. Creative illusions are at play in our ordinary conduct of daily engagements with reality, but the processes of creative illusion are hard-wired into the highest level of human organization. That makes them as real as the reality lying underneath. That is why Rank could say we cannot live without our illusions.

ARE HIGHER POWERS ILLUSIONS?

As was pointed out above, higher powers cannot be illusions because they are not filtered facts of a perceived reality. Higher powers are experienced at the more important level of subjectivity and unity.

The human is the only organism that universally exhibits a belief in, or asks questions about a power greater than itself—a power existing at a level transcending human species-specific activity. This higher power does not merely exist in another dimension of reality; it is somehow responsible as well for our well-being, if not for our being itself. This notion flows from an awareness unique to the human organism that we did not cause our own existence nor the existence of our environment. The human is the only organism that asks, How did I get here? Where did I come from? What is everything else doing here?

The notion of causality is innate and is rooted in the fact that we innately anticipate connection from birth. When the adult satisfies our needs we identify the adult's response as the cause of our satisfaction. A sense of causality is phylogenetically and ontogenetically developed. If we did not innately anticipate that this adult is the cause of our needs being met, we could not survive. If we did not have a notion of cause, we could not seek out connections. Other organisms anticipate connection and identify the cause of satisfaction, for example, the nursing calf, who "knows" the mother has milk for her, but the calf's sense of cause appears to be immediate and direct. For the human organism, on the other hand, the sense of cause is also symbolized. We can see this in early art where the genitals and breasts are exaggerated. The human, in other words, not only reacts to causative agents, but has the capacity to think about and symbolize them as *causative*. It is this innate anticipation of a causality upon which we depend that leads to religions, and beliefs in higher powers. The very notion of anticipation means that we cannot supply certain needs ourselves!

Belief in a higher power is not in the least unreasonable, but it has nothing to do with rationality—any more than does our anticipation of connection. Belief in a higher power is pre-rational, as are art and music. It is primitive and primordial. Belief, in the context of an organism-in-environment, is better understood as trust.

Are those who believe right, and others wrong? Those who believe in higher powers have chosen to accept an aspect of our reality that can in no way be denied to them. Those of us who choose to deny higher powers cannot do so on a rational basis, since rationality does not apply here. In other words, we cannot prove that higher powers either exist or do not exist.

(Thomas Aquinas, in his famous five proofs for the existence of God, was convinced that his rational capacity actually corresponded with reality. He was in that sense an Aristotelian realist. Aquinas' five proofs are based on the principle of contradiction and sufficient reason. For medieval philosophers, the principle of contradiction meant that a thing could not both be and not be simultaneously—that we cannot make a statement that simultaneously affirms and denies what we are saying. That God exists may be a logical necessity within Aristotelian realism, but our minds are simply not equipped to say that we have such correspondence with ultimate reality. We have certainly seen that in quantum mechanics. Our innate formative capacities transform information but they cannot describe for us the ultimate nature of that with which our formative processes co-respond.)

The matter of God's existence for the individual is a matter of internal experience, not rational argument. Probably no one today is convinced by the logical brilliance of the medieval scholastics. The experience of God's existence flows from the primordial trust of an organism that anticipates connection in a larger system of things.

Many of us do find that we are not compelled to believe in God, or a higher power. This is a matter of our particular experience, not a matter of right or wrong. It is safe to say that the human organism comes into the world equipped to fashion images of higher powers. How and whether we do so seems to be a matter of early developmental experience. We cannot deny higher powers on the grounds that they are not natural. On the contrary, it seems more natural to the human organism to look for higher powers transcending the self and its environment. Nor is it unreasonable to make a commitment to that aspect of our reality.

While the Enlightenment and rational science rejected the notion of God, or a higher power, we know now that that phase in human awareness has itself been transcended. We are heading inevitably into still another dimension of awareness. It is unlikely that we will return to the prescientific attitudes of trust, but we will rather move on into the post-modern scientific acceptance of our species-specific features, including a trust in larger connectedness. Trust in a higher power is a matter of choice—and a most reasonable one.

DISTRUST

Becker, along with Rank, equates neurosis with too much insight into reality without a sufficient offset of creative illusion. This is somewhat true, but I would add that the neurotic is focused upon a reality he fashioned in distrust. His anticipations of connection were shattered, and his world is filled with death equivalents. Through our formative capacities, we transcend the gross realities of bad breath, disease, and the stark facts of bodily eliminations—but only if our species-specific anticipations of connection in this world have been nurtured.

Becker's essay is a milestone in human psychology. He confronted the problem of mortality head-on—something the Freudians, the revisionists, and certainly American behaviorism has failed to do.

RELIGION AS ILLUSION

We look at a distinction here that is pertinent to any discussion about AA, higher powers, and religion. The distinction has to do with religion and belief in God.

Religion is not an illusion. Religions are visible symbols and signs created by our formative expressions of a belief in God. Religions are modes of symbolic human activity, but the notion of God, on the other hand, does not arise from our formative symbolic capacity. God is an expression of our impression that we are dependent, and are not the cause of ourselves. It is from this impression, or awareness, of ourselves that we and our environment take on the aspect of a creation—something that did not cause itself. Religion results from our formative symbolic features, whereas God results from our awareness of dependence. Our formative capacities create religions as expressions of a relationship with God.

Religions are proximate; belief in God is ultimate. Religions depend upon our formative capacities; belief in God depends upon our experience. Because religions are modes of immortality, however, they invite powerful attachments; therefore, someone suggesting that your formative life equivalent is wrong, is ultimately threatening you with a death equivalent. Thus we see the deep hatreds that can arise in religious conflict. People who believe in God violently attack one another's proximate expression of belief in the same God.

ATHEISM

We are not compelled to affirm the existence of a God. That is a choice, but atheism as a statement indicates a misunderstanding of our rational capacity to make that kind of statement. We cannot. Atheism as a poise, however, is a matter of indifference to the implications in dependence. Indifference to these implications is quite reasonable, since implications are always a matter of subjective acceptance. We can choose to believe or not to believe. We do not experience any compelling evidence about God unless we choose to.

INQUIRIES INTO REALITY

Once the fundamental control issue has been dealt with in Step One, there takes place in AA a process of learning, or of inquiring into one's newfound reality. This inquiry results in assimilation of Steps Two and Three.

We might ask, why does an inquiry into reality necessarily follow from the giving up of control in Step One? We can answer that by reminding ourselves that we are, as Dennett remarks, "anticipation machines." We innately anticipate meanings of life and death significance. A corollary of anticipation is inquiry. My cat anticipates food or something to play with. To that end, he prowls my house frequently, inquiring into what he anticipates in his environment. He "knows" beforehand what he is looking for. As a human organism, I am constantly anticipating life and life equivalents. I will find these in both form and connection. I can also find chaos and separation. As a result, I will be constantly inquiring into my environment for those meanings.

Giving up control exposes us to a larger context of inquiry, including ourselves as participants in a larger system. Thus, when the alcoholic has given up control, he or she naturally may be inclined to inquire into participation—even the transcendent, a most compelling mode of continuity—anticipating symbolic ways of uniting with life itself.

LEVELS OF INQUIRY

"The great irony of quantum mechanics," according to Morris Berman, is that as a Cartesian attempt to wipe out subjectivity once and for all, instead it "established subjectivity as the cornerstone of objective knowledge." Eric Jantsch says that rationality "constitutes the lowest level in a hierarchy of knowledge for human purposes." Jantsch believes that the rational approach "impoverishes and narrows down" reality. According to David Finklestein, Director of the School of Physics, Georgia Institute of Technology, experience is not bound by the rules of classical logic. He refers to a more permissive set of rules, quantum logic, which is not based on the way we think of things, but on the way we *experience* them. Gary Zukav says, "When we try to describe experience with classical logic—which is what we have been doing since we learned to write—we put on a set of blinders, so to speak, which not only restricts our field of vision, but also distorts it." In 1936, the mathematician John von Neumann and his colleague, Garrett Birkoff, published the paper that laid the foundations for quantum logic. In their paper they "demonstrated mathematically that it is impossible to describe experience with classical logic because the real world follows different rules." Jantsch adds, "Rationality, as it turns out, begins to play a role only after the knowledge has been obtained viscerally."

From the point of view of a cognitive scientist, Howard Gardner (*The Mind's New Science*), we have the following: "Empirical work on reasoning over the past thirty years has severely challenged the notion that human beings—even sophisticated ones—proceed in a rational manner, let alone that they invoke some logical calculus in their reasoning . . ."

Such statements affirm our position that we innately transform our perceptions into image-feelings of meaning before our rational capacities coherently organize these experiences.

Danah Zohar (*The Quantum Self*) supports this when she says, "All definite answers—all logic, all reason—are classical structures. They arise at the point where the wave function of thought collapses, that is, after the moment of choice." Zukav writes, "We are approaching the end of science. The end of science means the coming of Western civilization, in its own time, and in its own way, into the higher dimensions of human experience." Max Planck, the father of quantum mechanics, says, "Science means unresting endeavor and continually pressing development toward an aim which the poetic intuition may apprehend, but which the intellect can never fully grasp." In the same vein, G.F. Chew, Chairman of the Physics Department at Berkeley, says, "Our current struggle (with certain aspects of advanced physics) may thus be only a foretaste of a completely new form of intellectual endeavor, one that will lie not only outside physics but will not even be describable as scientific . . ."

One of the startling implications from quantum mechanics is that subject-object distancing, the rational-scientific view, is no longer a completely adequate probe into reality. Most vocal on this point is the physicist John Wheeler, of Princeton, who is fascinated by our participation in bringing about the "reality" of the electron through our measurements. In brief, it seems we are never simply Jantsch's man on the shore; we are also in the river at the same time.

Step Three: "Made a decision to turn our will and our lives over to the care of God . . ."

Step Three is the decision to turn over life and will to the care of the higher power. AA regards Step Three as the mature culmination of the first two. Acceptance of this Step—its realization in the individual's life—is the final repudiation of the Cartesian illusion of control. It is also the key to the peace of mind that its practitioners report. Popularly known as "turning it over," or "letting go," this Step is perhap most widely misunderstood by mental health professionals and authors. Critics are concerned about the irrational "submission" this step inculcates. This was a central concern of Kaminer in *I'm Dysfunctional, You're Dysfunctional* (reviewed on the front page of the *New York Times Book Review*).

In earlier chapters, I made use of the card game to illustrate the dialectical nature of human life. Games get their zest from the fact that they are always a playing out of the life-death polarity in the human organism. Let's take another look at the card game to help us with Step Three.

The Core Insight of Step Three

To enjoy a game of cards, the players submit to three conditions: First, there are fixed rules of procedure; second, the individual player has no control over the hands that are dealt; and third, the individual has no control over the decisions of the other players; each individual must respond in the game to the decisions of others (the dialectic). Any hope of controlling the outcome is thoroughly unrealistic. The individual simply recognizes and accepts the realities involved. Making responsible decisions within the confines of the nature of the game is what is important.

The much-maligned attitude of letting go—turning it over—is a simple recognition that the outcomes of complex dialectics—which is human life in an environment—result from the individual's participation in the system, and not from the individual's control of the system. This is the core insight of Step Three.

The card game is perhaps the best illustration of modern science's conclusion that humankind lives in an order of complexity, not in an order of control. That is why humans must begin to regard themselves more as participants than as individuals—and that is the message of AA. Once it is realized, the individual may experience renewed energy, creativity, and love.

TRANSCENDENCE

I suggested in the chapter, "The Basic Fault," that much of the quality of the image-feelings provided by alcohol has to do with transcendence. We could even argue that the experience of transcendence is of the essence of alcoholism. We can use Lifton's words here as appropriate: "The self feels uniquely alive—connected, in movement, integrated—which is why we can say that this state provides at least a temporary sense of eliminating time and death." The notion of transcendence might be understood as Jantsch's third level of inquiry, wherein the individual experiences itself as united with the flow of the river.

How is the state of transcendence to be recaptured by the recovering alcoholic? Lifton tells us that:

> [W]ildly, or gently, one must psychologically travel outside oneself in order to feel one's participation in the larger human process. . . . Psychological science should enter the domain it has tended either to ignore, further mystify, or else misrepresent by nervously and reductively invoking its own clinical terms instead of examining the phenomenology of man's experience of his larger connectedness. Depth psychology is capable of returning to an area it has mostly abandoned to the theologians. The formative, life-continuity paradigm provides a framework for addressing the domain of "ultimate concern" and charting some of the ecology of infinity . . .

AA's first three steps offer the recovering individual an opportunity to experience authentic transcendence. Turning oneself over to the care of higher powers provides the experience of "traveling outside oneself in order to feel one's participation in the larger human process." This language reminds us of earlier chapters when we discussed modern physics and the psychological implications of being a whole in a seamless web of interdependencies. Just as depth psychology—through a new paradigm of death and symbolic image feelings of continuity—can reclaim territory abandoned to the theologians, so AA has done just that, through its new paradigm of participation and responsibility within a larger view of human life. AA is urging nothing different from Lifton's modes of symbolic continuity—responsibility to family, nature, creativity, religion, and transcendence.

The Fork in the Road

Step One, admitting powerlessness over alcohol, is a fork in the road for the major outlooks on recovery. I generally refer to these differing streams as the you-are-not-in-control gang versus the you-are-in-control gang.

In the past several years, two self-help recovery groups for alcoholics have sprung up: Secular Organizations for Sobriety (SOS) and Rational Recovery (RR). Both of these organizations were founded as alternatives to AA. According to Charlotte Kasl (*Many Roads, One Journey*), these groups were founded "by pioneering souls who attended AA and left for various reasons, including dislike of the sexism, the powerlessness concept, rigidity, religiosity, the cult-like atmosphere, and the all-powerful God approach."

James Christopher, founder of SOS, has summed up his viewpoint succinctly when he says that his group prefers "the experience of an internal locus of control to the passivity of giving full credit to something or someone else." Because this is a virtually impenetrable form of the Cartesian mindset, it is a perspective not likely to mellow even in light of the postmodern shift to organic wholes in environment. It is rooted in the notion that life is lived in an order of control rather than in an order of complexity and interdependency.

These groups are not only repelled by the powerlessness concept, but they are particularly hostile to the notions of a higher power and turning it over. They assume a rational militancy in their rejection, relying on their understanding of what rationality is and its significance for them in human activity.

We find representations of these groups' beliefs in two accessible books, *SOS Sobriety* by James Christopher and *The Small Book* by Jack Trimpey. Both authors left AA because of a genuine discomfort with their perceptions of Twelve Step philosophy. They represent a number of recovering alcoholics who would prefer to tackle the problem of addiction without recourse to notions of higher powers and religious language.

Both Trimpey and Christopher display a profound misunderstanding of the nature of AA. They exhibit not the slightest acquaintance with the major intellectual shifts in this century. What is even more troublesome here is that both Trimpey and Christopher build their own programs upon a view that AA is wrong. They are angry about AA, as if it betrayed them. In both men's work, there is a lack of inquiry, and a misunderstanding of the rational features of the human organism. It goes without saying that no controlling image of the human organism is offered in either book. They both subscribe to a dualistic view of humankind—the warfare between the beast within and the self—and both are wedded to a Cartesian notion of control.

Christopher refers to Twelve Step philosophy as "shame-based" and "learned helplessness." Both of these misapprehensions about AA are rooted in a misunderstanding of AA's notions of control and surrender. One of the unattractive features of Trimpey's work is an encouragement of "AA bashing." Trimpey's book also offers a bizarre interpretation of AA's Steps as a conspiracy to sneak religion over on the unsuspecting! Both books are much too tainted with an unbalanced protestantism against AA, requiring too much attention to AA. This militates against an authentic autonomy for their own programs. While their programs may be designed to provide a comforting environment for those rejecting AA, it hardly seems a positive environment for the recovering alcoholic.

Neither book qualifies for consideration as an inquiry into the nature of either alcoholism or recovery, although both are peripherally interesting as a genuine complaint. Christopher explains that "many of us had not felt at home in AA with its twelve 'spiritual' steps, its 'program' for living." We are still a nation embedded in Cartesian worldviews. We have been raised on notions of self-reliance, subject-object distancing, independence, and scientific rationalism. AA makes no attempt to accommodate those worldviews.

The essential task of the final Steps four through twelve is the acceptance and practice of a new poise in life. The recovering alcoholic moved from defense and control when she assimilated the first three Steps. She must practice her new stance in environment. She must now be responsible and participate.

CONCLUSION

When quantum mechanics displaced the Cartesian view of the world as a giant machine, it became immediately apparent that another view was needed. Systems theory offers a view flowing from quantum theory. Systems theory is a rational and necessary response to the inevitable implications of quantum mechanics. Systems theory states: First, the world is a dynamic system of interacting and interdependent relationships. Second, our knowledge of the world differs from Cartesian rationalism. If the world is a system, then we are a part of it—not merely observers. Third, there are three levels of inquiry into reality. Systems theory illuminates the three levels: The rational first level is the poise of the observer, the organizer, the communicator. It is characterized by objectivity. The second level is connective, feeling, interactive. It is characterized by subjectivity. The third level is unitary. It is grounded in the first two levels, but transcends them. It is characterized by a profound awareness of unity. (The alcoholic yearns for this level of transcendence, but without being grounded in the first two.)

Following upon the discoveries of quantum mechanics and nonlocality, the notions of the whole, subjectivity, and participation have taken on fresh meaning. The age of the Enlightenment is receding. We see ourselves now as deeply involved participants in a system, with a capacity to organize and prioritize our experience. Subjectivity, feeling, and commitment to experience are ascendant. As a result, honesty and responsibility have become the indispensable characteristics of well-being in the quantum age. We look for wisdom rather than rationality.

The fellowship and program of AA have taken a place in the significant movements in this century. Some believe AA is part and parcel of the radical shifts in worldviews that have taken place in the sciences. For some seeking assistance with addictions, it is a most compelling way of finding a new life. For many others, perhaps even a majority, AA's principles will not be acceptable. As with alcoholism, Alcoholics Anonymous is a matter of choice.

14

The Treatment of Alcoholism

> To change a maladaptive habit, be it smoking or getting too little exercise or drinking too much alcohol, we cannot "treat," or compel, or reason with the person. Rather, we must change the person's belief system and then maintain that change. Time and time again, both evangelists and behavior therapists have demonstrated that if you can but win their hearts and minds, their habits will follow.
>
> —George E. Vaillant, *The Natural History of Alcoholism*

Strictly speaking, alcoholism cannot be treated, but the alcoholic can be assisted. This is not quibbling. The word treat implies an incorrect view of the nature of alcoholism. Treatment—a derivative from the Latin meaning *to drag* or *draw*—is a borrowing from medical intervention; it has a strong mechanical implication. It must be tolerated, however, in the context of alcoholism. Certainly there are consequences of alcoholism that should be treated. Eventually, in the decades to come, the language about alcoholism will change. We will expand our rational-scientific inquiries to include a more experiential mode of inquiry. In this book, I use the words treat and treatment as a convenience.

UNDERSTANDING THE PROBLEM

Nothing has been more important to the alcoholic than the life equivalents provided by the chemical. Nothing. He got himself into this condition through his choice to continue drinking in spite of consequences. If he wants to survive, he must choose to stop drinking. The core of the problem can be located in the choosing process of the human organism.

An alcoholic makes choices within the processes of the feeling complex. The feeling complex perceives meanings of life and death or their equivalents. The solution to the problem of alcoholism is helping the alcoholic develop new perceptions of life meanings without alcohol. The question for those assisting the alcoholic is whether changing the alcoholic's *behavior* alone restores the integrity of the feeling complex. This brings us to the heart of the treatment controversy. The nationwide treatment community, both clinical and academic, generally divides between the behavioral school—the habit-values model—and the Twelve Step model of Alcoholics Anonymous (AA). Sometimes this division is confused because the Twelve Step model is identified with the medical model in rehabilitation programs. Medicine has nothing to do with the core of the problem. The medical model invariably relies upon the Twelve Step regimen.

CONTROL

The core insight of AA, that which makes AA what it is, is the awareness of limitation. The control issue sharply separates the rational school from the pre-rational Twelve Step program. The rational school wants to restore the individual's power, to give him tools, to convince him that he is in control of his destiny. The pre-rational school believes the alcoholic seized control that does not belong to him by nature.

In most of our daily activities, we control in the Cartesian sense. We control cars, we control the cooking of our food, we control our budgets, we control the temperature of our homes, we control spaceships to the moon. These are appropriate Cartesian aspects of our natural capacities, but when we use alcohol, we are attempting to chemically control our meaning-feeling feature. Our well-being as organisms is based on meanings of *connections* (on the realization of symbolic modes of continuity). These are various kinds of relationships. We *participate* in them. We negotiate them through a dialectic. We cannot control them. *The basic appeal of alcohol is the feeling that we are controlling our connections.* The basic thrust of treatment is convincing the alcoholic that he cannot—that he participates in life, but does not control it.

Treatment programs divide into two camps. One uses the you-are-not-in-control perspective of AA—the pre-rational, subjective viewpoint. The other uses the you-are-in-control perspective—the rational, objective

viewpoint. The rational, behavioral approach generally ignores the more important pre-rational, subjective view.

The Twelve Step model can include a rational habit-values approach, but the habit-values model, on the other hand, is generally hostile to the Twelve Step approach. We can summarize this chapter with the following statement: The rational model teaches one how *not* to drink. The AA model offers a way of life *without* drinking. Let's look into these differences.

THE RATIONAL SCHOOL

This school suggests to the alcoholic that he can use his reasoning capacity to give up his destructive habit. He can identify his core values and see that alcoholism is an unreasonable way to go. This school suggests that he has *learned* this self-destructive *habit,* and that to remedy this, he can learn coping skills; he can learn to recognize triggers and cues; and he can learn to use guidelines, signposts, and maps to avoid traps and anticipate setbacks. If he chooses, he can even reframe the earlier experiences that led to self-destructive behavior.

Much of the rational approach is actually *training.* (When I applied for a job many years ago to teach Dale Carnegie courses, the director told me their customers were not there to learn, but to be trained. She turned me down for the job, asserting that I would be inclined to educate them rather than train them.) Another word is *programming.* The question then arises, can rational training and programming (behavior) affect the specific level where alcoholism originates—choice? Training and programming provide techniques, but do they provide meaning? The alcoholic changes most successfully when he becomes aware of meaning. He is a participating organism seeking connection in the larger arrangement of things. Meaning for the human organism always has to do with connection. Values have no meaning until grounded in connection.

Training and programming work best if the individual is grounded first in connection. This implies that the alcoholic gives up control and defense and accepts his limitations in an interdependent world. He must see limitation as a positive feature of an organism in an interdependent world.

THE PRE-RATIONAL MODEL

Rational programs counsel the alcoholic to admit that his behavior is unreasonable, that it is illogical, that it works against what he really desires for himself and others. Some alcoholics are moved by the approach to reason. Many are not. Fundamental human action is neither rational or logical; it is *experiential*. For instance, a drunk driver kills someone and changes his life. His changing is not a rational approach; it is pre-rational. He does, however, go about reorganizing his life in a rational manner. What drives his new life is not his reason but his experience. The Twelve Step program of AA is the major pre-rational approach. It is not theoretical, academic, or contrived in any way. It is a statement of the actual experience of recovering alcoholics. Alcoholics bring to the recovery process issues around distrust, self-dependence, and confusion. They have tried to control these feelings with alcohol. The question is whether the rational school can reach the core issue—control and defense.

GROUNDING AND CENTERING

The rational, Cartesian approach is neither grounded nor centered; the pre-rational approach is quantum-age. The quantum-age has grounded the Cartesian age. *A quantum-age outlook (participation and interdependency) can properly ground a rational poise.* In this sense, in approaching an understanding of the human organism, we gain the more complete picture first by grounding humankind in our pre-rational nature. *We can describe grounded people as those who are secure in their innately anticipated connections.*

Jantsch (*Design for Evolution*) says:

> A grounded man knows what he needs and what is good for him, because he knows in a very basic way, not dependent upon logic, what is natural for him. And this—in an evolutionary perspective— is the all-important question which perplexes all rational creative planning today so that it trickles off into vague philosophizing. *For there is no way to find out rationally and logically what is good for man and his systems*—as much as we may strive for an empirical consensus. Static notions such as happiness have eluded us in spite of all our attempts to satisfy material needs and desires. The individual does not know what is good for him if he is not well grounded—and much less can the members of a human system determine rationally and logically what is good for the system.

A centered person, according to Jantsch, puts his center in himself—not into another person, an outside authority, or some impersonal mechanism. He is a self-regulating whole in a larger system of wholes. Second, a centered person is a balanced person. The notion of balance has become increasingly important in the study of living organisms. Living organisms "defy" the

Second Law of Thermodynamics, which states that all equilibrium systems eventually run down and stop. Living organisms are nonequilibrium systems. Rather than run down (like a clock) they maintain a state far from equilibrium (through metabolism). Hence they must maintain balance. Balance provides stability in a nonequilibrium state. Nobel laureate and chemist Prigogine has described this process as "order through fluctuation." Jantsch says these are new approaches to recognizable old themes, but they are up-to-date approaches because Western societies have become "grossly unbalanced," tending toward the "ego trip" side. Put another way, we have gravitated toward individualism, and away from participation. Participation requires balance.

We talked about anticipation earlier. From the very beginning, the human organism *anticipates* naturally and innately what it needs. Humankind does not rationally and logically anticipate what is good for it, but is given the capacity to rationally pursue what it anticipates. Here we see the problem with aborting our treatment of the alcoholic at the rational level of habit and behavior. The human is an organism anticipating continuity of life through connections—within such symbolic modes of continuity as family, work, church, art, and so on. There is nothing rational about this primal enterprise, but we organize these pursuits rationally and logically.

What is needed, then, is a vision of recovery that is geared to grounding and centering: first, to grounding the innate anticipations of the human organism-in-environment—his sense of what he is; and second, to centering his sense of entitlements—the difference between what he needs and what he wants (balance). After this is done, we can look to rational behavioristic exercises to assist in the recovery project.

RATIONAL VS. PRE-RATIONAL INQUIRY INTO REALITY

We have come to the point in this narrative where a further illumination of the rational approach is necessary. I have been stressing a pre-rational approach, and saying that rational (behavioral) programs are not fully adequate to the problems besetting organisms-in-environment. Downgrading rationality is a heresy in a scientific, positivistic, technological world.

It took some years after quantum physics stunned the scientific world for the shock to wear off and for the fog to begin to lift. Gradually, scientists probed this new reality, shaking their heads, trying to piece together a brand new coherent view of the real world. Einstein never did stop shaking his head—going to his grave unhappy with the implications from this unassailable new knowledge. Quantum theory, however, has been the most rigorously tested and spectacularly successful theory in the history of science. Where to go with its meanings and significance? An imperative question loomed: *If the Universe can no longer be a giant Cartesian clockwork, then what is it?* For the last three decades or so, physicists, historians of science, and philosophers have been wrestling with this question as they developed their new model of the universe that conforms with quantum theory and nonlocality—a model of systems.

SYSTEMS THEORY

We are all wholes—systems—within a larger system of wholes. When I see a cat, a tree, a rock I am looking at a system that manifests itself materially as a cat, tree, or rock. In a real way, my perception of things as they appear is an illusion. I see things as I am designed to see them, so that I can deal with them at their material level from my own material status. (The real illusion is that of individualism, of separateness; the reality is relationship and interdependence.)

We are all in the system, but we do not participate at the rational level! We participate at the pre-rational, subjective level. We are not just observers. Quantum mechanics has done away with separability. We are integrated participants. Quantum mechanics, therefore, posed an enormous problem for epistemology—the study of how we know reality. The rational inquiry into reality was based on objectivity, but quantum mechanics had done away with objectivity. Ultimately there is no separation between knower and known. Systems theorists, wrestling with the consequences of quantum theory, were confronted with the inseparability of knower and known. Very gradually, the nature and validity of subjective experience was re-examined. Finally, the word subjective was dropped in favor of simply *experience.* We are an integrated part of the system. *We experience reality!*

After centuries of disdain, human experience has been brought back into scientific repute. Morris Berman calls this the "reenchanting" of the world. We are one again with nature.

THE GOAL OF REHABILITATION: PRE-RATIONAL CHANGE

The most important idea in recovery from alcoholism is not treatment, but change on the part of the alcoholic. The change must be at the subjective and pre-rational level. In our scientific, technological, medically oriented society, we believe all our ailments can be treated. We are just beginning to realize, however, that many of our medical complaints can be alleviated by changes at the species-specific level—our attitudes (which can be defined as our inventory of image-feelings), our lifestyles, our beliefs.

Rehabilitation is best described as a regimen to promote change; therefore (sometimes unknown even to the treatment community itself) AA is the principal remedy. The support activities of medical and psychological programs are organized around a Twelve Step regimen.

There are three immediate goals for rehabilitation centers. The most important is to assist the individual to surrender. Surrender—acceptance of limitation—is the indispensable poise from which the alcoholic will begin to change. The second goal is to promote the natural healing processes, and the third is to provide a caring and hopeful environment. In the rehab, the core regimen is organized around the natural healing process. In most treatment centers, the natural healing program is the Twelve Step program of AA.

CHANGE AND THE NATURAL HEALING PROCESSES

Rationalistic and behavioristic approaches to recovery are not natural healing processes; they are an aid to natural processes. So let's discuss now what is meant by natural healing processes. Although this is a term used by authors Vaillant and Peele, it is likely that neither author understands the dynamics of the healing process in the same way that I do. Actually, a definition of natural healing processes is off limits for behavioral psychology and sociology, because natural healing processes are pre-rational and subjective.

As has been pointed out, there is a basic fault in the human organism. We do not share it with the other animals. We are vulnerable at the very core of our nature because we can be shamed. We can experience death equivalents because of broken connections and fantasy bonding with those we need. The organism's response to shame and fantasy bonding is distrust and self-dependence. If a natural healing process is to take place, distrust and self-dependence must be replaced by their opposites. First, the alcoholic accepts his dependency—his need for connections. He accepts help—and simultaneously he must begin to trust those offering him help. This gives rise to image-feelings of authentic connection, a process that must be gently encouraged.

The trick in the self-healing process of recovering from alcoholism is the acceptance of, and a commitment to, a new system of image-feelings. The alcoholic has for many years been living with fantasy connections, harboring anger, distrusting, self-dependent, confused in his relationships. For many years, only alcohol suffused him with life equivalent image-feelings of connection, or numbed him from the painful confusion of separation and shame. It is sad to hear biopsychiatrists reasoning that the problem is largely physiological because they can find no premorbid mental disturbances. What they are missing is the basic fault. (The basic fault is nowhere described in psychoanalytic literature, simply because psychoanalysis has not discovered the fundamental model of the human organism-in-environment.)

Any treatment program for the alcoholic, therefore, must offer first, and above all, an environment of commitment to meanings of connection. He or she must see them, feel them, hear them.

SURRENDER

The alcoholic became an alcoholic by trying to control his image-feelings—his interface with his environment—with a chemical. The primary job of the rehabilitation center is to help him see that he is limited, that many things do not come under his power—especially alcohol. The rehabilitation center must be alert to the beaten alcoholic's *compliance* with these suggestions of limitation. Compliance is not *acceptance,* although compliance can be the first step in acceptance. Alcoholics who relapse have failed to assimilate the notion of limitation. Some authors examine relapse from the angle that the alcoholic cannot stand discomfort and *loses* control; I take the angle that he cannot stand the discomfort and *takes* control. Many alcoholics have difficulty realizing that taking a drink is taking control, as this view places the responsibility squarely at the appropriate level of human organization.

DENIAL

Hand in glove with the control issue, the alcoholic is afflicted with a mind-set of denial. This can go deeply into the psyche of the afflicted person, so much so that many of us still feel vestiges of denial in the later stages of recovery and sobriety. ("It's been ten years now. Surely I could have a glass of wine with Saturday night dinner.") Denial is so powerful because alcohol became the source of life itself. To admit that alcohol was a problem was to invite death. The intractability of denial has been regarded as a prominent symptom of alcoholism, but it cannot be thoroughly understood without a model of the continuity of life and the feeling complex. Most of us can admit readily that our bad habits are bad habits. The alcoholic cannot admit that about his habit. Even when he can, he may hold reservations. As a result, he may relapse after many years of abstinence. There is probably no greater indicator of the level of human organization at which alcoholism occurs than the phenomenon of denial. Denial is clearly not occurring at the physical level, nor is it driven at the level of habit.

Without doubt the most important achievement in the natural healing process for the alcoholic is surrender. The healing process cannot begin as long as the alcoholic has any belief left that alcohol can successfully deliver image-feelings of more life, or numb the pain of separation.

Remember, the alcoholic is generally a heavily defended person. He has probably from the early years of his life been self-dependent. To use Ernest Becker's words: He becomes a little god in the *causa sui* project—father of himself. Whatever means he finds to survive will become life equivalents for him. When alcohol comes into this scheme of things, he has probably found the strongest and most vivid life equivalents he has ever experienced. He is not about to surrender easily.

Many experts are irritated by the notion of surrender and limitation. They believe this is exactly the opposite of what the alcoholic needs to hear—that he should be told to take control and forget about negatives like limitation. They believe the problem can be resolved by a clear-cut application of rational processes, but the fundamental remedy is surrender and acceptance of limitation, to be followed by the natural healing process.

The efficacy of surrender, or acceptance of limitation, flows from the nature of an organism-in-environment. If an alcoholism expert lingers still (as virtually all do) in a Cartesian worldview, surrender and acceptance will not be a congenial notion. Once we understand the new worldviews of modern science about wholes and interdependencies, however, surrender and acceptance actually become the rational way to go.

ABSTINENCE

I cannot leave this chapter on treatment without a word about the suggestions by some authors that alcoholics can safely return to social drinking, or moderate drinking. This suggestion occurs principally among academics and sociologists—almost never among clinicians.

Let's concentrate for a moment on the phenomenon of stopping. Stopping can either mean a temporary abstinence or a permanent abstinence. Whichever, it means breaking a destructive behavior permanently. Some psychologists may suggest we can return to social drinking. They are assuming we have stopped for now—that we have broken the destructive habit. If it is important to me, or a challenge, to return to social drinking, however, *then I am not indifferent to alcohol*. The essential characteristic of the social drinker is *indifference*. If returning to social drinking, or controlled drinking, is important, as it is to moderation groups, then we are not indifferent to the mood changes in drinking. I see that as a warning. My daughters, for instance, could not care less whether they ever had a drop of alcohol. They are as indifferent to alcohol as they are to chewing gum. That indifference will never be available to me in the same sense that it is to them. I have a history that is part of my core. Even if I trained myself to thoroughly reframe those scenes that lead to alcohol abuse, I can never be sure my historical responses will not be re-awakened. Remember, we are historical organisms, unlike other animals. It is not possible to change our behavior so deeply that we can begin a new history *on a blank slate*.

People wanting to return to moderate drinking want to resume controlling their feelings with a chemical. They want to believe that by joining a moderation group, or undergoing reframing, they can resume chemically changing their moods at will. The enormously high risk in this is that alcohol in the blood tends to relieve one of species-specific choice. None of us is exactly the same person after a drink or two.

If I have a history of using alcohol to the point that my life became unmanageable; if I have a history of returning to its use repeatedly in spite of consequences; if I have a history of being uncomfortable living without alcohol for protracted periods, then it is too high a risk to return to altering my moods with alcohol. If at some point in my recovery, I choose to celebrate my daughter's wedding with a glass of champagne, I am challenging my own system of beliefs. If I choose to drink again, then I must have a good reason to discard the belief system that relieved me of alcoholic behavior. Why do I want to change again? If it becomes important to me to be able to drink again, that alone is a danger. Most people are thoroughly indifferent to drinking, while others do not like the idea of taking any mood changers and will not take alcohol even ceremoniously. What is there about me that would like to return to social or moderate drinking? These suggestions of a safe return to drinking spring from Cartesian control theories. Once we understand the feeling complex, through which an organism negotiates with the environment, we can see the dangers for a historic symbolic animal in returning to chemical control of forms and feelings.

RELAPSE

> Alcoholism Counselor: Have you ever stopped drinking?
>
> Patient in treatment: Me? Stopped drinking? Oh, yeah, sure. Hundreds of times. (AA joke)

A major concern of those engaged in the treatment of alcoholism is the prevention of relapse. A most influential book on this subject is *Relapse Prevention*, by G. Alan Marlatt. Marlatt's work is a comprehensive representation of the rational point of view about addiction. Marlatt takes a different approach than I do to the nature of relapse.

Relapse can be described as a return to drinking after a sustained decision to stop drinking. Relapse presumes that the relapsing person had made a decision to completely cease his self-destructive behavior.

Relapse Prevention talks about the two factors in relapse: (1) the external determinative factors in relapse. Determinative factors are a matter of cognitive assessment. (2) The self-judgments that lead to relapse in the face of external determinants. These self-judgments are about self-efficacy.

Both perspectives are rational and objective.

Cognitive assessment implies a rational weighing of factors leading to a decision to drink or not drink. These factors can be evaluated as being unreasonable, illogical, and militating against the individual's basic plan to stop drinking. (This approach is also recommended in AA, where we are advised to "think the drink through.") This approach enlists only level one of inquiry, however—ignoring level two where decisions are enacted. The cognitive assessment approach is more effective for people already grounded and centered at level two of inquiry.

Self-Efficacy: Relapse Prevention describes self-efficacy as a judgment about how well one can organize and execute courses of action to deal with prospective situations. In *Relapse Prevention*, a feeling of poor self-efficacy is the individual's belief that he "just can't do this," but this is not what is happening. When an individual says, "I just can't do this," he is actually saying he *chooses* not to do it. What appear to be manifestations of poor judgment about the self are in fact more than that. Granted, the shame-based person may have a poor opinion of himself, but the poor opinion has not been formed for him by the shaming circumstances. He formed it himself in paradoxical defenses early on. What he must learn in recovery is that he is choosing to continue these defensive postures. Self-judgments about self-efficacy turn out to be essentially controlling postures, developed as defenses in shaming situations early on. *Relapse Prevention* surveys relapse from the Cartesian rational cause-and-effect point of view and teaches behavioral techniques to confront risky causative situations. The quantum-age view is taken in AA, where it is common knowledge that a relapsing person is "taking back his own will." AA recognizes that cognitive assessment is not sufficient without surrender. What *Relapse Prevention* sees as losing control in the face of overwhelming circumstances, AA sees as taking back control.

When Marlatt speaks of motivation and commitment, he speaks of motivation as being "determined by a wide range of factors including the payoff matrix of the immediate and long-term benefits and costs involved, the events precipitating the decision to quit at a particular time, the individual's history and outcome of prior attempts to change." Here we see once again behavioral observations of factors surrounding the action of an organism. The appropriate question always is: *Why does the individual choose to succumb to these factors?* How much more beneficial to understand what motivation is for an organism-in-environment, instead of merely some behavior determined by a wide range of factors. *Relapse Prevention* avoids the nature of human activity in favor of behavioral observations.

As we have seen, we need no longer be reluctant to develop models of human nature because they delve into the unseen and unmeasureable aspects of human organization. Just as psychologists followed the physicists into behaviorism, they can now safely follow them into levels of discourse about the internal dynamics of organisms.

THE CORE OF RELAPSE

When a person decides to take a drink again—a "slip"— what should be learned is that she made a choice. He believed he could control his feelings again with alcohol. The matter should not be left by the counselor as a mere mistake, and we just try again. The slip should be used to reinforce his conviction that he cannot successfully control his moods with alcohol. (Cueing situations, triggering situations, and the so-called high-risk situations, are not determinative of relapse. Species-specific human behavior is never "triggered" or "cued.") We are not talking about a question of "I can't do this" (self-efficacy, as Marlatt would have it), but rather a matter of feeling,

"I don't want to do it this way." The alcoholic will believe that he lost control, that he could not do it, because that is the way he has been trained to look at failure in a Cartesian worldview. In fact, what the alcoholic actually did by taking the drink was take control of his feelings at the time; he made a choice. Understanding relapse in this way is of crucial importance. It keeps the nature of the problem and the solution squarely where it belongs—at the species-specific level of human organization.

Poor feelings of self-efficacy do not determine anyone to take a drink. Taking a drink is a decision to control poor feelings of self-efficacy. As we say in AA, the drink was taken before the person encountered the high-risk situation. That is why coping skills are not the answer. Coping skills presume that a problem has arisen, but the problems arise because the principles are not fully assimilated. It is not coping skills that are needed as much as a commitment to a new worldview appropriate to the organism-in-environment.

Self-efficacy implies control rather than a sense of participation. Self-efficacy is a rational view ungrounded by the pre-rational. When the alcoholic says at a given moment, "I can't do this. I am incompetent to handle this," he is actually reverting to his shame-based poise of control. The notion of *can't* is a cloak for a choice of the other. We are trained in the belief that greater forces are at work that are difficult to resist, whereas in reality we are choosing what is felt to be a greater good at the moment. The self-disgust that follows the choice to relapse is not from a feeling of incompetence or failure but from feelings of guilt and shame because of the choice to revert to the older, self-destructive responses. Rather than feeling inferior to forces at work upon us—the self-efficacy notion—we are feeling guilt and shame about the choice we made.

Why do we relapse, or lapse? A relapse or a lapse is rarely the result of an impulse (or as Marlatt might say, a particular moment of incompetence in the face of a particular high-risk situation, which a coping skill could salvage). Relapse assumes the alcoholic has sustained a period of not drinking. If he has been choosing not to drink (behaviorism), he remains quite vulnerable, but if he is choosing a different belief about life (the pre-rational), he is far less likely to relapse.

Relapses do not always occur under high-risk situations; this is Cartesian thinking. Relapse occurs most of the time as the result of a collapse of the belief system that initiated the attempt to stay away from alcohol. This collapse is generally gradual. The alcoholic in AA calls this erosion "stinking thinking." We are historical organisms. No matter how much we reframe, no matter how many coping techniques we learn, unless we build up the new belief system, we will remain highly vulnerable to relapse. For coping skills and strategies to work, they must flow from an appropriately grounded choice to use them. The battle is won or lost before the coping techniques are brought to bear. The alcoholic must understand the nature of his failure in this way. If a person fails to handle a particular high-risk situation, his fundamental grounding should be explored before his behavioral techniques.

HABIT

We should recall from Chapter 12 that *Relapse Prevention* describes fundamental human behavior as habit. Working from this mechanical assumption, it is literally impossible to develop a model for specifically human activity. Addictions are habits in the behavioral point of view, not specific human choices. Habit, of course, lends itself to the rational, mechanical, objective point of view. The habit theory remains unaware of the higher levels of inquiry two and three from systems theory. Within a Cartesian mindset, habit is the only way to describe addiction.

In *Relapse Prevention*, the active role of the organism is not illuminated. The individual chooses to relapse because the meaning-feelings he is experiencing are not providing the life equivalents he needs. In AA, we do not confront the decision to drink head-on. We never force ourselves to choose between drinking and not drinking. We decide to put off the drink and choose to go to a meeting or call a friend. This is the basic decision; it can be supplemented by coping skills and strategies. This practice allows into play the important subjective levels of meaning—authentic connection.

THE JOURNEY

A highlight of *Relapse Prevention* is the analogy of a journey as the daily effort to beat an addiction. Marlatt likens striving toward recovery to a journey to a mountain. It is not wise to teach that life is a journey through an order of control. The basic fault with *Relapse Prevention's* notion of a journey is that it rests entirely on the idea of rational control *without grounding or centering in pre-rational reality*. Further, it fails to recognize that addiction is a pre-rational choice to control feelings, not merely a bad habit. Something is awry at the pre-rational level. Bad habits are symptomatic. In Marlatt's journey, the goal is to stop the addictive habit. In the pre-rational journey of AA, the goal is a way of life without addiction. The journey is better thought of as a participation by an organism subjectively engaged in connections with its environment.

Relapse Prevention speaks of "setbacks" on the journey. We simply pick up, try again, or try something different. Here again, we see the rational notion of setback. It is something encountered in the linear cause and effect of the journey. We objectify it, reason it out of the way. Precisely what is a setback for an organism-in-environment? *Setbacks will always be an attempt to resume control.* The struggle to assume control is a failure to surrender in the first place to a limited role in a larger system.

What are the origins of self-efficacy judgments? That would appear to be a key question. Generally they occur from comparisons with others, poor performances, and criticism from others, but what is actually taking place for the subject? It is easy enough to observe that he is judging himself poorly in comparisons, but why? Let's try to get beyond the behavioral description into the dynamic level of human action. How does poor self-judgment arise for the symbolic-affective organism-in-environment? We know that poor self-judgment arises from the basic fault, a matter of shaming in primary relationships from early development. We also know, that poor self-judgment in a specific instance or in a global sense, yields image-feelings of death equivalents. A sober alcoholic, when faced with poor self-judgment, may yield to the alcohol which provided image-feelings of life in connection, or the numbing of death equivalents in separation. As we saw, this yielding is actually an attempt to control his death equivalent feelings. It would seem important then, that not only rational, behavioral remedies are called for, but an awareness by the subject of the reasons he has chosen to control his feelings with alcohol rather than with a newfound system of meanings. How his organism works in the environment is crucial self-knowledge. Behavioral techniques could be more effective in an aware subject. Behaviorism cannot explain the alcoholic to himself, but once he understands what he is, behavioristic techniques can work wonders.

It is dangerous for an addict to feel he is in control—an impression he can receive from behavioral successes. He is not in control—no more than the player in the card game. *Instead of feeling pleased that he is in control, the recovering alcoholic learns to feel pleased that he is behaving responsibly,* in a participatory system of things. He is playing his cards to the best of his ability, thereby pleasing himself and others in the game. Once he knows that, he can take delight in the behavioral techniques that help him organize himself in his environment.

TREATMENT SUCCESS RATES

Let's pause for a moment on the notion of success. What standards are we going to use to measure success? This has become an increasingly important question, because insurance companies and other agencies are demanding higher success rates—lower recidivism—and the follow-up studies to prove them.

Treatment programs are better evaluated from the soundness of their principles and their staffs than they are from so-called success rates in follow-ups. That human "success" can be measured is another Cartesian idea. The best parents cannot guarantee the future conduct of their children. Treatment centers can guarantee the soundness of their programs and their administration, but they cannot guarantee the number of favorable outcomes of their treatment. That is, of course, a thoroughly unscientific thing to propose. Or is it? Alcoholism is not curable, human nature cannot be fundamentally altered, and there is no way of training a human being to behave unalterably in the future. Rehabs are not machine shops where the alcoholic can be re-built and a ten-year warranty pasted on his forehead. The matter comes down to showing the alcoholic a way of changing his life, not getting rid of his human nature. Proposals to change one's life must be based on the best current understanding of what a human being is.

Rehabilitation centers are promoting change in the individual—recognition of fundamental facts about his life—and offering him a new life style, and principles of behavior. We cannot track success as we would with medical intervention. Should we close up churches whose members divorce more frequently than others? Should we choose among religious affiliations those who produce the fewer number of bank robbers? What statistical tables tell us which colleges better prepare us for all-around living? In all cases like these in life, we examine the end product as well as we can, but rely more heavily on the principles, goals, and quality of the institution.

Follow-up studies on results: Who knows? That absenteeism and performance on the job have improved may not tell the whole story. Someone who has not had a drink in three years may be eating too much, ruining his relationships, gambling, oversexing, or engaging in other self-destructive behaviors, but he shows up for work every day on time. Has he become a workaholic? Is he smoking more than ever? Is he neglecting his family? Following up on treatment for alcoholism is not like following up on treatment for cancer or high blood pressure.

For those readers who are curious about alcoholism treatment, I recommend *The Treatment of Alcoholism*, by Edgar P. Nace, M.D. The book was written for doctors but is also most helpful to the interested layperson.

TREATING THE DISEASE

I find the disease concept wanting in three ways: First, it has Cartesian causative connotations and denotations in the same sense that medicine has; second, the notion does not imply the species-specific nature of the disorder, which is human choice; and third, the notion does not in itself suggest the appropriate relief, which should flow directly from the implications of the description.

Tempers flare when the notion of disease is debated because none of the participants has troubled to define the subject; in truth, they cannott. Casting the disease concept in a less favorable light takes away nothing of the power and gravity of alcoholism. On the contrary, describing alcoholism as a disorder striking at the very core of the afflicted person suggests a far more serious malady than does disease. Disease tends to separate the malady from the person. Disease suggests something "you get" rather than something "you do." The disorder should be presented to those suffering from it with all the gravity belonging to disease, as Vaillant seems to acknowledge.

In the behavioral-psychological treatment of alcoholism, we witness an attempt to transform behavior by an appeal to the rational capacity of the organism. A strong appeal is made to values and responsibility, but no model is available to explain the innate processes from which values and principles emerge in an organism-in-environment. This leaves the proponents of behavioral change unanchored in a sea of tautologies. They can only offer charts, maps, and lifebuoys without appealing to the level of human organization where choices originate. In offering their behavioral guides, they cannot appeal to the specific issues of an organism-in-environment attempting to control. They cannot get to the issues of distrust, self-dependence, and confusion.

Treatment centers offering the Twelve Step strategy are currently the most suitable for attacking the malady of alcoholism, but the treatment centers are just the beginning. As one person remarked, they are the "boot camp" for AA, or whatever spiritual regimen one wishes to pursue in sobriety. In addition, two other programs are powerfully effective as supplements to AA.

Albert Ellis has written *Rational Steps to Quitting Alcohol*—a wonderful book for straightening out "stinking thinking." It is an axiom in AA that "stinking thinking" ushers in a relapse. Ellis, in this book, offers a clear picture of what he calls our irrational beliefs. He bills his book as an alternative to AA. I would rather see it billed as a supplement to AA. Ellis does not subscribe to the AA notion of powerlessness, but he does quite rightly emphasize the element of choice in the addiction. Ellis prefers to remain with the rational aspect of human organization when assessing the notion of addiction; his books are therefore particularly helpful to those who have already grounded their experience in a Twelve Step program. Ellis's misunderstanding of AA is irrelevant—and is to be expected from an author unacquainted with the implications arising from quantum mechanics and systems theory.

Another effective program is offered by Bandler and Grinder in their book *Reframing: Neuro-Linguistic Programming and the Transformation of Meaning*. It is a rationalistic approach but with a difference. Unlike most psychologies whose methodologies rest on observation and experiment, neuru-linguistic-programming assumes the existence of the unconscious, or the cognitive domain. It also relies upon innate feelings to prompt behavior change. However, it is not the least interested in internal processes, but simply in what is observable emerging from these hidden aspects of human organization. It works on the belief that a "part" or a portion of the person is responsible for unwanted behavior, and that a programmer can assist the person in accessing that part of himself or herself. The basic idea is that every behavior, even poor or unwanted, is intended to accomplish some good for the organism. As Bandler and Grinder say, "The heart of reframing is to make the distinction between the *intention* of the behavior and the behavior itself. Once that is done, then the programmer can help the client find new, more acceptable behaviors that satisfy the same intention." This is classic rationalism. It fails to fully enlist the subjective level two, which calls for feelings of limitation and participation in the greater system. As a rational technique, however, it works wonderfully for those fully grounded and centered at level two.

The ascendancy of quantum-age systems does not mean rational behavioral techniques are useless. On the contrary, they can be very helpful to people grounded and centered, those operating at levels two and three of inquiry. It is my proposal throughout this book that a plan of recovery from self-destructive behavior must first of all satisfy the primordial and primary need of an organism to participate in an order of complexity, not objectify in an order of control.

We have learned that the human is an organism-in-environment. It is a species-specific characteristic to participate in the dialectic with the environment. Our fundamental image-feelings are formed or "expressed," as we saw, in a continual participation. It is essential, therefore, that recovery must be a restoration of authentic participation. Toward this end, the recovering alcoholic must develop her or his sense of participation—with others, with the environment, with the world. This is not a rational project, although it must be approached coherently and consistently. Here again, the organic impulse to participate will be pre-rational, but expressed and presented to the self in rational terms. One of the responsibilities of the treatment center is to introduce this sense of participation. It must be experienced rather than taught—thus the necessity for frequent group work. Attempting to turn the alcoholic around with common sense lectures on values and rational analysis will not enable him to experience the dynamics of an organism-in-environment.

Treatment programs in the United States have come in for a barrage of criticism in recent years. Stanton Peele is one of the loudest voice in the assault against the treatment "industry." Peele's thrust is twofold: (1) the disease concept is a fraud; and (2) the principles of recovery fostered by the treatment industry (Twelve Step programs) are self-defeating.

First, the disease concept is *not* a fraud. It is a heartfelt belief. The industry does not (until now) have the conceptual tools (nor does Peele) to describe such a deadly affliction. Second, Peele's criticism of Twelve Step programs is uninformed and irresponsibly distorted.

Treatment centers are here to stay. While many alcoholics hit a natural bottom, which drives them on their knees to AA or to a change on their own, there are many more who need to be confronted by their bosses and their families. These alcoholics are in denial; they still believe that their lives are not unmanageable because of alcohol. These alcoholics, in particular, are the people who need in-patient and out-patient treatment. There are also thousands of others who recognize that they are in trouble and turn to their employers, friends, clergy, and doctors for help; they need the treatment centers. Then there are the thousands of disenfranchised who have turned to alcohol; they need structured programs reaching out to them. There have been no offerings from the critics of treatment to deal with these situations.

The job of the treatment center is threefold: (1) to help the alcoholic to surrender, that is, to recognize limitation as natural for an organism-in-environment; (2) to help the alcoholic begin a process of change and acceptance of responsibility; and (3) to provide an atmosphere of acceptance and caring.

Two appendices follow—one discussing codependency, and the other elaborating on the concepts of guilt and shame. Both have a contemporary significance that those interested in recovery from alcoholism will find pertinent. The vast majority of the public and academia are still uninformed about the profound shift in awareness that has begun—the opening of the quantum age. Some believe that this is only another beginning; already, books like Michael Talbot's *Beyond the Quantum* are appearing. In this new intellectual atmosphere, further illumination of such concepts as codependency, and shame and guilt will be useful.

Appendix A

Codependency

Power through sacrifice of self lies at the core of co-dependence

—Timmens Cermak M.D., *Diagnosing and Treating Co-Dependence*

At a convention of mental health professionals in Texas, a psychiatrist rose to the podium to address the thousand or so attendees. In short order he was electrifying them with his surprise attack upon the recovery movement, expressing his weariness with notions of powerlessness and turning-it-over-to-higher-powers stuff. According to the *New York Times* report, his audience came to their feet in wild applause when he demanded, "Whatever happened to good, old-fashioned resilience?" And self-reliance? And self-empowerment? And self-control? The psychiatrist was venting a growing professional irritation with the grass roots notions of codependency. As one well known Harvard psychiatrist said in the *New York Times Book Review,* the codependency movement is "pop-psychology run amok."

Codependency is a prodigious phenomenon springing out of the treatment programs for alcoholism. Although this book is aimed at illuminating the nature of alcoholism and addiction, codependency is so closely linked in both the clinical and popular mind with alcoholism and the Twelve Step movement, that it would be useful to look at the nature of codependency in these pages. Further, many clinicians working with alcoholics are heard to say, "Scratch an alcoholic and you'll find a codependent."

The notions of codependency have been articulated by several pioneers in the field. These notions were born in clinical practice and not in academia. Although codependency has attracted a large number of definitions or descriptions, each differing slightly, it is an authentic insight—occurring at the experiential level—into a real social problem. Very simply, it came about when clinicians observed that family members of alcoholics needed special help as well as the alcoholic. They were seen as codependent with the alcoholic. In short order, this codependency was observed in nonalcoholic familes as well.

The following authors are the strongest voices describing codependency: Charles Whitfied, M.D., Timmen Cermak, M.D., Terry Kellogg, Sharon Wegscheider-Cruse, Robert Subby, Anne Wilson Schaef, Janet Woititz, and Claudia Black. Codependency was introduced to its widest audiences by Melody Beattie and John Bradshaw. Beattie wrote a best-selling book, *Codependent No More*. Bradshaw drew millions to his books on family systems and shame through his national television series and endless lecture tours around the country.

In the likelihood that many readers are not acquainted with the condition of codependency, the following description—from "Diagnostic Criteria for Codependency," by Timmen L. Cermak, M.D., appearing in the *Journal of Psychoactive Drugs* (1983)—should be helpful:

* Continual investment of self-esteem in the ability to influence or control feelings and behavior in oneself and others in the face of obvious adverse consequences

* Assumption of responsibility for meeting others' needs to the exclusion of acknowledging one's own needs

* Anxiety and boundary distortions in situations of intimacy and separation

* Enmeshment in relationships with personality-disordered, drug-dependent, and impulse-disordered individuals

* Exhibitions of any three or more of the following behaviors: constriction of emotions with or without concomitant dramatic outbursts; depression; hypervigilance; compulsions; anxiety; excessive reliance on denial; substance abuse; recurrent sexual or physical abuse; stress-related medical illness; or a primary relationship with an active substance abuser that lasts for at least two years without the individual seeking outside support.

For the purpose of offering the shortest introductory notion about codependency, I prefer to describe it as any behavioral patterns organized by the self around the maintenance and stability of the family system at the expense of the autonomy and spontaneity of the self. I speak of family systems here, because it is my belief that although codependent behaviors appear in adult relationships later in life, and even in the larger systems of society, the individual internalizes codependent responses during developmental years in the family system.

Having defined codependency, let's immediately deal with the increasingly popular idea that codependency is another patriarchal male attempt to assign women a dependent role. A codependent person, young or old, male or female, is any person who subordinates his or her own autonomy and spontaneity to maintain stability in significant relationships. It is true that the majority of persons attending codependency self-help groups are women, and this has been unnecessarily alarming for some observers. A female majority is appropriate for two reasons: first, women have found, on their own, that codependency groups are enormously helpful in breaking out of the male-dominated system; and second, women more than men are ready to recognize the importance of their feelings. Women have been assertive enough recently to realize that codependency groups are empowering, not subordinating.

A major occasion for the misapprehension about women in codependency groups is the wide misunderstanding of cause and effect in codependent relationships. Such misunderstanding is symptomatic of the Cartesian worldview. It is perpetuated in books such as Kaminer's *I'm Dysfunctional, You're Dysfunctional,* and *The Culture of Recovery* by Elayne Rapping. Kaminer's book is characterized by rational Cartesian inquiry, subject-object distancing, and an expectation of cause and effect. People committed to Twelve Step principles, however, have moved into quantum-age inquiry, which is characterized by pre-rationality, subjectivity, and an expectation of participation in a system. I believe these distinctions lie at the heart of Anne Wilson Schaef's work on codependency. Rapping's book is subtitled, *Making Sense of the Self-Help Movement in Women's Lives.* The question is, for whom does Rapping hope to make sense—for herself, or for those of us in the movement? We do not need anyone to make sense of it, thank you. Rapping's book is a typical reaction of the rational viewpoint to an outbreak of more significant pre-rational inquiries.

DECONSTRUCTING-RECONSTRUCTING

It is not possible to assess quantum-age experience from a Cartesian point of view. Making sense, of course, is a rational exercise. Let me give an example. Some time ago, Anita Hill spoke at Georgetown University before a gathering of lawyers. She told the group that the rational male senators deconstructed her experience and reconstructed it to fit their own model of what happened. The male senators simply "made sense" out of Hill's story. This is an unrecognized problem for authors who set out to explain other people's experience to them. That is why the perspectives of Kaminer, Rapping, and Stanton Peele, for instance, miss the mark when describing AA. They bring their own rational models to the phenomenon and judge it accordingly.

The key disagreement I have with both Kaminer and Rapping is their insistence that their understanding of recovery principles is correct. They do not, however, understand recovery. They work out of the cause-and-effect mentality: If you want to lose weight, go after the people who made you get fat. Do not be a victim. Direct your energies to the oppressors, defy the existing order, organize and write your congressperson, and you will lose weight. If you fight the justice system tooth and nail, you will get your abusive husband sent away. That will ensure that your next marriage will be a good one. Get mad enough to confront the external causes that make you so miserable.

In quantum-age systems theory we no longer work out of an order of control, or cause and effect. We are not reactive agents in the system; we are responsive participants. Failure to understand this leads to the kind of rational deconstruction of recovery that we find in Rapping and Kaminer's books. Both Kaminer and Rapping's work need a considerable amount of page-by-page commentary and correction, which are outside the scope of this present book. I do not suggest deconstructing their viewpoints to suit mine—as they have done—but simply correcting what they misunderstand about mine. Rapping winds up her book with an eloquent declamation that we do not need Higher Powers. *She* does not. But is it okay if I do? And Einstein? And Heisenberg? And Bateson?

Another misapprehension about self-help groups is that they focus exclusively on the self without taking into consideration the social environment that creates codependency. Some voices, angry with the apparent self-absorption of the codependency movement, believe our energies should be at least equally addressed to the oppressive society. The answer is that societies with oppressive hierarchies came into existence precisely because individuals were not sufficiently self-aware to stop them. That awareness, thanks mostly to feminism, is reaching critical mass. It may well be that the codependency movement, like a mortgage, is self-liquidating. I can think of no more powerful a threat to the oppressive society than the liberating dynamics of the codependency movement.

The codependency movement receives high negatives in some quarters because of the exploitative nature of television shows. These confessional shows may have some use in awakening people to the existence of real social problems. However, none of them concentrate upon the spiritual remedies of the Twelve Steps. Sharing one's problems in Twelve Step groups is always preparatory to undertaking a program of change. It is unfortunate, but typical, that TV offers only the entertaining aspects of real social problems.

I will deal with two subjects here: first, the nature of codependency, and second, the remedy for codependency.

THE NATURE OF CODEPENDENCY

Let's establish first the nature of codependency from our controlling image, then show how it differs from addiction. I will then introduce two authors with the most recent opposing views, one agreeing with me, the other disagreeing. Anne Wilson Schaef finds the Twelve Step approach the most effective remedy, while Charlotte Kasl believes it is necessary to "move beyond" the Twelve Steps to find wholeness.

The definition of codependency offered here will evoke strong objections from some authors who take the prevailing Cartesian point of view about human behavior—in the belief that codependency is caused by oppression in a strict cause-and-effect relationship. As we saw with the treatment of alcoholism, we can divide the opposing camps into the you-are-in-control camp, and the you-are-not-in-control camp.

ADDICTION AND CODEPENDENCY

First of all, let's compare addiction and codependency. Both addictions and codependency are species-specific human activity that seeks to maintain or restore connection. Addictions are behaviors that control image-feelings directly, by manipulating the feelings directly, as with alcohol, sex, or gambling. Codependency is human behavior that controls image-feelings by directly manipulating the environment. Addictive behaviors are primarily aimed at changing one's mood; codependent behavior, at stabilizing the environment. The addict is little concerned with those about him; the codependent is concerned with little else except those about him. Both addiction and codependency are defensive and controlling, and originate in developmental shaming.

The feelings are at stake in both behaviors, of course, but the addict changes feelings without adapting to others, while the codependent changes (or stabilizes) feelings by adapting to others. This difference is not highlighted in the literature on codependency. Codependents are primarily concerned with feeling safe rather than with feeling better. Codependents maintain connection by subordinating themselves; addicts maintain connection by medicating themselves, or getting into addictive behaviors. In addiction, the immediate object is the self; in codependency, the immediate object is relationships.

The distinction between the two is important because the individuals' different modes of controlling in addiction and codependency require different acknowledgments and behavioral changes. Although codependency is best not described as an addiction, I take it up here because it does appear to clinicians that most alcoholics are also codependents.

We can describe codependency most satisfactorily as paradoxical defense. Paradoxical defense, as we have seen in shame, is the effort to control one's significant connections by subordinating one's authentic needs in order to stabilize life equivalent image-feelings in connections.

We should also take up the question of whether codependency is a disease. The disease concept prevails among authors in the field. Disease, conventionally understood, is a matter of mechanical cause and effect. Therefore, dysfunction at the species-specific level of human organization cannot be described as disease in the conventional sense. At the specifically human level, disorder is a more acceptable term. Codependency is a disorder brought about by our responses to oppression or shaming during developmental stages. It is better described as the disorder of paradoxical defense and control, and not as disease. We must not confuse a specifically human response with a mechanical cause-and-effect reaction.

THE PREVAILING VIEW

Because the notion of codependency grew out of the attempt to assist the alcoholic and his or her family, the most popular remedy for alcoholism was also brought to bear on codependency—the Twelve Step program of Alcoholics Anonymous.

I have referred to the AA viewpoint about changing human behavior as the you-are-not-in-control viewpoint. It is the prevailing viewpoint of the codependency movement. This is precisely the irritant that caused such an eruption at the Texas convention mentioned at the beginning of this appendix, and lately has more and more commentators wagging their heads. Most impassioned has been Wendy Kaminer's complaint in *I'm Dysfunctional, You're Dysfunctional*, wherein Kaminer eloquently decries the "dumbing down" of national discourse in the culture of complaint fostered by the flourishing Twelve Step programs. Kaminer is ultimately concerned about the flabbiness of an electorate comprising victims who have turned themselves over to higher powers—no trivial concern, of course. Many reporters and columnists have welcomed Kaminer's kind of refreshing return to common sense. Her view of Twelve Step principles, however, is mistaken.

CODEPENDENCY: INTERNALIZED OPPRESSION SYNDROME?

In her book *Many Roads, One Journey*, Charlotte Kasl offers us the most interesting opportunity to look at the vociferous opposition to the Twelve Step view of codependency. No other currently popular book so clearly delineates the nature of the opposition to Twelve Step programs as does Kasl's work. Kasl found the Twelve Step programs for codependency personally repugnant, and set about "moving beyond the Twelve Steps."

Instead of the word *codependency*, Kasl proposes that we use the term *internalized oppression syndrome*. Kasl does not like the term codependency because it suggests that the victim is playing too great a part in his or her own oppression. She complains that Twelve Step groups insist the victims should "own their stuff," instead of looking at the oppressor. Indeed, in her survey of the various definitions of codependency in the literature, she discovers that Robert Subby is "at last" bringing in the causative factor. Subby is one of the first to talk about oppressive systems.

When it comes to offering a formal definition of codependency, Kasl tells us that "codependency is a disease of inequality." This is a sociological definition. Oppression and inequality are hallmarks of codependent relationships. But those words remain a description of human behavior, not of human action. What are the dynamics in codependency for the human organism-in-environment? Before we decide to focus on either the oppressor or the victim, or the relationship between them, we should attempt some model of the human organisms involved. In this book, I have proposed the model of a symbolic-affective organism exercising choice in environment. Application of this model results in a dialectical rather than mechanical description of codependency.

The term *internalized oppression syndrome* offers nothing that is not already recognized and accepted by the codependency movement. As a matter of fact, the movement is much maligned precisely because it is seen as a "culture of complaint," that is, a segment of society seeing itself oppressed and victimized, railing against and blaming parents, society, the church, and so on. John Bradshaw, the leading spokesman, preaches ceaselessly to the nation about the oppressive rules of society, the "poisonous pedagogy" that Alice Miller blames for Nazi Germany. Every codependent seeking to get better feels angry, oppressed, abused, and betrayed. The message of Bradshaw and others is to shift the blame (but not the feelings) from the parents to the larger system—just what Kasl is saying. Bradshaw is almost universally criticized in the press for blaming parents or society for his troubles, no matter how often he clearly states that he is not blaming parents. He insists that he is attacking the system and the rules of patriarchy.

The description of codependency as internalized oppression needs further illumination. There is no doubt that external factors are at work in oppression. What we must recognize is that internal factors are also at work. External factors do not stamp internal responses upon the affected organism. (As even Skinner recognized, the same external forces do not always produce the same effects; therefore, he had to give a significant role to the organism, coming up with his notion of operant conditioning.)

What the codependency movement has recognized is that, facing oppression, the respondent individual has assumed defensive postures and controls that are not in its own best interests. This can be seen as a form of paradoxical defense, such as that which we see in shame. Codependency theory focuses on the self-destructive defensive responses of the self as attempts to control the environment rather than focusing upon the controlling role of the environment. Kasl would have us look to the external forces rather than the nature of the response of the individual. Kasl's view is classic Cartesian-Newtonian mechanics. Kasl winds up viewing the co-dependent as victim of oppression rather than shame-based actor in the dialectic. Until the shame-based individual understands his or her role in the codependent situation, it is not likely the person will make the internal changes necessary to take action against oppression, and significantly, to recognize and avoid a repetition of codependent responses.

We distinguish between types of oppression. There is physical oppression in terms of physical force and constraints, and there is oppression in terms of relationships with others that affect the organism's fundamental needs and claims. Codependency is concerned with oppression of the second kind. As we have shown, human action can never be adquately described exclusively in terms of external influences and causes; such thinking obscures the level of individual organization at which the second kind of oppression must be described. Recall that the human is a responsive organism, not a reactive organism. This realization has been the genius of the codependency movement, borrowed from the notion of responsibility in AA.

Internalized oppression syndrome is an action-reaction dynamic. In this new age of wholes in environment, it is better to focus on the nature of response rather than reaction. It is better because human relationships are a dialectic. Although helpless as a child, the human does develop defenses. Eventually the child will participate as an adult in the dialectic. If the adult recognizes what went wrong for him or her in the developmental years, he or she can then set boundaries in the dialectic. In this way, a new system is introduced; but this cannot happen unless the individual focuses on what went wrong for the individual as a responsive organism.

Kasl does not deal with the role of choice in internalized oppression, but this is the level at which the problem must be described and discussed—in the same way that we discussed choice in the matter of alcoholism. Are we to assume that all choice is removed in internalized oppression, and that a strict cause-and-effect determinism takes its place? Specifically human action does not take place that way. The problem calls for the same description of choice that we gave to alcoholism. There is simply no way of avoiding this if we consider the codependent a human being.

Most common-sense behavioral approaches carry helpful suggestions and insights about our responses to reality, but all good behavioral psychology is incomplete. It fails to anchor the individual in reality as an organism-in-environment. Behaviorism cannot deal with issues arising from shamed image-feelings (distrust, self-dependence, confusion). This requires an understanding of the individual's species-specific defenses and controls during a shaming developmental environment.

There will always be a tendency on the American scene to put the individual back into control. Books about control in the self-help sections have enormous appeal because they encourage attitudes and techniques that restore control to individuals who believe they have lost it. These books extend the illusion of control fostered by Western science for hundreds of years. To the extent that control theories *do* encourage difficult choices, they are helpful. We have, after all, seen millions of successful people throughout Western history who thoroughly believed they were in control of themselves and their environment. There is a growing consciousness now, however, on a global scale, that controlling—including patriarchy and hierarchy—has also gotten us into a lot of trouble. What we are learning today is that an attitude of participation rather than control brings about satisfactory results but with a bonus—both psychologically and practically.

You-are-in-control theories are particularly questionable for people who have ruined their lives with their attempts to control. Controlling approaches are not good medicine for recovering addicts—given that controlling is the essence of their problem—nor are they good for any people whose addictions have rendered their lives unmanageable. They must first of all give up control. That puts them in a position of making responsible choices within a participatory reality. Recovering alcoholics in AA shun a language of control. They prefer instead the language of responsible behavior. After awhile, control notions become meaningless for them. As we have tried to show, there is a deep basis for this in the human organism. We are embedded in a vast interdependency of relations—of connections—as we know now from physics. From the subatomic reality that supports each of us, there is a furious activity within patterns and connections. No wonder that at the macroscopic level of our own organic patterns we anticipate connections.

We have no control over our births or our deaths. We have no control over the organic patterns that make us what we are. With regard to managing our behavior, we can make choices, but we can never control outcomes. Even the nature of the subatomic world reveals only statistical certainty about outcomes. We can only choose to participate. That is the message of the Twelve Steps.

What is distinctive about Kasl's notion of codependency is an attempt to impose strict cause and effect upon the dynamics involved in oppression. This is radically different from the vision of Bradshaw, Schaef, and others. What Bradshaw and Schaef have recognized is that a strict cause-and-effect interpretation works against changing both the self and the system. One has to understand system in order to grasp the codependency viewpoint. In human systems, unlike mechanical systems, cause and effect do not constitute the essential dynamic. Within the human system, there often is a genuine victim-and-oppressor dialectic, but in the human system, the victim is not billiard ball B. The victim develops defenses and controls against the oppression. These are almost always self-destructive because the victim prefers the bonds of the system to separation, and is unable to independently process the meanings in the oppressive events.

The change that is required must begin with the victim. No revolution is ever begun by the oppressors; that is, the victim must recognize what happened in the system and how she or he responded, and then take steps to confront the oppressors. In this view, it is essential that the victim recognize the self-destructive nature of the response, realize that he or she is now able to change that response, and if possible, explain his or her new response to the oppressors in the system. In this way, the system can be changed. The victims, having recognized the dynamics of the system, can choose not to pass on the sickness of their system to the next generation.

So we have a choice. We can follow Kasl and others, and focus upon the oppression in the system. We can take positive steps to eliminate the oppression itself. We can take steps to empower ourselves. There is nothing unreasonable about that. In the Cartesian view of dynamics, it makes sense. It is good, old-fashioned action-reaction. Alternatively, we can adopt the quantum-age systems view of the codependency movement, focus upon changing our responses from the defenses and controls we set up as children (so that the system would not desert us), and establish appropriate boundaries with oppressors. This is the codependency movement's idea of empowerment.

The favorite word of Kasl, working out of the illusion of the old worldview that the human organism struggles in an order of control, is empowerment. We know now that we struggle in an order of complexity. That is to say, even though the victim is helpless (cannot escape from the oppression) during the developmental years when codependency takes root, that victim is not defenseless. There is a process of control and defense developed and internalized by the individual. This internalized process must be illuminated and acknowledged during the adult years.

(In cases of severe abuse, such as incest, the victim may be both helpless *and* defenseless—in other words traumatized. In this case, none of the species-specific features of the organism can be brought into play. In such cases, Twelve Step groups must focus upon re-establishing the trust of the victim in interpersonal connections before the principles of the Steps can become efficacious.)

Timmen Cermak, M.D., strikes right at the core of codependency. In his book *Diagnosing and Treating Co-Dependence*, Cermak writes: "Power through sacrifice of self-lies at the core of co-dependence." This fundamental insight is not understood or acknowledged in *Many Roads, One Journey*. What Cermak is stating is the fundamental perspective accepted in all Twelve Step groups: The issue is personal controlling, and not simply oppression. We can see the immediate introduction of the word control into Kasl's "Sixteen Steps to Empowerment." For example, in her first step, Kasl offers: "We affirm we have the power to take charge of our lives and stop being dependent on substances or other people for our self-esteem and security."

The sixteen steps of empowerment offered by Kasl are useful affirmations, so to speak, but they do not engender a change in understanding one's place as a human organism-in-environment. To "take charge of our lives" we must first understand what taking charge means for a participating organism in a larger system of things—a concept that is missing throughout Kasl's work. In Twelve Step philosophy, "taking charge" of one's life is seen from the point of view of the new sciences—of an organism in a vast system of interdependencies. In Kasl's empowerment point of view, taking charge of one's life is seen from the Cartesian point of view of cause and effect. Take your choice. However, if it comes to a question of who is "moving beyond" whom, you might want to take another look.

Kasl is unaware that her sixteen steps are not an improvement upon AA's Twelve Steps, but instead they are a fundamentally different philosophical perspective. Kasl refers to her sixteen-step alternative as a "sixteen-step empowerment model." Kasl's steps can stand on their own as self-affirmations. They do not deal with dynamics, however, and thus *Many Roads, One Journey* is a mixing of apples and oranges. The Twelve Step principles of AA have no common starting point with the sixteen steps of empowerment. The sixteen steps cannot be said to move beyond a place where they have never been.

Rather than moving beyond, Kasl is suggesting a radically different starting point. In essence, the sixteen steps of empowerment constitute a radical paradigm shift from the AA convention. This requires a new model, which she does not offer. The problem here is that Kasl is unaware that she has radically changed paradigms. One of the results of this confusion is that the author presents us with the bizarre suggestion that AA groups should sit down and kick around different wordings of the Twelve Steps!

As we have seen, AA absolutely shuns the empowerment notions that attract so many people. Such notions are the residue of Cartesian-Newtonian illusions of control. Books like Kasl's are telling people that they have discovered something better, something superior, without at the same time displaying an understanding of what they think they are moving beyond!

The failure to grasp the revolution of the twentieth century is revealed in one sentence in *Many Roads, One Journey*—what we could call the master paradigm of the book: "The Steps simply are not designed to create a sense of personal power." First of all, the statement is wildly contrary to the experience of millions in 114 countries. Second, the core meanings of limitation and participation have entirely eluded Kasl. As Bateson, Denzin, Berman, and others have pointed out, the Twelve Steps of AA offer the human-in-environment a new epistemology—our species-specific way of seeing ourselves in environment—that becomes the source of wholeness, serenity, freedom, and creativity.

ALCOHOLICS ANONYMOUS AND SPIRITUAL MATURITY

In *Many Roads, One Journey*, Kasl attempts an appraisal of the spiritual maturity of AA and its members. Her foray into this area affords us an opportunity to discuss the spirituality of AA in the quantum age.

Kasl bases her survey on James Fowler's book *Stages of Faith*, a well received attempt in 1981 to correlate spiritual maturation with the natural psychological development (stages) of the human being. Fowler offered the following stages of faith:

1. Infancy (Undifferentiated Faith)
2. Early Childhood (Intuitive-Projective Faith)

3. Childhood (Mythic-Literal Faith)

4. Adolescence (Synthetic-Conventional Faith)

5. Young Adulthood (Individuative-Reflective Faith)

6. Adulthood (Conjunctive Faith)

It is risky for an author to equate spiritual maturity with psychological stages of development. (In his book, *Will and Spirit*, Washington professor of psychiatry and spirituality, Gerald May, M.D., takes up what he calls "The Fallacy of Staging.") Throughout Christian history, some of the simplest of souls have been noted for their sanctity. Further, there is the universal view among theologians that the human has little to do with the level of spiritual awareness one is awarded by the divinity. The notion of grace—free gifts from God—figures essentially in traditional Western theology. However, Fowler does acknowledge grace at any stage of psychological development. He sees grace at work in the innate psychological gifts throughout human development. Overall, Fowler's work is carefully thought out, highly intelligent and illuminating.

There are some caveats, however. Staging is fraught with the danger of compartmentalizing and linearizing the development of a whole. We cannot forget that at most stages of human development, authentic species-specific characteristics are operative. These specific characteristics are engaged with the environment throughout stages of organic development. As Fowler himself says:

> I also ask you to keep in mind that each stage has its proper time of ascendancy. For persons in a given stage at the right time for their lives, the task is the full realization of the strengths and graces of that stage. . . . Each stage has the potential for wholeness, grace and integrity and for strengths sufficient for either life's blows or blessings.

Kasl sees AA operating at early childhood and childhood stages of psychological maturation. "The Twelve Step model operates primarily at levels two and three of faithing—the literalist and the loyalist." This is a subparadigmatic exercise of inquiry on her part. The appropriate paradigm for describing AA is the three levels of inquiry in systems theory. People committed to the Twelve Steps are operating at levels two and three in systems theory.

From the beginning, Bill Wilson and the early members insisted upon the open-endedness of AA spirituality. Wilson was always searching. In no way can the dynamism of AA's practice of spirituality be tied to "literalness" or "loyalty" at fixed stages. Kurtz says, "It is no accident that Wilson's favorite image, repeated literally thousands of times in letters to people who sought his advice, depicted sobriety as a kind of Pilgrim's Progress."

The Twelve Steps actually propose the ideal poise from which the human organism-in-environment undertakes spiritual progress. In this sense, the Twelve Steps are primordial. As fundamental spirituality, they are pre-religious. Their epistemology of self in the world forms an indispensable base for development in any authentic spiritual process. Psychological and spiritual "empowerment" notions, without this correct epistemology, are antithetical to authentic spirituality. Gregory Bateson was one of the first great thinkers of our time to spot this truth at work in AA.

KURTZ COMMENTS ON ALCOHOLICS ANONYMOUS:

Discovering an ancient spirituality in a room full of drunks may seem strange, even paradoxical. Who would expect, walking into a smoke-filled room in a church basement to encounter wisdom carved out by ancient Greeks, early Christians, Zen teachers, and Jewish scholars? Who would have thought that in the fellowship of AA one would hear the voices of Aeschylus, Buddha, Saint Augustine, the Baal Tem Tov, William James, and Carl Jung? To study AA "is to mine the rich vein of wisdom that runs through all the centuries and culminates in modern times with the fellowship and program of Alcoholics Anonymous."

A somewhat different view indeed from Kasl's drunks stuck in childhood stages two and three of faithing! Kasl says:

> While AA claims to be a spiritual program, it fits with levels two and three of faithing, operating from an external locus of control, often becoming rigid and dogmatic. SOS and Rational Recovery, which claim to be secular, correspond more to levels four and five of faithing, because they teach people to think for themselves, honor differences. . . . So, for me, SOS and RR have a spiritual component, while AA is more a religious program based on sin and redemption.

Such a summary is surprising. Kasl is here consigning about a million of us to a low-level psychospiritual status without knowing us or what we believe, while at the same time elevating two secular programs, built upon a vivid hostility to religion and spirituality, to a high level of spiritual maturity! Kasl misunderstands both the nature of AA and the nature of the strictly rational programs she admires. SOS and Rational Recovery choose to remain at the rational level of inquiry, with only objective-behavioral remedies for addiction. The more important subjective and unitary levels are ignored. (Trimpey and Christopher find Twelve Step groups operating at levels of "cult" and "superstition.")

AA is not interested in teaching people to "think for themselves." The point is not to enshrine thinking for yourself in recovery, but instead to accept—or reject—a proposed model as it is presented. If one adopts a model, or controlling image of the subject, then thinking for oneself can have meaning within the meaning of that paradigm. If one rejects the controlling image, then thinking for oneself has meaning outside that paradigm, and moves on to differing meanings within other viewpoints. AA is based on a worldview embodied in the first three Steps, as was explained in Chapter 13. This view can be boiled down to a profound sense of participation and responsibility as human organisms-in-environment. AA invites individuals to participate with it in this new worldview. AA does not invite individuals to think about other models. This is precisely the confusion that Kasl got into when she first felt stirrings of rebellion at Twelve Step meetings. She could not understand why her own views— paradigmatically contrary—could not be accepted within the group's Twelve Step paradigm. This confusion maintains throughout her criticism of the Twelve Steps.

AA does not operate from an "external locus of control." It operates from the interior locus of a self-regulating whole, a symbolic-affective organism-in-environment. Nor does AA operate at levels two and three of faithing. AA operates at the full range of spiritual experience of which the human organism is capable. From the psychological aspect, AA's inquiry into reality corresponds to the three levels of inquiry described by Jantsch in *Design for Evolution*. From the spiritual aspect, AA operates according to the conventional purgative, illuminative, and unitive stages, which are clearly paralleled in the Twelve Steps. In quantum-age systems theory, AA operates at the fundamental spiritual level—grounded and centered.

The AA model is to be judged not on the numbers of people at the highest levels of faithing, but on the authentic spiritual integrity it provides at every level of faithing. Would Kasl have us speak of Honesty 2 and Honesty 3, or Charity 4 and Charity 5? This is a basic risk in staging faith.

BEYOND THERAPY, BEYOND SCIENCE

A book far richer (in terms of my model of the human being) on this subject is *Beyond Therapy, Beyond Science*, by Anne Wilson Schaef. Schaef is an internationally known pioneer in codependency theory. She is an advocate of Twelve Step philosophy. She has also taken the time to thoroughly acquaint herself with the radical changes in the physical sciences. There is more of a raw honesty in Schaef's work than in *Many Roads, One Journey*. Schaef says:

> It is no wonder that so many people see the Twelve Step program of Alcoholics Anonymous as the best program for recovery, because its support of self-defined spirituality reconnects a person with his or her own universe. If one really works that program, one has to take ownership of all aspects of one's life and become participatory in one's universe.

Schaef adds:

> At the same time, I find it fascinating that a bunch of high level physicists and philosophers (at the top of the scale of influence in the society) and a bunch of recovering addicts (often at the bottom of the scale of influence) are taking the leadership in a major shift in consciousness that is currently happening globally.

Kasl, in *Many Roads, One Journey*, is unacquainted, unfortunately, with the significant shifts in the scientific worldview. Schaef would disagree with Kasl's internal oppression syndrome. She writes:

> The real issue for women is not to challenge the system only on the basis of what it does to women . . . the real issue is to divorce ourselves from the system. . . . We cannot support a mechanistic scientific world view and say that we support women's (human) rights.

If the problem (codependency) is reduced to an internalized oppression model, as it is in Kasl, there is the great danger, as Schaef warns, that instead of changing the system, the oppressed will simply struggle for a piece of the action.

Schaef says:

> It is important to recognize and remember that women are victims of a culture that devalues females. Yet, if a woman stays stuck there and does not move on to quit focusing upon the culture—knowing that only she can heal what is inside her—and does not begin to own the choices she has made and do whatever she needs to do to heal, she will never have self-esteem. Self-esteem does not come from someone else. It comes from confronting and working through the

reality of our own lives. In my experience, the Twelve Step program of AA does a much better job of facilitating this move toward self-esteem beyond victimization than does psychotherapy.

CONCLUSION

Our society is still a long way from assimilating the impact of the scientific revolution of the twentieth century. Science, with systems theory, has struck a mortal blow to the old order. It is my belief that feminism will continue to be the greatest thrust forward, preparing us for the new consciousness emerging from quantum-age systems.

Appendix B

Shame and Guilt—The Difference

Guilt means I *made* a mistake; shame means I *am* a mistake!

—Recovering alcoholic

In the earlier years of my recovery in Alcoholics Anonymous, it was necessary to come to terms with the past, particularly in Step Four, which suggests that members take a moral inventory of themselves. Questions often arose as to the difference between shame and guilt. Some noticed while pondering their past that a difference between a sense of shame and a sense of guilt came up for them. One night a friend of mine, a minister and psychotherapist, came into the meeting grinning broadly. He was quite elated. He told us he had discovered the difference between his feelings of guilt and shame. He said, "Guilt means I *made* a mistake; shame means I *am* a mistake!"

The difference between shame and guilt is an important difference for those interested in the nature of addiction and recovery. For those working such a program of recovery from addiction as the Twelve Step program, it is essential to tease out the strands of guilt from the shame in the fabric of their feelings. They are addicts because of their shame, but they are guilty because of their behavior. This has been a critical revelation for many in the course of getting well. Shame and guilt must be addressed differently.

In Chapter 11, "The Basic Fault," we saw that shame originates when necessary others break connection with us through abandonment, abuse, or neglect. Guilt originates, on the other hand, when the self breaks connections with others.

It is only recently that a sharp distinction between shame and guilt came to the forefront. If you recall from Chapter 11, shame is now regarded as the principal factor in human disorder. Because of the importance of this distinction, I wish to take up two significant viewpoints that differ from mine. Throughout this book, I have looked to prominent and respected interpreters who offer differing positions about the subject of my inquiries. In the case of shame and guilt I will comment on the ideas of Ernest Kurtz and Gershen Kaufman.

Kurtz is the most generally acclaimed interpreter of the experience of AA (*Not-God*). Gershen Kaufman has achieved an ever-widening influence as an interpreter of affect theory (*Shame*).

Affect theory has been hailed as a milestone breakthrough in psychology. It came to national attention in 1991 with a cover article in *U.S. News and World Report*. Its main thrust is aimed at those within the psychological convention who choose not to acknowledge the emotions because they are not empirically verifiable. Affect theorists made the emotions "real" for the psychological community. They have done away with behaviorism's belief that the inner processes are unverifiable. Books that are particularly informative about affect theory are Silvan Tomkins' *Affect, Imagery, Consciousness,* and *The Face of Emotion* by Carroll E. Izard. Both of these works demonstrate a prodigious scholarship.

For more than three decades, psychologist Silvan Tomkins labored arduously to restore emotion to its proper primacy in human behavior. He was a voice crying in the wilderness for much of his career. Academic psychology was firmly in the grip of Cartesian mechanists. It was Tomkins' genius to observe that facial expressions gave physical indications of a truly biological nature of emotion. Tomkins was able to associate the movements of more than thirty facial muscles precisely with the registration of emotion—meaning that emotions could be concretized. They could be observed, measured, and predicted. In the Cartesian world, things can be real only if they are observable and measurable.

Along with affect theory, there has been energetic activity in neuroscience to find the mechanisms in the brain for feelings and emotions. To establish a theory, you must find the mechanisms. The essential triumph of affect theory is establishing the reality of the emotions through their physical mechanisms. The effort now is left to neuroscience to locate the precise mechanisms that give rise to emotions.

Affect theory is Cartesian, and has no bearing on the species-specific behavior of wholes, but the phenomenology, in a work like Tomkins', is of general academic interest. The reason I delve into this view of emotion is to respond to Kaufman's conclusion that guilt and shame are the same affect.

Affect theorists do not list guilt in their repertoire of demonstrable emotions. Accordingly, in the preface to his third edition of *Shame*, Kaufman disparages the belief of the recovery movement that there is a difference between shame and guilt. Kaufman says, "[W]hen we are concerned with this dimensional quality of inner experience, it makes little difference to distinguish shame from guilt. The affect is still the same in each, and the affect is the principal component of the overall experience." It seems of no consequence, therefore, that people experience shame and guilt differently.

I do not accept that the affect is the principal component of the overall experience. It is the subjective expression that is the principal feature of the overall experience. Kaufman identifies the emotion with the biological activity itself. The same neurons may be involved in both shame and guilt, but the point is I feel shame, or I feel guilt, regardless of what my neurons are doing. (Does that remind you of Hofstadter's cheeseburger/pineapple cheeseburger confusion in Chapter 5?) There is a real difference between shame and guilt.

I would normally not take an interest in theoretical underpinnings of such obvious and universal experiences, but in *Shame* Kaufman chooses to object to a distinction that is vital among us recovering folks. Kaufman says:

> Other perspectives continue to view shame and guilt as two dis-
> tinctly different affective states. Implicit in these mistaken notions
> is the assumption that shame is always about the self, whereas guilt
> is always about the actions of the self. It is consequently believed,
> both in our culture and in our science that in shame the focus is on
> the self, whereas in guilt the focus is only on the actions involved.

(Willard Gaylin suggests somewhat the same thing when he says that in guilty fear we dread the results of our actions, while in shame we fear exposure.) In these murky descriptions we see the failure to adequately describe the subjective experience. In both shame and guilt the focus is always upon the self; in both shame and guilt the emotion or feeling arises from broken connection.

In shame the self experiences disintegration, loss of identity, falling apart, and the sense of being worthless, but in guilt a person retains her identity, a sense of who she is, a sense of being grounded and centered to a degree, and an ability to evaluate the situation. In both states, shame and guilt intermingle and ebb and flow, but one does predominate now; the other, then. What we have to keep in mind is that guilt can flow in a grounded and centered ego state, but shame flows in a confused, diminished, shattered ego state.

It is not the relativity of language in describing inner experience that is the problem lurking here, as Kaufman suggests. It is the lack of a controlling image, or model, of the human organism-in-environment. Kaufman states his preference for a free-floating perspective, but this is going to result in subparadigms looking for a master paradigm. This free-floating perspective puts Kaufman in a poor position from which to make dogmatic pronouncements about the "mistaken assumptions" of other perspectives— which he does about the recovery movement.

Affect theorists argue that an identical subsystem of components services both subjective states of guilt and shame, and that guilt, therefore, is not an emotion discrete from shame. My argument is that the emotions of shame and guilt are subjectively discrete, and have radically different subjective origins. Affects must be described as primarily subjective, and the failure to do so ignores the primary role of subjective experience in species-specific actions of the human. The affective features of the human organism are organized around mortality—at the immediate and symbolic levels of perceived life and death equivalent meanings. Affect theory ignores entirely the organism's primary need to negotiate its existence in environment, as what it is, for as long as it can. For the human organism, this negotiation is organized specifically around the life-death tension. Affects must be described primarily at that level of organization where species-specific negotiations occur.

Affect theorists *do* affirm subjective experience and consciousness. This is what makes the theory appealing when compared with conventional behaviorism. Affect theory, however, remains at the level of Cartesian ideas of separable parts and forces, even while recognizing that the human being is not a machine. As the physicist Capra states, "[T]he notion of separate parts, such as atoms or subatomic particles, is an idealization with only approximate validity. These parts are not connected by causal laws in the classical sense."

What affect theory misses is that the human being is a whole, a symbolic organism negotiating in a dialectic with its environment. This requires a hierarchy of organization within the whole, but no ultimately separable functions. Remember, wholes can never be analyzed into parts, although we can describe aspects of the whole.

PERCEPTION

Affect theory provides no confrontation with the nature of perception. We know that information comes in through light and sound waves and is somehow transformed in the brain into images. An acknowledgment of the difficulty in describing this activity does not appear. Kaufman proposes "special activators" (an empty term) for the occurrence of various kinds of feeling or emotion. Who or what is pushing the buttons? Who or what is interpreting the meanings in perception for this mechanical action of emotion? It is likely that, at the level of transformation, the entire process of image-feeling-emotion is initiated and completed by the whole. The models for the nature of emotion should be organized around the level of these perceptions rather than around separate subsystems.

Kaufman is drawn into the affect theorists' classical view of the organism when discussing the difference between shame and guilt. Affect theorists are lured by the observable stability of mechanical phenomena such as facial reactions. They are attracted to this Cartesian viewpoint because they have no notions of the whole. They are misled into believing that emotions are "reals," or discrete subsystems—a belief that can be quite jarring to those of us who understand the major paradigm shifts of this century.

As physicist Fritjof Capra explains, the dramatic shift that took place in physics in the 1920s was a shift from the view of the world as a collection of separate entities to the view of a network of relationships. What affect theory sees as parts, entities, or "reals" as they put it, is instead a stable pattern in a network of relationships. These patterns take on the aspect of reals precisely because of their measurable stability. As Capra points out, however, whenever you delineate parts out of the whole, "you make an error." It is the separating out of the subjective level of the whole and the "reality" of the affects that constitutes the central mistake in affect theory. We see this in the use of language such as "components," and "discrete," the Cartesian viewpoint. Modern physics, however, tells us that these parts we observe do not have intrinsic properties; all observable properties flow from relationship. That is the fundamental insight from modern physics and the 1925 revolution in quantum mechanics. The mistake of affect theory is the attempt to assign intrinsic value to the "components" of emotion, as if they were separable from subjective experience.

We do not talk anymore of real structures as ultimate in nature or organisms, but rather of *processes*. Structure is what biologists call the "compositional" perspective. Affect theory has a compositional view of the feelings and emotions; they insist upon discrete physical reals for emotions. In their viewpoint, these physical components are called upon for use (in Cartesian connections) by a chain of physical events in the organism. An unknown separate part interprets meanings that activate the mechanism. (Kaufman's term is "special activators." How do special activators decide what is a shyness event and what is a shame event?) At another point in the chain, the physical units of emotion, packages in the brain, are dishcharged into the system, in varying amounts, at varying degrees of density and intensity, and so forth.

Specific organic activity is not compositional in nature, but is a process, orchestrated by the whole. Our task is to describe (we cannot analyze wholes) the level of organization where specific organic activity originates.

The recent interest of quantum physicists in the nature of consciousness and relationships is of enormous help in understanding the nature of emotion. For one example, Danah Zohar and Ian Marshall, writing in *The Quantum Society*, refer to Robert Bellah's *The Good Society*. Bellah and his team write, "Infants who do not get attention, in the sense of psychic interaction and love, simply cannot survive, even if they are fed and clothed." It is not a discrete physical emotion or feeling that kills them. It is the subjective experience of separation. Zohar picks up on this to say that a quantum understanding of the physical dynamics of consciousnes can help us understand emotions. She says that "consciousness literally depends for its continued existence upon a constant input of relationship. In quantum terms we are our relationships. We are relational wholes, some of whose qualities only come into existence when our being overlaps those of others." These quantum mechanical inquiries into the nature of the human organism make it clear that we cannot describe the nature of emotions as some kind of reals in themselves. Shame and guilt are relational in nature and must be described at the relational level.

At the heart of the insistence by affect theorists upon the emotional features of the organism as separate reals, lies the philosopher's or the classical scientist's difficulty with "an entirely abstract world having any influence on the physical world"—to quote Roger Penrose. Organizational principles of wholes partake of the abstract world.

(For those readers interested in this most important question of the reality of the abstract world and its influence upon the real world, readings in quantum mechanics are most enlightening. Perhaps most interesting of all are the books written by Werner Heisenberg, author of the uncertainty principle, and a founder of quantum theory—*Physics and Beyond*, and *Physics and Philosophy*. Heisenberg is a leader among those quantum scientists who believe that Plato was right, that our real world is a shadow of an abstract world of mathematical forms—but they add that it is a fundamentally unified world. In this regard, physicist David Bohm (*Wholeness and the Implicate Order*) sees our world as an "unfolding" of an implicate order of abstract reality.)

When Kaufman is dealing with the subjective or phenomenological, as in his chapters on splitting and disowning, he is most instructive and illuminating, and very helpful to my own understanding of what went wrong for me. The Cartesian view of affect theory, however, does not account for the compelling phenomenology of emotion. With the implications flowing from the new physics, we see subjective experience of the whole as primary and our classical scientific analyses as secondary.

In affect theory, the affects as reals exhaust their own actuality, and therefore the subjective experience is secondary. Guilt and shame can be "proven" to be the same. If you take the point of view of modern science that organisms must be described as organisms-in-environment, however, then the principal feature of shame and guilt will be described not at the level of the affects themselves but at the level at which the organism negotiates in its environment. At this level, shame and guilt are different—and thus the recovery movement's view of shame and guilt, focusing upon broken connections of a whole in environment, is more congruent with modern science.

In his new preface, Kaufman attempts to demonstrate that the notion of shame predominates over that of guilt in Western literature, using the example of Hester Prynne in *The Scarlet Letter*. Public exposure in this story is an essential ingredient in Hester's feelings. We can guess that she experienced a predominant sense of shame rather than guilt. We must then look at the Irish movie, *The Informer*, where the hero is tortured by his private sense of guilt. No one broke connection with him; he betrayed his friends, who trusted him. This is not to say, however, that internalized shame from earlier shaming scenes was not intermingled with his terrible sense of guilt.

In *The Man in the Gray Flannel Suit*, the hero did not feel predominantly shame because he had a lover and child overseas during the war; he identified with them and loved them. He did, however, experience terrible guilt before his wife when he was back home. At no time in the book does the hero lose a sense of his identity, his centeredness or grounding. A sense of personal disintegration is not the dominant mood. He has caused a deep conflict for himself and others. There is little to be ashamed of, but there is guilt and conflict in abundance. Again, of course, the characters may bring to the conflict any shame from internalized scenes in their own pasts, but shame is not the dominant feeling of the book.

Ernest Kurtz (*Shame and Guilt*) finds a difference between shame and guilt. He does not argue from a theoretical point of view but rather from an experiential point of view. Kurtz makes no mention of any theories about the nature of shame and guilt. I would like to offer my own observations about Kurtz's explanations.

Kurtz suggests that the distinction between shame and guilt is the difference between failure and transgression. Okay as far as it goes, but let's look more closely. To illustrate his ideas about shame and guilt, Kurtz employs the game of football. Guilt is a question of boundaries; shame is a question of goal lines. Guilt occurs when the sideline boundaries are violated; shame occurs when the goal line is not reached. "Guilt thus indicates an 'infraction'; shame, a literal shortcoming."

We do not feel guilt about infractions, violating boundaries, breaking rules, or disobeying morals, however. What we feel, if anything at all, is fear of getting caught and punished. We can only feel guilt about breaking rules if by doing so we perceive we have somehow broken connections. Boundaries, rules, laws, and morals are constructs to support cultural modes of symbolic immortality, or a sense of continuity. If they are perceived as life equivalents because they safeguard the culture and the individuals it embraces, then they may evoke feelings of guilt, but the essential requirement for guilt is a perception of broken connection, not broken rules or morals. Robbing a church poor box may be accompanied by a fear of getting caught, but the thief will not feel guilt unless he is aware of the effects upon others. He is breaking connection—compassion—with others.

In the football illustration, players who cross the boundary lines feel only frustration, anger, and disgust—not guilt. However, if guilt has been internalized because of earlier developmental scenes when rules were broken, there is the possibility that guilt could be evoked in crossing boundary lines.

A familiar situation is deciding to go through a red light in the middle of the night with no traffic in sight. If I have any feelings about breaking this rule, it will be fear of getting caught. If I have internalized feelings of having harmed someone by going through a red light, however, then I may experience some guilt at going through the light. And if there is even some shame tinging the guilt at going through the light, it will originate in some developmental scene where infractions of rules were treated as shameful.

Looking at Kurtz's model of the football field, we see that shame is described as falling short, failing to reach the goal. Failing to reach goals, however, results in disappointment, anger, frustration, bitterness, even sorrow—but not shame. It may result in shame, and even guilt. But goal-failure will result in shame only if the individual is shame-based. In other words, somewhere in the developmental stages, failure to reach goals, or live up to parental expectations, led to an abusive breaking of connection by the parents—and paradoxical defense by the individual. Any failure to achieve in the future could therefore be tainted by shame. Again, the essential nature of the experience of shame must orginate in broken connections, and not in failures to reach goals.

Kurtz's book, *Shame and Guilt*, is an excellent exposition of the importance of distinguishing between shame and guilt for recovering folks. It is especially significant in explaining the dynamics of the fellowhip's Twelve Steps. I have heard a saying in Alcoholics Anonymous that it is the aim of the program to move the individual from shame to guilt. This is clearly the fact when one examines the first three Steps—the break from shame—and then the remaining Steps, which deal with guilt.

Select Bibliography

Bateson, Gregory. *Steps to an Ecology of Mind.* New York: Ballantine Books, 1972.

——*Mind and Nature: A Necessary Unity.* New York: E.P. Dutton, 1979.

Becker, Ernest. *The Denial of Death.* New York: The Free Press, 1973.

Bergstein, T. *Quantum Physics and Ordinary Language.* Humanities Press, 1972.

Berman, Morris. *The Reenchantment of the World.* Ithaca: Cornell University Press, 1981.

———. *Coming to Our Senses: Body and Spirit in the Hidden History of the West.* New York: Bantam New Age Books, 1990.

Bohm, David. *Wholeness and the Implicate Order.* London: Rutledge & Kegan Paul, 1980.

Boulding, Kenneth. *The Image.* Ann Arbor: University of Michigan Press, 1956.

Capra, Fritjof. *The Tao of Physics.* Boston: Shambhala Publications, 1991.

———. *The Turning Point: Science, Society, and the Rising Culture.* New York: Bantam Books, 1983.

Cassirer, Ernst. *An Essay on Man.* New Haven: Yale University Press, 1944.

Davies, Paul. *God and the New Physics.* New York: Simon & Schuster, 1983.

Eagle, Morris N. *Recent Developments in Psychoanalysis: A Critical Evaluation.* Cambridge: Harvard University Press, 1984.

Firestone, Robert W. *The Fantasy Bond: Effects of Psychological Defenses on Interpersonal Relations.* New York: Human Sciences Press, 1987.

Flanagan, Owen. *The Science of the Mind.* Cambridge: The MIT Press, 1984.

Gardner, Howard. *The Mind's New Science: A History of Cognitive Revolution.* New York: Basic Books, 1985.

Heisenberg, Werner. *Physics and Beyond: Encounters and Conversations.* New York: Harper & Row, 1971.

———. *Physics and Philosophy.* New York: Harper & Row, 1971.

Herbert, Nick. *Quantum Reality: Beyond the New Physics.* Garden City, N.Y.: Anchor Press/Doubleday, 1985.

Jantsch, Erich. *Design for Evolution: Self-Organization and Planning in the Life of Human Systems.* New York: George Braziller, 1975.

Kuhn, Thomas S. *The Structure of Scientific Revolutions.* Chicago: University of Chicago Press, 1970.

Kurtz, Ernest. *Not-God: A History of Alcoholics Anonymous.* Center City, Minn.: Hazelden, 1979.

Langer, Susanne K. *Mind: An Essay on Human Feeling.* Baltimore: Johns Hopkins Press, 1967.

Laszlo, Ervin. *The Systems View of the World: The Natural Philosophy of the New Developments in the Sciences.* New York: George Braziller, 1972.

Lewontin, R.C.; Steven Rose, and Leon J. Kamin, *Not in Our Genes: Biology, Ideology, and Human Nature.* New York: Pantheon Books, 1984.

Lifton, Robert Jay. *The Life of the Self: Toward a New Psychology.* New York: Basic Books, 1983.

———. *The Broken Connection: On Death and the Continuity of Life.* New York: Basic Books, 1983.

Mayr, Ernst. *The Growth of Biological Thought: Diversity, Evolution, and Inheritance.* Cambridge: The Belknap Press of Harvard University Press, 1982.

Neisser, Ulric. *Cognition and Reality: Principles and Implications of Cognitive Psychology.* New York: W.H. Freeman & Co., 1976.

Peat, F. David. *Synchronicity: The Bridge Between Matter and Mind.* New York: Bantam New Age Books, 1987.

Zohar, Danah. *The Quantum Self: Human Nature and Consciousness Defined by the New Physics.* New York: Quill/William Morrow, 1990.

Zukav, Gary. *The Dancing Wu Li Masters: An Overview of the New Physics.* New York: Bantam Books, 1979.

General Bibliography

Abrams, Jeremiah [ed.]. *Reclaiming the Inner Child.* Los Angeles: J. P. Tarcher, Inc., 1990.

Adler, Mortimer J. *Intellect: Mind Over Matter.* New York: Macmillan, 1990.

Anthony, Dick; Bruce Ecker, and Ken Wilber. *Spiritual Choices: The Problem of Recognizing Authentic Paths to Inner Transformation.* New York: Paragon House Publishers, 1987.

Bandler, Richard, and John Grinder. *Reframing: Neuro-Linguistic Programming and the Transformation of Meaning.* Moab: Real People Press, 1982.

Barzun, Jacques. *A Stroll With William James.* Chicago: The University of Chicago Press, 1983.

Beattie, Melody. *Codependent No More.* San Francisco: Harper & Row, 1987.

Becker, Ernest. *Escape From Evil.* New York: The Free Press, Div. of Macmillan, 1975.

Bellah, Robert N. et al. *Habits of the Heart.* New York: Harper & Row, 1985.

Berger, Milton M. [ed.]. *Beyond the Double Bind: Communication and Family Systems, Theories, and Techniques with Schizophrenics.* New York: Brunner/ Mazel, 1978.

Berger, Peter L., *The Capitalist Revolution: Fifty Propositions About Prosperity, Equality, and Liberty.* New York: Basic Books, 1986.

Blane, Howard T., and Kenneth E. Leonard [eds.]. *Psychological Theories of Drinking and Alcoholism.* New York: The Guilford Press, 1987.

Blum, Kenneth. *Alcohol and the Addictive Brain.* New York: The Free Press, 1991.

Bowlby, John. *Separation* (vol. 2) *Anxiety and Anger.* New York: Basic Books, 1973.

————. *Loss.* (vol. 3) *Sadness and Depression.* New York: Basic Books, 1980.

Bradshaw, John. *Healing the Shame That Binds You.* Deerfield Beach, Fla.: Health Communications, Inc., 1988.

Brown, Norman O. *Life Against Death: The Psychoanalytic Meaning of History*. Middletown: Wesleyan University Press, 1959.

Burns, David D. M.D., *Feeling Good: The New Mood Therapy*. New York: Signet, Penguin Books, 1981.

Carpenter, Finley. *The Skinner Primer: Beyond Freedom and Dignity*. New York: The Free Press, 1974.

Carruth, Bruce, and Warner Mendenhall. *Co-Dependency: Issues in Treatment and Recovery*. New York: The Haworth Press, 1989.

Cermak, Timmen L., M.D. *A Time to Heal: The Road to Recovery for Adult Children of Alcoholics*. Los Angeles: J. P. Tarcher, Inc., 1988.

———. *A Primer on Adult Children of Alcoholics*. Deerfield Beach, Fla.: Health Communications, Inc., 1989.

———. *Diagnosing and Treating Co-Dependence*. Minneapolis: Johnson Institute Books, 1986.

Chopra, Deepak, M.D. *Quantum Healing: Exploring the Frontiers of Mind/ Body Medicine*. New York: Bantam Books, 1989.

Christopher, James. *SOS Sobriety: The Proven Alternative to 12 Step Programs*. Buffalo: Prometheus Books, 1992.

Cohen, Sidney, M.D. *The Chemical Brain: The Neurochemistry of Addictive Disorders*. Irvine: Care Institute, 1988.

Dawkins, Richard. *The Selfish Gene*. New York and Oxford: Oxford University Press, 1976.

Denzin, Norman K. *The Alcoholic Self*. Newberry Park, Calif.: Sage Publications, 1987.

———. *The Alcoholic Society: Addiction and Recovery of the Self*. New Brunswick, N.J.: Transaction Publisher, 1993.

Donovan, James M. "An Etiologic Model of Alcoholism," *American Journal of Psychiatry*. 143 (1986):1-11.

Edelman, Gerald M. *Neural Darwinism: The Theory of Neuronal Group Selection*. New York: Basic Books, 1987.

Ehrenberg, Otto, and Miriam Ehrenberg. *The Psychotherapy Maze: A Consumer's Guide to Getting In and Out of Therapy*. New York: Simon and Schuster, 1986.

Ellis, Albert. *Growth Through Reason: Verbatim Cases in Rational-Emotive Therapy*. Palo Alto, Calif.: Science and Behavior Books, 1971.

Ellis, Albert, and Emmett Velten. *When AA Doesn't Work for You: A Rational Approach to Recovery*. Fort Lee, N.J.: Barricade Press, 1992.

217

Ferguson, Marilyn. *The Aquarian Conspiracy: Personal and Social Transformation in the 1980s.* Los Angeles: J.P. Tarcher, Inc., 1980.

Filstead, William J.; Jean J. Rossi, and Mark Keller [eds.]. *Alcohol and Alcohol Problems: New Thinking and New Directions.* Cambridge, Mass.: Ballinger Publishing Company, 1976.

Fingarette, Herbert. *Heavy Drinking: The Myth of Alcoholism As a Disease.* Berkeley: University of California Press, 1988.

Fitzgerald, Kathleen Whalen. *Alcoholism: The Genetic Inheritance.* New York: Doubleday, 1988.

Fossum, Merle A., and Marilyn J. Mason. *Facing Shame: Families in Recovery.* New York: W.W. Norton & Co., 1986.

Fowler, James. *Stages of Faith.* San Francisco: Harper & Row, 1981

Fox, Vincent. *Addiction, Change, and Choice: The New View of Alcoholism.* Tucson, Ariz.: See Sharp Press, 1993.

Friel, John, and Linda Friel. *Adult Children: The Secrets of Dysfunctional Families.* Deerfield Beach, Fla.: Health Communications, Inc., 1988.

Gaylin, Willard, M.D. *Feelings.* New York: Ballantine Books, 1979.

Glashow, Sheldon L. *Interactions: A Journey Through the Mind of a Particle Physicist and the Matter of This World.* New York: Warner Books, 1988.

Gleick, James. *Chaos: Making a New Science.* New York: Viking, 1987.

Gold, Mark S., M.D. *The Good News About Drugs and Alcohol: Curing, Treating, and Preventing Substance Abuse in the New Age of Biopsychiatry.* New York: Villard Books, 1991.

Goldberg, Arnold, M.D. *The Psychology of the Self: A Casebook.* New York: International Universities Press, 1978.

Goodwin, Donald W., M.D. *Is Alcoholism Hereditary?* Second ed. New York: Ballantine Books, 1988.

Gould, Stephen Jay. *Ever Since Darwin.* New York: W.W. Norton & Co., 1977.

Griffin, David Ray [ed.]. *The Reenchantment of Science, Postmodern Proposals.* Albany: State University of New York Press, 1988.

Herbert, Nick. *Elemental Mind: Human Consciousness and the New Physics.* New York: Penguin Books, 1993.

Hofstadter, Douglas R. and Daniel C. Dennett. *The Mind's I: Fantasies and Reflections on Self and Soul.* New York: Basic Books, 1981.

Huxley, Aldous. *The Perennial Philosophy.* Cleveland: The World Publishing Company, 1962.

Izard, Carroll E. *The Face of Emotion*. New York: Appleton-Century-Crofts, 1971.

Jellinek, E.M. *The Disease Concept of Alcoholism*. New Haven: Hillhouse Press, 1960.

Johnson, George. *Fire in the Mind: Science, Faith, and the Search for Order*. New York: Alfred A. Knopf, 1995.

Kaminer, Wendy. *I'm Dysfunctional, You're Dysfunctional: The Recovery Movement and Other Self Help Fashions*. Reading, Mass.: Addison-Wesley Publishing Co., 1992.

Kasl, Charlotte Davis. *Many Roads, One Journey: Moving Beyond the 12 Steps*. New York: Harper/Collins, 1992.

Katz, Stan J., and Aimee E. Liu. *The Codependency Conspiracy: How to Break the Recovery Habit and Take Charge of Your Life*. New York: Warner Books, 1991.

Kaufman, Gershen. *Shame: The Power of Caring*. Rochester, Vt.: Schenkman Books, Inc., 1992.

Kissin, Benjamin, and Henri Begleiter [eds.]. *Clinical Pathology, Vol. 3, The Biology of Alcoholism*. New York: Plenum Press, 1974.

Kohut, Heinz, M.D. *The Analysis of the Self: A Systematic Approach to the Psychoanalytic Treatment of Narcissistic Personality Disorders*. New York: International Universities Press, Inc., 1971.

Kurtz, Ernest. *Shame and Guilt, Characteristics of the Dependency Cycle*. Center City, Minn.: Hazelden, 1981.

Langer, Susanne K. *Philosophy in a New Key: A Study in the Symbolism of Reason, Rite, and Art*. Cambridge: Harvard University Press, 1979.

Lasch, Christopher, *The Culture of Narcissism*. New York: Warner Books, 1979.

Laughlin, Charles D., Jr., John McManus, and Eugene G. d'Aquili. *Symbol, and Experience: Toward a Neurophenomenology of Human Consciousness*. Boston: New Science Library, 1990.

Lewis, Helen Block. *Shame and Guilt in Neurosis*. New York: International Universities Press, 1971.

Lieberman, E. James, M.D. *Acts of Will: The Life and Work of Otto Rank*. New York: The Free Press, 1985.

Lifton, Robert Jay. *The Future of Immortality, and Other Essays for a Nuclear Age*. New York: Basic Books, 1987.

Mahler, Margaret, Fred Pine, and Anni Bergman. *The Psychological Birth of the Human Infant*. London: Maresfield Library, 1975.

219

Marlatt, G. Alan [ed.]. *Relapse Prevention: Maintenance Strategies in the Treatment of Addictive Behaviors*. New York: The Guilford Press, 1985.

May, Gerald G., M.D. *Addiction and Grace: Love and Spirituality in the Healing of Addictions*. San Francisco: HarperSanFrancisco, 1988.

———. *Will and Spirit*. San Francisco: HarperSanFrancisco, 1982

May, Rollo. *The Meaning of Anxiety*. New York: W.W. Norton & Co., 1977.

———. *Love and Will*. W.W. New York: Norton & Co., 1969.

McCord, William, and Joan McCord. *Origins of Alcoholism*. Stanford: Stanford University Press, 1960.

Milam, James R., and Katherine Ketcham. *Under the Influence: A Guide to the Myths and Realities of Alcoholism*. New York: Bantam Books, 1981.

Miller, Alice. *Thou Shalt Not Be Aware: Society's Betrayal of the Child*. New York: New American Library, 1984.

———. *For Your Own Good: Hidden Cruelty in Childrearing, and the Roots of Violence*. New York: Farrar, Straus & Giroux, 1984.

———. *The Drama of the Gifted Child: The Search for the True Self*. New York: Basic Books, 1981.

Moody, Paul Amos. *Genetics of Man*. New York: W.W. Norton & Company, 1967.

Morgenbesser, Sydney, and James Walsh [eds.]. *Free Will*. Englewood Cliffs, N.J.: Prentice Hall, Inc., 1962.

Nace, Edgar P., M.D. *The Treatment of Alcoholism*. New York: Brunner/Mazel Publishers, 1987.

Nelkin, Dorothy, and Lawrence Tancredi. *Dangerous Diagnostics: The Social Power of Biological Information*. New York: Basic Books, 1989.

Pagels, Heinz. *The Cosmic Code: Quantum Physics As the Language of Nature*. New York: Simon & Schuster, 1982.

———. *The Dreams of Reason, The Computer and the Rise of the Sciences of Complexity*. New York: Simon & Schuster, 1988.

Peele, Stanton. *The Meaning of Addiction: Compulsive Experience and Its Interpretation*. Lexington, Mass.: Lexington Books, 1985.

———. *Diseasing of America: Addiction Treatment Out of Control*. Lexington, Mass.: Lexington Books, 1989.

Peele, Stanton, and Archie Brodsky. *Love and Addiction*. New York: New American Library, 1976

————. *The Truth About Addiction and Recovery.* New York: Simon & Schuster, 1991.

Penrose, Roger. *Shadows of the Mind: A Search for the Missing Science of Consciousness.* Oxford: Oxford University Press, 1994.

Perls, Frederick S., M.D. *Gestalt Therapy Verbatim.* Layfayette, Calif.: Real People Press, 1969.

Pierce, Benjamin A. *The Family Genetic Sourcebook.* New York: John Wiley & Sons, 1990.

Pittman, Bill. *AA: The Way It All Began.* Seattle: Glen Abbey Books, 1988.

Pribram, Karl [ed.]. *On the Biology of Learning.* New York: Harcourt, Brace & World, Inc., 1969.

Progoff, Ira, *The Dynamics of Hope: Perspectives of Process in Anxiety and Creativity, Imagery and Dreams.* New York: Dialogue House Library, 1985.

Rachlin, Howard. *Introduction to Modern Behaviorism.* San Francisco: W.H. Freeman and Company, 1970.

Rank, Otto. *Truth and Reality.* New York: W.W. Norton & Co., 1936.

————. *Will Therapy.* New York: W.W. Norton & Co., 1936.

Rapping, Elayne. *The Culture of Recovery: Making Sense of the Self-Help Movement in Women's Lives.* Boston: Beacon Press, 1996.

Restak, Richard M., M.D. *The Brain.* New York: Bantam Books, 1984.

Reynolds, G.F. *A Primer of Operant Conditioning.* Glenview, Ill.,: Scott, Foresman and Company, 1968.

Rieff, Philip. *The Triumph of the Therapeutic: Uses of Faith After Freud.* New York: Harper & Row, 1966.

Roebuck, Julian B., and Raymond G. Kessler. *The Etiology of Alcoholism: Constitutional, Psychological, and Sociological Approaches.* Springfield, Ill.: Charles C. Thomas Publisher, 1972.

Royce, James E. *Alcohol Problems and Alcoholism: A Comprehensive Survey.* New York: Free Press, 1989.

Schaef, Anne Wilson. *Beyond Therapy, Beyond Science: A New Model for Healing the Whole Person.* San Francisco,: HarperSanFrancisco, 1992.

————. *Co-Dependence: Misunderstood-Mistreated.* San Francisco: HarperSanFranciso, 1986.

Secretary of Health and Human Services, Alcohol and Health. "Seventh Special Report to the U.S. Congress, National Institute on Alcohol Abuse and Alcoholism." Rockville, Md., 1990.

Subby, Robert, and John Friel. *Co-Dependency: An Emerging Issue.* Pompano Beach, Fla.: Health Communications, 1984.

Talbot, Michael. *Beyond the Quantum.* New York: Macmillan, 1986.

———. *The Holographic Universe.* New York: Harper Perennial, 1991.

Tasman, Allan, M.D., Robert E.Hales, M.D., and J. Frances Allen, M.D. [eds.]. "Review of Psychiatry," *American Psychiatric Press.* Washington, DC, 1989.

Taylor, Shelley E. *Positive Illusions: Creative Self-Deception and the Healthy Mind.* New York: Basic Books, 1989.

Thune, Carl E. "Alcoholism and the Archetypal Past: A Phenomenological Perspective on Alcoholics Anonymous," *Journal of Studies on Alcohol,* Vol. 38, No. 1, 1977.

Tocqueville, Alexis de. *Democracy in America.* New York: Anchor Books, Doubleday, 1969.

Tomkins, Silvan S. *Affect, Imagery, Consciousness, Vol. I, The Positive Affects.* New York: Springer Publishing, 1962.

Tomkins, Silvan S. *Affect, Imagery, Consciousness, Vol. II, The Negative Affects.* New York: Springer Publishing, 1962.

Tomkins, Silvan S. and Carroll E. Izard [eds.]. *Affect, Cognition, and Personality, Empirical Studies.* Silvan Tomkins New York: Springer Publishing, 1965.

Trimpey, Jack. *The Small Book* [Rational Recovery Systems]. New York: Delacorte Press, 1992.

Twerski, Abraham, M.D. *Addictive Thinking, Understanding Self Deception.* San Francisco: Harper & Row, 1990.

Vaillant, George E. *The Natural History of Alcoholism: Causes, Patterns, and Paths to Recovery.* Cambridge: Harvard University Press, 1983.

Vaughan, Clark. *Addictive Drinking: The Road to Recovery for Problem Drinkers and Those Who Love Them.* New York: Penguin Books, 1982.

Weil, Andrew, M.D. *Natural Health, Natural Medicine, A Comprehensive Manual for Wellness and Self-Care.* Boston: Houghton Mifflin Company, 1990.

Weinhold, Barry K., and Janae B. Weinhold. *Breaking Free of the Co-Dependency Trap.* Walpole: Stillpoint Publishing, 1989.

Werner, Heinz. *Symbol Formation: An Organismic-Developmental Approach to Language and the Expression of Thought.* New York: Wiley, 1963.

Whitfield, Charles L., M.D. *Healing the Child Within.* Deerfield Beach: Health Communications, Inc., 1987.

Wilson, Edward O. *Sociobiology: The New Synthesis*. Cambridge: Harvard University Press, 1975.

Wison, James Q. *The Moral Sense*. New York: The Free Press, 1993.

Wright, Robert. *The Moral Animal, The New Science of Evolutionary Psychology*. New York: Pantheon Books, 1994.

Wurmser, Leon, M.D. *The Hidden Dimension: Psychodynamics in Compulsive Drug Use*. New York: Jason Aronson, 1978.

Zohar, Danah, and Ian Marshall. *The Quantum Society: Mind, Physics, and a New Social Vision*. New York: William Morrow & Co., Inc., 1994.

Acknowledgments

Many, many people deserve my thanks for the role they played in my recovery from alcoholism and in the writing of this book. But writing this book was actually a solitary enterprise. I needed to read hundreds of books and articles and journals over several years before I could start to put it together. My approach to addiction is unprecedented and no collaborators crossed my path along the way.

My friend of fifty-five years, John Robben, began the process for me about twenty-five years ago with the publication of his book, *Coming to My Senses*. John called me at my office high over 42nd Street one morning to tell me to buy *The Denial of Death* by Ernest Becker. A transforming author for me, Becker also introduced me to Robert Jay Lifton's *The Broken Connection*, the most important contribution to psychology since James and Freud. This book could not have been written without Lifton's ideas.

Ed Gormley has been a friend for more than twenty-five years. Ed hired me as a bartender when I needed to be hired. He fired me when I needed to be fired. A playwright and author, Ed encouraged me to write my own books. Ed took this book into the mainstream for me, lifting my spirits a thousandfold.

Don Wigal indexed this book for me. Theologian, entrepreneur, publisher, writer, bottomless source of information, Don was the first person I ever allowed to talk to me about my alcoholism. Don was clever enough to refer to it as my "lifestyle" rather than my drinking. He suggested a way out which I jumped at, and have consequently stayed alive to tell the tale.

Paul Lanier has been another close friend of twenty-five years. In Paul I saw the world I wanted to inhabit. Brilliant, polished, kind, and gentle, Paul somehow always lived above the mean and trivial, dreaming wonderful dreams for all of us. Paul wrote his questions, suggestions, and advice on literally every page of my manuscript. That is generosity.

Joe and Kathryn Schenkman, my publishers, run their business in a remote valley in Vermont. Joe keeps a warehouse of more than three hundred titles in print for his authors. I took to the Schenkmans the moment I met them. They are true Renaissance people—curious, warm, and talented. I knew I was in good hands, and that has been proven with the publication of this book.

Paul Fargis, owner of Stonesong Press in New York, published John Robben's book in 1973, and has been a powerful friend to both of us since that time. Both John and I talk often of what Paul has meant to us, about his unique generosity and good will.

Evan Holstrum edited this book for me. I have never met anyone more responsible and careful. Evan rewrote some paragraphs for me, and asked questions which caused me to rethink some parts.

My sister, Peggy, has lived with me for fifteen years, putting up with the crudities of the always distracted male of the species. Peggy deals with the turmoil of life with grace and compassion, sometimes sacrificing herself in the bargain so that others may thrive. Peggy taught our aged mother how to enjoy being loved and touched during the final months of her life.

And finally there is Pat, my dear friend of sixteen years. Pat has tirelessly and courageously nudged me along the path of recovery, not always finding me willing and comprehending. Most of the important things I have done in recovery she has inspired.

There are so many others! I am now experiencing the discomfort known to most authors at being constrained to limit their acknowledgments. Thank you all.

Index

Index 229

Other Titles of Interest

Shame: The Power of Caring
GERSHEN KAUFMAN
263 pp., 1992
Cloth $22.95 (ISBN 0-87047-052-3)
Paper $14.95 (ISBN 0-87047-053-1)
Shame has crippling effects on the human psyche, but until Gershen Kaufman's breakthrough study was first published over a decade ago, this basic human experience was virtually neglected as a factor in mental health. Since then, there has been an explosion of interest in the topic. In this revised and expanded edition, Kaufman clarifies the role shame plays in connection with dysfunctional family systems, childhood sexual abuse, and addiction recovery. In this third edition he extends shame theory in relation to aging and disability; the school and work settings; culture and gender; and sexual orientation and gay/lesbian identity. The final chapter explores how affect in general and shame in particular manifest themselves in war and international relations.

The Chase: The Compulsive Gambler
HENRY R. LESIEUR
323 pp., 1984
Paper $18.95 (ISBN 0-87073-643-4)
Those who must gamble are studied here in the context of the social forces they face. A distinguished social scientist takes the reader into poolrooms, racetracks, bowling alleys, and football stadiums, showing how increased involvement and reduced options interact as a spiral. An excellent tool for sociologists and clinicians studying the cause and effect of addiction.

Work Abuse: How to Recognize and Survive It
JUDITH WYATT AND CHAUNCEY HARE
392 pp., 1997
Cloth $29.95 (ISBN 0-87047-110-4)
Paper $19.95 (ISBN 0-87047-109-0)
Work abuse is the dehumanizing of people through patterned ways of interacting at work. This includes systematic denial that the abuse is happening, as most abusive managers consider such poisonous treatment to be "the way the world works." Work abuse can affect a whole organization or it can be focused on one individual scapegoat. Our society as a whole tends to reinforce this attitude, placing the blame on the traumatized victim. When the abuse cannot be

redressed at work, it often reappears at home as addiction or family violence. Intended for individual workers and their families, therapists who help them, and manager and union leaders responsible for work systems, this book explains how and why work abuse happens and offers a practical plan for healing. Includes in-depth case studies, exercises, and worksheets to guide the reader.

The Dynamics of Power: Fighting Shame & Building Self-Esteem
GERSHEN KAUFMAN AND LEV RAPHAEL
147 pp., 1991
Cloth $19.95 (ISBN 0-87047-050-7)
Paper $11.95 (ISBN 0-87047-051-5)
As an outgrowth of Kaufman's work on shame, this book's comprehensive educational curriculum for psychological health and self-esteem has professional, educational, and personal relevance. The principles and tools in this book directly combat addiction, violence, and stress-related disorders by reversing the very conditions responsible for them: shame and powerlessness.

Addicted to Suicide: A Woman Struggling to Live
MARY SAVAGE
144 pp., 1979
Paper $14.95 (ISBN 0-87073-907-7)
A highly subjective, intensely personal story. For those concerned with supporting and caring for suicidal people, as well as for those not "obsessed with death."

Harassment Therapy: A Case Study of Psychiatric Violence
DON STANNARD-FRIEL
183 pp., 1981
Paper $13.95 (0-87073-160-2)
Stannard-Friel focuses not on the mental patient but the therapist. In the broadest sense, the topic of this book is the organized violence found throughout society, especially as it relates to the "bad behavior" of "good people."

The Women of Psychology Vol. II: Expansion and Refinement
EDITED BY GWENDOLYN STEVENS AND GARDNER SHELDON
240 pp., 1982, illustrated
Paper $18.95 (ISBN 0-87073-446-6)
This invaluable sourcebook reveals facts about women psychologists that have been largely neglected or ignored by male historians. A stimulating supplement to psychology and women's studies courses.

To order any of these titles please send your check or money order (include $3.00 for shipping for the first title; add $1.00 for each additional title) to the address below. Write or e-mail for a free catalog.

Schenkman Books, Inc.
118 Main Street
Rochester VT 05767
schenkma@sover.net

web site: www.sover.net/~schenkma/